PATRIARCH

Of

OVINGTON

BY

SALLIE LEE SHORT

Library of Congress Cataloging-in-Publication Data

Short, Sallie Lee, 1932-
   The Patriarch of Ovington/Sallie Lee Short
TXu459-277

DEDICATION

Dedicated to the memory of my only son

Michael Anthony Short, and my eight daughters Jacqueline,

Carita, Paulette, Shelia, Marilyn, Regina, Panthea, and Greta.

I hope that my book and other writings will inspire them to

pursue their goals fulfilling their dreams.

ACKNOWLEDGEMENTS

I would like to thank Mrs. Sarah Maxwell, Director of the Learning Lab at Nashville State Technical School in Nashville Tennessee. When I first started writing my book she offered the technical assistance I needed to help me get started with my book.

I would like to thank Mrs. V-Ann Buckingham for the many hours she devoted of her time. She spent many hours typing and transferring my book from a floppy disk to a more updated Version of Work Perfect.

I would like to thank my sister, Beulah Hardin for encouraging me to write my poetry, and to pursue the publishing my book.

I would like to thank my close friends, the administration, faculty, and staff at Nashville State Tech that encouraged and assisted me in anyway to complete my book.

My special thanks to my daughter Greta Duncan for the many hours she devoted in helping me. She and her husband Michael A. Duncan MD have shown great generosity assisting me financially to get my book published.

Most of all I thank God for giving me the wisdom, strength, and knowledge to write this historical drama "The Patriarch of Ovington."

PATRIARCH
Of
OVINGTON

Born in Ovington Tennessee, Thomas Theodore Ovington was an only child of Willie Monroe and Laura Crawford Ovington. The town was located in East Tennessee Mountains, and was named after Thomas' ancestors.

As the protagonist of the story, Thomas was always able to meet adversity with a strong demeanor. His father, Willie Monroe, was a harsh character and continually abused both Thomas and his mother. Thomas grew up unhappy and as a result of this, animosity existed between him and his father.

Willie Monroe had a mistress, a woman half his age, whom the town called "Precious"." Thomas hated her. When he was in his late teens and very handsome, Precious lusted after the younger Ovington. She found him alone on the mountain, stripped him of his clothing, and seduced him.

Thomas, ashamed by his weakness, made up his mind he would leave Ovington. He kissed his mother good-bye, and he traveled down the mountain until he came to a town called Lawsonville, Tennessee.

Thomas befriended the Cannon's, James and his daughter Beth Marie. He loved James like a father. After James Cannon died, Thomas and Beth were married.

Thomas made plans to move home to Ovington after the death of his father. He hired John Smithson, an architect who owned a big construction company, to build a beautiful home in which he and his wife could live. In nineteen hundred twelve, Thomas moved Beth and her servants to Ovington.

A few of the main characters that provide the story with much of its charisma/excitement are Doctor Newman and his wife Betty, Constable Harrison, the Bollings, Sarah, and Roscoe Bennett, a dynamic evangelist.

Thomas was known for his natty attire, one of the most esteemed men in the eastern part of Tennessee, and looked upon as a leader of this town.

CONTENTS

1

arah could feel the warmth of the early spring as she sat on her front porch to greet the residents of Ovington when they came by to see her. The winters in the East Tennessee mountains were very harsh, and now that Sarah was older, she was confined to her house most of the winter months.

Smelling the honeysuckle in the air as she looked out into the stillness of the early morning, this was the time of the year that Sarah loved. She looked up at the Ovington's house, the "Big House" as most of the people called it, built by the late Thomas Theodore Ovington at the top of the mountain. With all of its surrounding beauty, this estate was known to all who visited this community.

The Ovington house had been Sarah's home for many years and she still loved to sit and observe the daily routine of the estate as if she still lived there. Sarah would sometimes wonder what the outside community was like. She had never lived outside of this community since she was born in the Ovington house after the mother she never knew expired when she was five minutes old. Sarah was left to live on the mercy of the people in this community.

The family bloodline had ended for the Ovington name. Thomas Theodore Ovington's long and troublesome life had ended, and he was the last of the Ovingtons, a proud name in this community. He had been a small, but powerful, man, a person who was industrious to this community, but memories of him lived on; he left a community profitable, because he loved these people.

Thomas Theodore Ovington was known all over Eastern Tennessee. He was a man of "personality" and wealth. His wealth was acquired when he married Beth Marie Cannon, the daughter of the late James Cannon, a wealthy tycoon businessman and a big stockholder in the railroads. James Cannon trusted Thomas as his son, and had befriended him when he came to his home a very poor, hungry and a broke young man after leaving home to be on his own.

Ovington was a dirt-poor community when young Thomas fled because of animosity toward his father. He was so unhappy and had suffered for years because of his father's abuse toward him and his mother. His father had taken up with a mistress with whom he openly had an affair. This caused his mother mental anguish. This same woman, after having the father, came after the son, Thomas. She saw how very handsome he had grown to be and how lonely he was. This sinful woman was the "Darling of Ovington." They called her "Precious." She was no good; she managed to break Thomas' mother's heart. She had enough nerve to come after the son when she had gotten tired of his father. Precious understood Thomas' feeling. She exposed her voluptuous body to him when she found him in a semi-intoxicated frame of mind. She fondled him to the point he could not control his feelings. She taught him to love her as she tricked him into having coitus with her; exposing him to a feeling he never knew existed, and he had great problems afterwards.

Fleeing in shame from his home and the community, he returned years later only after the death of his father, and saw the condition of the people he loved that lived in a valley off from Ovington. This valley was called "Hidden Valley," some called it "Little Valley" because of a small number of people who lived there. These people were identified by a heritage that no one was really sure of, but they were believed to be decendants of Indians. These people were very fair skinned, with long black or dark brown hair, and they had high cheekbones in their smooth round faces, very closely resembling the American Indian people.

Little Valley had always been a part of the small community, which was named the Ovington Community years later. It was situated below the mountain, that was covered by the thick and towering trees that lined the road above, leading a half-mile down into the isolated homes of the people that lived there for many years.

The people in this valley were very friendly with the White Hill people, sometimes called "hillbillies," but the people in the valley called them "White Hill" people. During the many years the two races of people were friends, there was an intimate relationship among them that resulted in copulation between the men and women, which later resulted in a mixed race of people.

Someone gave a formula to some of the men in valley for making their own liquor, called moonshine. Making moonshine was a way of life for some of these people, because it was often sold off the mountain.

The Tucker family was the biggest family in Little Valley, and the most feared, because there were a lot of men in this family. The family commander was Grady James Tucker; he had six sons (Clarence, David, Roy, Barry, Frank and Albert) and two daughters (Helen and Lottie). The Tuckers were fearless men, they were skilled trappers, they knew the mountain terrain, and how to survive on the most dangerous parts of the mountain.

Some of the people that lived here were afraid of the danger they often faced when they would venture out into the wilderness. Grady Tucker would visit around this community often, whether it was to deliver some of his moonshine, or just visit his relatives or friends.

Barry was the youngest, and his father's favorite son. Grady Tucker rarely went anywhere without Barry. From the time he was able to walk, Barry was on his father's shoulder, or running behind him somewhere. Grady was close to all of his sons, but he was partial to his youngest son, and the other weren't jealous or didn't seem to be. David was the seventh child, and the most aggressive among the eight children. He was the smallest, and the one that was a loner; he never went with any of the other family members as they would travel through the mountain. He preferred to go alone. One day, David left home to visit his relatives. He told his father he was going to visit his cousins, but he was never seen or heard from again by his family.

Barry was the handsomest, and charming as well. Everyone knew that he was his father's favorite son. Barry would travel with his father through the mountain. Sometimes they would visit the Sloans. Grady was known to sell some of his moonshine, and he would take some of it to the Sloan's for sale, or sometimes just to be sociable with the couple. The Sloans were heavy drinkers. Jerry and his wife Sadie were the worse when they would take to the bottle. Sadie would often flirt with some of her husband's male friends, just to make him mad, and he often got into a mean mood, and there would be a big scene out of Jerry.

Barry became fond of this family and he would visit them alone sometimes. He would get a kick out of how the couple would act whenever they drank too much. On one occasion Barry went alone to visit the Sloans. It was a bad time to get involved when the couple were fighting. Barry tried to talk to Jerry when he was treating his wife real bad, and using his fist to beat up on the poor woman. Barry only tried to talk to Jerry about not harming his wife, when Jerry got into a real bad mood and stabbed Barry with a pocketknife. Barry hemorrhaged to death.

The elder Tucker was so devastated by this act of violence to his youngest son that he became physically sick from this tragedy. He never recovered completely from the shock, and he soon died. The Tucker family was so grieved by all of this hurt to their family, that it wasn't long before Jerry was found dead also; no one knew the person, or persons, responsible for his death.

Albert was the most disappointed of the Tucker children, because he had no sons, he only had four daughters. Lillian was the oldest, Minnie, Frances, and Mattie the youngest, but he taught his girls to be as rough as any boy on the mountain. Albert would take his girls with him wherever he went, often taking them into the wilderness to hunt, and he taught them to use a gun and knife as good as he would use one. The girls weren't afraid to travel the mountain together, like some of the other women in the valley.

Elaine, Albert's wife, had died after she delivered Mattie. Having gone into labor alone with only the girls at home, Lillian was only twelve when Elaine went into labor with Mattie. Lillian was very frightened as her mother cried out as the pains wracked her body. She travailed with labor for a long period of time as she instructed Lillian how to prepare for the birth of her child.

The minutes seem like hours as Lillian tried to help her mother. After a long and frightening time for Lillian, Elaine finally delivered her baby and named her Mattie. Elaine was smiling as she held Mattie in her arms, but she suddenly became quiet, and Lillian knew something was wrong with her mother.

When Albert came home to find his wife gravely ill, he was devastated. Elaine was bleeding and unable to speak to him. Albert knew his wife was near death. Albert ran to get his mother and some of the neighbors, but they were unable to save Elaine. Albert and his mother were very concerned about the baby. They knew she had come through a hard labor and birth. They gave special care to the tiny baby to make sure she was all right before they left Albert alone with his small family.

Albert's mother offered to take the baby, and raise her if necessary. Albert refused to allow her to take the infant. He promise he would care for his children himself. Albert had a hard time caring for his girls. When Mattie was old enough, he took her with him to work. He taught all of his girls how to survive in the mountain. The girls were smart and they did as their father instructed them. They were taught what to look for in the mountain, and which was the most dangerous. They always went with him regardless of the danger they faced.

There were many dangerous animals and many poisonous snakes that roamed the mountain. Most of these men were good hunters, but being careless sometimes got them killed. Some would not watch where they stepped. Reptiles known to be dangerous to men had bitten many in these parts.

The death rate was high among the babies and small children because of the extreme poverty in the small valley. There was little work to do, but the men preferred to work around their area, rather than to travel off the mountain to find work because of the indifference of some of the people they encountered. The Hill people were real friendly with the valley people, but some of them accused them of being no good and lazy, and refused to have anything to do with them. So the valley people just sort of stayed in their own little family circle and tried not to venture too far from home.

Some of the people in the valley would have a moonshine still in operation from time to time and would make a little moonshine to drink, or to sell if they could find someone who wanted it bad enough. They had customers that they would deliver to for many years. The Tuckers were the biggest moonshiners, and the Williams were another family that made a lot of moonshine.

The Williams were not too friendly with their valley neighbors, the Tuckers, and sometimes they would get into violent arguments with each other. They weren't as close to each other as some of the other families. In fact, they were rivals with the bootlegging business.

2

The Ovington family and a few other families fled up the mountain during the latter part of the Civil War. Headed by Joseph Clyde Ovington and his small family, he was the leader of these people that had decided to migrate to a new area, and this site was the ideal place to settle, since Joseph Ovington had been a leader in the War. He knew this area, liked the place and decided to move his family up the mountain and start over, he loved the area that much. Joseph saw the beauty of the surrounding grounds and knew this would be the ideal place for him and his family to start over after the bloody war.

Another family who were friends of the Ovingtons were John Jacob Crawford, a great officer in the Civil War, who was badly wounded and unable to do very much for himself. Joseph talked John Jacob into moving to this community with him, as well as a few other families, when he explained to them the beauty of this land.

The trip up the mountain was dangerous and many of the people were hurt, became sick, and a few died before they were able to reach the site where they had agreed to settle. John Crawford was unable to do very much, but he survived the trip better than some of the others. The women were worn out, and the children were half sick and fussy, and the men were weak and slow in clearing the land and building shelter for their families. They seemed to have contracted some sort of fever.

The families had been on the mountain approximately a month, when some of the men from Little Valley came up to help the people with shelter, and they helped them care for the ones that were sick. This act of kindness from these people in the Little Valley to the new residents made them close to the people who had come when they really needed help, and to get them through these hard times in a new and strange place.

The first few years were hard on the new residents. Some of them weren't able to stand the hard years, and they soon left the rugged mountain area, and went back down the mountain to their former home. But all of Joseph Ovington's family stayed, and they named this community Ovington. Over a period of years, other families moved to this area, building up the community.

Willie Monroe Ovington was a descendant of Joseph Ovington. He was a genuine mountain man, a tall man of heavy build, with lots of reddish-blond hair, and a deep voice that would scare the life out of you, if you didn't know him. Most of the Ovingtons died out, and Willie Monroe was the only one left. This man was known to be mean if he didn't get his way, and most of the people stayed out of his way.

Laura Crawford, like Willie Monroe, was the last of the Crawfords. The two families had been marrying into each other's families for years, so it was no surprise when Willie Monroe and Laura were married. The Ovingtons only had one child; that was all Laura wanted when she found Willie Monroe to be so abusive. Their only son was named Thomas Theodore, a name that Laura liked so well; of course, Willie Monroe wasn't too happy since he wanted the child to be named after him. Thomas was Laura's whole life. She was smart, could read and write, and she taught Thomas all that she knew, since there were no school nearby at this time.

Willie Monroe wanted his son to be like him, and he would take him into the most treacherous parts of this mountain. Knowing he was frightened, Willie Monroe wanted to toughen Thomas to live on this dangerous mountain, but Thomas would run home to Laura frightened and crying his eyes out. Willie Monroe would accuse his wife of babying his son, and called Thomas a sissy for being so frightened when he would try to take him out into the mountain wilderness. Laura would try to comfort Thomas, but as he grew older, he began to have animosity toward his father for the abuses he felt like his father was guilty of, by the way he treated him.

Willie Monroe and Laura were not close, and had not been in love as most couples are when they marry. The two married because both of Laura parents were dead, and she felt like no woman should be alone, and the residents encouraged the two to marry. Laura was brought up with love in her family, and she was very protected by her father, since she was the only child. Laura was a very intelligent woman, and among the few that knew how to read and write in this community.

The Ovingtons soon acted like they were strangers to each other, they weren't very sociable, and they became unpopular among the other residents. A new couple moved to the Ovington community, Howard and Margaret Daniels, who became friends with the Ovingtons. They liked Laura real well, but they weren't too fond of Willie Monroe. They would visit the Ovingtons often, and soon they were close, but Laura was the one that kept the friendship, because they could not stand the way that Willie Monroe would talk to them at times.

The Daniels had no children, and when Howard's brother died leaving three children alone, the Daniels took the only girl, and another brother of Howard took the two boys. The girl's name was Rose Ann; she was their pride and joy, and they spoiled her beyond words. Howard and Margaret called her "Precious." Rose Ann was about six years old when she came to live with the Daniels.

Most of the community sooned starting calling Rose Ann by the nickname "Precious," too She was indeed precious—a beautiful child, she was always smiling, with dimples in each of her cheeks. Her black hair was curly, and her smooth skin was always scrubbed clean.

The Daniels remained friends with the Ovingtons, Precious was always over at the Ovington's house, but Thomas wasn't too fond of Precious, he could see that this child was spoiled, and always wanted her way, so he never had anything to do with Precious. Over the years, Precious developed into a real beauty; her body matched the beauty of her face. She was getting to be a real headache, as she began to be a big flirt with the men.

The Daniels provided the best as they could for Precious, but she was getting bored with nothing to do. She would tease the men in this community, and she began to go out with some of them. Precious soon got herself a real bad reputation, and she was the talk of the town. Precious would come to the Ovington's house as often as she stayed in her own house. She would try to be friends with Thomas, but she wasn't very likeable to him, and he had nothing to do with her.

Now it was different with Willie Monroe, who began to notice this beauty, and tried to talk to her. The gossip grew wild as Precious began to mess around with Willie Monroe. She was in her late teens, and she walked with a wiggle that drove the men wild with desire, but how she bothered to even look at Willie Monroe was mind-blowing to these people. Most of the most faithful men in his community wanted to slip around with Precious.

When the ladies of this community felt threatened by this little hot number they all called Precious, the irate women went to the Daniels' house and tried to tell them about their wayward child. The Daniels listened in disbelief, refused to believe their stories, and ordered the women from their home.

The gossip about Precious' loose ways didn't hurt her as she continued to tease and flirt with the men of this community. Somehow the affair between Precious and Willie Monroe continued as she ceased to date anyone else, but the outrageous Precious still liked to flirt, but no one would pay her any attention anymore. Most men feared Willie Monroe, and would not take a chance of antagonizing him. Laura always thought of Precious as a child, and she didn't believe the stories of her husband and this girl, who she had known since she was six years old. But Laura began to hear stories of the two meeting at various places around the little community, and this made more trouble in the Ovington house, and more sorrow for the unhappy Laura, and Thomas only felt more sorrow for his mother.

Thomas didn't think too much of the gossip, nor did he pay any attention to his father; he was always a child that loved his mother, and he wasn't too fond of his father, because of the way he was treated as a child by Willie Monroe. He remembered the times his mother was abused so badly, and how she would cry for hours, she was always protective of Thomas whenever she thought his father was abusing him as well.

On one of Thomas' bad days, he was walking past the old shed on his parents' land. The shed only contained a lot of junk, things they had no use for – when Thomas heard a noise coming from the shed. He was curious, and he went to the shed and looked in. Thomas got the shock of his life; he never would have dreamed he would see his father and this woman they called Precious engaged in coitus together. His Father never bothered to stop this act of fornication as he looked up into his son's shocked face.

When father and son met one another again, Thomas only looked at his father with hate in his heart. Willie Monroe tried to talk to his son, but the two began to argue, and Willie Monroe slapped his son so hard, he fell to the ground. Thomas ran up the hill, the one place he was always afraid to venture out into, the rugged and dangerous hill of the mountain. The places that had not been cleared were the most dangerous to the people that did not know how to take care of themselves.

These were bad times for Thomas, once he was so frightened of the mountain, but now he found peace among the wild as he sat alone. He began to consider this place his favorite place whenever he was unhappy. Thomas was able to see over into Little Valley. He would see the people as they went about their daily jobs of taking care of their families. He would see some of the people at various times as they would come up into the community to visit, or do odd jobs for some of them. As Thomas watched over into the valley, he observed the people and became curious about them. He could see they were a little different, they stayed to themselves, but the thing he observed was they always seemed to be happy and were close to each other, and he made up his mind to visit this valley, although none of the residents of Ovington ever went to this valley except to get some of the men to work for them.

On one of the unhappy days when Thomas was feeling alone, he was so curious about these people in the valley, he decided to visit, and get acquainted with the people. He was known by most of the people as the son of Willie Monroe. Thomas was a loner, and he rarely visited anyone, he stayed around his mother most of the time. Of course, the residents of Ovington didn't visit the Ovington's house anymore, since Willie Monroe was considered such a disgrace to this community. Laura was too afraid to venture too far out into the mountain, she stayed home most of the time; she knew how the neighbors felt about her family, and she was ashamed of the way her husband had disgraced the Ovington name.

Thomas finally got enough nerve to visit the people in Little Valley. He was curious about them, they looked friendly, and he was hoping he could be friends with them. They looked at Thomas with curiosity, knowing he was the son of Willie Monroe, but they were a little shocked to see him visit in their valley since no one that young would come into their home just to be friendly, especially an Ovington, since Willie

Monroe was such a bad man to deal with at times.

The Tuckers, who were still the largest family in the valley, welcomed him, but still looked at him with curiosity, wondering what he wanted. Thomas was a little nervous himself, and almost ran from all of the stares by these people, but he told them he had come to visit and to get a chance to know them. Once the tension was gone, he made himself at home.

Of the four Tucker daughters, three had passed, and only the youngest, Mattie, was still living. She was the matriarch of the Williams family. Mattie had married Derrick Williams, and they were the parents of eight children.

Mattie, being the youngest of the Tucker girls, was always babied by her father and sisters. None of her other sisters were ever married, and after the death of their father, they were protective of their youngest sister Mattie.

Lillian was the oldest, and she was the midwife in this valley, and she was the meanest among the girls. She was known to fight a man, and most of the time she would win, and none of the men in this valley would marry her. Although Lillian and her other two sisters were never married, they dated and were involved in some very sensuous love affairs.

Thomas would visit many of the residents in Little Valley, once he got to know them, but the Williams were the ones he was partial to, they were his favorite family. He loved Mattie and her family. Mattie was a big woman, she loved to cook, and would invite Thomas to eat with them. Thomas was so amazed at so many people in one house, but he enjoyed being with this family.

Mattie would spoil Thomas, he loved the way she would make over him, and he loved the family's closeness, the good times he would have whenever he would visited them. Mattie, being a big woman, could be rough with her family if they got out of hand. Thomas would remember the time he was playing with two of Mattie's boys, Grady and Steve; when the playing got rough, Steve threw the piss pot at his brother, drenching Thomas along with his brother. The incident was hilarious to Thomas, but now Mattie was furious, and she got downright violent with her sons.

Derrick Williams' family and the Tuckers did not get along too well, being rivals with the bootlegging business. The white people around the mountain, always came around to check out the still operation, and when they would need some of the moonshine to tide them over, they would come into the Valley and have them to make up a lot for their families or sometimes they sold it for their own gain.

Everyone was surprised when Mattie and Derrick married, since Mattie was a Tucker and Derrick was a Williams. There were bad times for the two families at first, but the tension soon ceased when Mattie and Derrick began to have children, and they soon were close to each other.

When Thomas became close to the Williams, he would visit them often, and he loved Mattie so much, he trusted her enough to talk over his problem with her. After he had another bad fight with his father, Thomas was in a depressed mood, and he decided to visit Mattie. She knew Thomas was having problem with his family, and she decided he needed some of her "medicine," as she called the jug of moonshine, that was always kept under the kitchen table.

Thomas reluctantly took the small cup she offered him, and he sipped the liquor, and soon began to relax, although he felt rather dizzy. This warmth he felt from this jug of moonshine gave him the courage to face the bad times he had in his home.

Thomas would look at his mother sometimes, and the tears would fall down his cheek, he could see the lines in her face, and he knew she was failing fast. The once beautiful Laura, the daughter of a beautiful set of parents, she was a intelligent woman, but the way his father had broken her spirit, caused Thomas to crave for the moonshine to ease his suffering as he could see his mother had lost her will to live.

Mattie had lots of children and grandchildren, but she believed in discipline, and she ruled her children along with her husband Derrick. He was sort of henpecked, but there was no back talk, or sassy children in her house, and she advised Thomas to ignore the trouble between his parents, and not to get involved, but the two families were different, and the conditions were far apart, and hard for Thomas to ignore.

Thomas always seemed to get into many fights with his father, and he began to go into Little Valley often to get a little of Mattie's medicine, he had learned how to handle the liquor a little better, and he finally persuaded Mattie to give him a jug for him to take home. Mattie gave him a whole jug, and he hid this jug under his bed; he would sip from this jug when he was depressed or in a bad mood.

As Thomas began his late teens, he experienced feelings that frightened him – the feeling of passion as his body would cry out for love of a woman. But he didn't understand these feelings, and he had no one to talk to, since he and his father weren't close, and he was too ashamed to talk to his mother.

Thomas had grown into a tall, handsome man. He had the dark hair and slim body of the Crawford family. His lean body walked with a fast pace, since he was known to climb the hills up the mountain, and he went into Little Valley quite often. Although Thomas was a very handsome young man, the girls were indifferent to him, because of his father's involvement with Precious, which was no secret anymore.

The loneliness was unbearable for Thomas, and he worried about his mother Laura, who had slipped into a world of her own. Laura would stare into the open space at nothingness for hours at a time. She had ceased to pay any attention to Willie Monroe. Thomas spent many lonely nights remembering the shameful way his parents carried on, and his father's cruelty to his mother, which was the cause of her condition. Willie Monroe began to worry and feel guilty about the way he treated his wife, but he loved Precious, and he refused to give her up.

Precious was the most beautiful woman in Ovington. She never had to work, unlike the other women who had to work to help their men, and do other heavy work. Precious spent her time looking pretty, and trying to get the men to notice her as she strolled around this community.

After a long and shameful relationship with Willie Monroe, Precious began to tire of him; he was getting old, and the bulge around the middle was becoming unattractive to her. Precious began to slip out with other men, but they were few, because most of the men were still afraid of Willie Monroe. Precious soon noticed Thomas, the handsome man no one had claimed, and she set her trap to get him. Precious knew Thomas hated her, but she began to watch his movements. He only went two places around this community: to see his friends in Little Valley, or to his favorite place up in the mountain. Unlike most of the woman in Ovington, Precious wasn't afraid to go into the mountain alone.

Thomas had a bad day, and he went to get his jug that Mattie always supplied for him; he was feeling low, and decided to go to his favorite place in the mountain. He drank a little too much of his moonshine, and the tears started to flow when Precious approached him.

There was nothing but hate for Precious by Thomas and his mother, but Thomas was almost drunk, or he would never have allowed her near him. Precious laid down beside Thomas and started to caress his body, making sure she kept Thomas occupied enough as she teased him with foreplay. She stripped him of his clothing, and he was aroused to the point he couldn't control himself. The poor lad who never had the pleasure of a woman, and didn't understand this feeling that he had no control over. Precious covered her body with his as she taught Thomas the movement that sent shock and feelings through his body that he never knew existed as he gave in to her voluptuous body, trembling and crying at the same time.

Thomas soon realized the shameful thing he had done, and he ran out into the most treacherous part of the mountain. He wanted to be bitten by one of the poisonous snakes that slithered throughout the mountain, or be harmed by one of the other dangerous animals. Looking out into open space, Thomas could see the thickness of the trees, branches, and rocks. He was a little frightened of what was ahead for him, but he made up his mind, he could not stay in this community, named for his family any longer. Thomas slowly made his way home, and he knew he must leave Ovington.

Thomas went into Little Valley to see Mattie, he had to tell her he had decided to leave Ovington. Mattie started to cry, and she begged him to stay. Thomas was close enough to the Williams to be one of their sons. Thomas loved the times he would slip down into the valley at night, and he would stay up half the night raising hell with the others, whenever they would get the jug of moonshine, and they would try to sing and do all sorts of silly things, and of course, Mattie was right there with them. The Williams gathered around Thomas, and joined Mattie in a tearful good-bye. They all loved Thomas, he was a part of their family, he had eaten and joined in the family gatherings for a long time, and it would not be the same without him. He promised them he would come back one day to see them, and he slowly left Little Valley.

Willie Monroe saw Thomas as he was coming up the hill into Ovington; he spoke to Thomas, and tried to be nice to Thomas for once, but Thomas could see his father was thinner, and his skin was pale, he looked awful. At that moment, Thomas felt sorry for his father, but remembering the past, and the unhappiness his father had caused him and his mother, he quickly disregarded that feeling.

As Thomas walked away from his father, he mumbled that he was leaving Ovington. Willie Monroe had heard rumors that Thomas was leaving the mountain. He knew he had not treated his son as a father should, but he was a stubborn man, he did not try to persuade his son to stay, he only wished him well, he showed no love, or regret that he was leaving.

Laura came out of her little world long enough to help Thomas collect his few belongings, and cried as she helped him pack. Thomas embraced his mother, felt the thinness of her body, and the tears were wet on his cheeks; he knew his mother would be put to rest soon. Thomas hated to leave his mother with his father, but he felt like it would be easier if he did not see his mother suffer in her last days. Laura cried, and she begged him to take care of himself as Thomas kissed her for the last time.

Precious heard the news that Thomas was leaving, and bold as she was, she went looking for him. When Precious found Thomas, she begged him to take her with him. Spewing with anger, he lashed out at Precious, calling her Rose Ann, the name she was given when she was born, because there was nothing Precious about her. Thomas advised her to never come near him again, and the look of anger, and the hatred Rose Ann could see on Thomas' face made her run from him frightened.

Thomas did not bother to see any of the other residents around Ovington, he knew what the people thought of him and his family. He had tears in his eyes as he slowly left Ovington, and he began his trip down the mountain.

3

Thomas, making the long and treacherous trip off the mountain, had no idea where he was going. He stopped at many places along the way for work so that he could eat. Only a few of these places were able to help him. The people were very poor and lived in shacks. He was given poorly cooked food in some of the poorest stables. As Thomas traveled down the mountain he became tired, and weary. His health was failing from walking such a long distance. He had cried so many tears. Thomas was suffering from many stings bites made by insects. A couple of times his feet had been cut by rocks with sharp edges. Thomas didn't know at the time, but he was only 40 miles from his homeland. Suddenly, he came upon this beautiful farmland that belonged to the Cannons. This was the most beautiful scenery he had ever seen in his life.

Thomas was very hungry, and he looked as though he had not eaten for a while. He was afraid to go inside of the neat picket fence. He had never seen so many animals. There were many cows, horses, and other animals that grazed on the beautiful farmland. Thomas could see people at various places on the farm. He went inside the fence to see if he would be welcome, so that, he could find work.

The house that sat on the Cannon's farm was amazing. Thomas discovered that this was the home of James Robert Cannon, and his daughter, Beth Marie Cannon. They lived in the big farmhouse located on the land. This house was of the finest constructed material, and one of the biggest he had ever seen. He stood in astonishment as he looked at the farm. He had never seen a house so big, certainly not in Ovington. This town that Thomas had stopped in was called Lawsonville.

Thomas first talked to Jay about employment. Thomas asked for food, and whether help was needed. Thomas was introduced to a huge man called Samuel. Most of the workers called him Sam. When Thomas asked for a job, Sam looked at him for a long time. Sam thought Thomas was too small for this type of work. He finally decided to give him a job. Sam seen to it that Thomas was fed, since he looked, as though he was starving. Sam wanted to be sure that Thomas was strong enough to do farm work, which wasn't easy.

Thomas cleaned up and he was given food. He was shown around the farm. His duties were assigned to him. The work was difficult since, Thomas never really worked. He had never done any hard physical labor. Thomas didn't want to return back home to the mountain, so he did his best. There were many things he had to learn about farming. It didn't look like he would ever get caught up with his work.

Thomas had been on the Cannon farm for over a month before he had a chance to meet James Cannon. As Thomas spoke to this man, James could see that Thomas was a little different than most of the other workers. Thomas was nervous when he first met James. He tried to be on his best behavior, and was very careful with his language. He tried to speak intelligently as his mother had tried to teach him. He refrained from using the slang language that many people in this part of Tennessee commonly used.

James was impressed that Thomas could read and write. He even noticed that Thomas was able to carry on an interesting conversation. James asked Thomas about himself and his family. He invited Thomas to have dinner with him and his daughter sometime. Thomas felt nervous about having dinner with the boss, and his daughter. He had never been around such high-class people. The Cannon family had such a beautiful huge farm home that Thomas felt uncomfortable having dinner with them.

There was a big turnover with the workers at times, but James let his overseer take care of the workers. He only got involved when there were real big problems. James would see Thomas from time to time, and he always enjoyed talking with him. Thomas could sense that James Cannon was fond of him. James thought that Thomas had the potential of being a big businessman as himself. He didn't think that Thomas would have any problems running a farm like his.

James Cannon decides to replace Samuel. He liked Samuel a lot, but James knew that Samuel spoke abusively to the employees he supervised. Samuel had fired two men for no good reason. James decided that he had to replace him, and he asked Thomas to take this position. Thomas didn't take the position right away, but he later did. Of course, this new position made Thomas nervous. He had never been the boss of anyone. He didn't know what his new duties would be.

Thomas tried to do a good job, but the men didn't respect Thomas as a boss. He stayed nervous most of the time. Thomas was too soft-hearted to be a supervisor. He wasn't used to ordering anyone to do anything, or threatening to fire them if their work wasn't up to par. Thomas didn't last very long on this new position. He decided that this job was not for him, so he soon resigned.

James was very fond of Thomas, and he treated him like a son. Thomas had reminded him of his deceased son. James had missed his son so much before Thomas came to the farm. He thought that having Thomas around was like his son being with him again.

James encouraged Thomas to enroll in school. Lawsonville was a small town, but there were few outstanding buildings. One of them was a nice school, since they believed in having a good school. Thomas was advised to get some type of business training, and enrolled in some of the business classes that they offered. At first, Thomas had many problems keeping up with the rest of the competitive students. The training he received from his mother was what helped him to pass his courses. Thomas was fortunate to finish his education in business. He was elated when he received this degree. He quickly found a job in the business field.

Thomas was hired by the only bank in Lawsonville. Their weren't many white-collar jobs in Lawsonville, but with James' help, Thomas was given a job at the bank. Being able to read and write wasn't enough in this busy, complex, and hectic pace of the business world. Thomas was glad that James had advised him to educate himself in the business field, because this job was so stressful that he was glad he had been trained to handle himself in a job that deals with the public.

The Cannons were the wealthiest family in upper East Tennessee. James Robert Cannon had migrated from the East. He had decided to move to Tennessee after having trouble with other big stockholders and financiers in the railroad business. There were many abuses in the railroad business, including a lot of favoritism among other big stockholders, especially among the shippers. James Cannon was an honest man; he loved to make money, but he detested crookedness within a business.

After losing his wife and only son back East, James decided to move to this part of Tennessee. He had been through every part of the country. He had traveled abroad with his small family, but this part of Tennessee was the land that he loved, with all of its beauty. Seeing the beautiful mountains, the forest of trees that seemed to never stop growing, he wanted to move to this part of Tennessee that he loved so much.

James loved animals, and had always wanted to have enough land so that he could raise as many animals as he wanted. This was his choice, and he bought acres of this land, and built up the surrounding ground adjoining his home that he occupied with his daughter.

This change in James' life was the best thing he could have done. James and Beth Marie were the only two left of the family of four. James' son, Louis, and his wife, Martha, had died before they moved to Tennessee. Beth was a small woman, no raving beauty, but she had class written all over her. Beth was James Cannon's heart. She was spoiled, and she ruled her father; he let her do as she pleased. She had dated some back East, but in Lawsonville, she wasn't very popular, and had never married. When James decided to move to Tennessee, Beth decided to move with him, although she was grown, and didn't want to leave Eastern New York that she loved so much. Missing her mother and brother, her father was all that she had left.

James came from a family of business venture people. He was highly educated, a whiz with figures; he knew how to make a dollar, and invested it wisely. He made large investments with railroad stocks and bonds, and he invested in some import of various trade goods. If James thought a business would make money, he would take a chance, and always succeeded; he was a tycoon when it came to business and making money.

The Cannon's house had servants consisting of Fred Hudson, and Anna Lee Jackson, two black employees who came from back East with the Cannons. They were the only ones to live in the main house beside the Cannons.

Fred had worked for the Cannons nearly 30 years, doing various jobs, mostly inside the house. He was used to doing any and everything for the Cannons, he had been with the family so long, he wasn't used to anyone else, and didn't want to be with anyone but the Cannon family. Anna was employed with the family some 20 years or more when Beth was just a baby. There had been two other Black servants in the Cannon household, but they died before the family had moved to Tennessee.

James was getting on in years, about 68, and had begun to worry about Beth. He knew he had enough money for the rest of her life, but being an unmarried woman, he was concerned about her welfare; she needed someone to take care of her. Beth was well educated and a very smart woman, she had been sociable back East, but she wasn't very likeable in Tennessee. Most of the women in Lawsonville considered Beth too fancy for this part of the country, and she talked much too proper.

Beth was unhappy, staying inside the house most of the time, beside her father. She only talked to Fred and Anna. Beth played the piano well, and had been a classical pianist back East. This was a comfort to her to be able to play some her favorite songs when she was lonely. Beth would have the Phaeton that James had brought her some years ago, hitched by two of the finest Cannon horses on the farm, and she would ride to the main section of town to shop occasionally at the few stores in Lawsonville, or ride around the countryside to ward off boredom.

Knowing her father's health wasn't up to par, Beth had given some thought to her father leaving her all alone, but she had some distant relatives back East. Beth wished they would move to Tennessee to be company to her and her father. The relatives never accepted the invitation that the Cannons sent to them to visit their home.

Fred and Anna had their own duties. Fred was older, but he wasn't sure about his age. He loved the Cannons, and was willing to move to Tennessee, though his family all lived back East. Anna Jackson was alone, she claimed to have been married once, but said her husband left one day, and never returned to her, or let her know his whereabouts. Beth was curious about Fred and Anna sometimes. Although they slept in different parts of the house, Beth suspected there was a love affair between them. Beth would see them giving each other a sign that seemed to be some sort of a code to meet, and she assumed they were meeting secretly.

Beth would see Thomas at various times, and knew he was shy and felt uneasy around her. But she liked this handsome young man. He seemed intelligent, and she knew her father liked Thomas very much. Beth decided to invite Thomas to dinner and had Fred to drive her to the little rooming house where Thomas was staying. Thomas was surprised to see Beth, and after small talk between the two, Beth asked

Thomas to join her and her father for dinner as a guest, not as one of the farm hands. This invitation was a surprise to him, but he accepted. The dinner was the beginning of a friendship between Thomas and Beth.

The biggest building in Lawsonville was the County Court House. Of course, there was a small tavern that was a popular place for the men to hang out in this rather dull town. The bank, where Thomas worked, was his life. James would have liked it better if Thomas had stayed on the farm and become the overseer of his huge farmland, since he was getting old and he needed someone to take over; he wasn't able to cover the grounds as he once did when he moved to this place. Thomas loved his job at the bank, and he thanked James for helping him gain employment suitable for him, he loved this man as a father, and he visited him regularly. Thomas liked Beth, but she was no beauty. She was so high class, and seemed to be above the people in Lawsonville. But he was nice to her, and always went to have dinner with the Cannons when he was invited, but he never considered this woman to be the one he would marry.

Thomas, like the Cannons, was different than most of the residents in Lawsonville. Their ways were more intelligent, and their attire was different than the simple ways that the people dressed, and their lifestyles were very simple. Most of the residents were just plain, talked very slowly, and used non-intelligible languages at times.

Most of the residents in Lawsonville liked James. Even though he was wealthy, and most of the people knew this, he treated the people very kindly. But Beth was one to turn up her nose at these people when they had moved to Tennessee, and they had not forgotten this. Although Beth had tried to change her ways, since she was so alone with only Fred and Anna to talk to, and sometimes they could not be found. Beth had to find ways to ward off boredom; she would play her piano for hours, the kind of music that drove Fred and Anna crazy, since the classical arrangements she was trained to play weren't their kind of music.

Thomas would see someone from Ovington occasionally; he would ask about his family, and the residents in Little Valley. There were times he missed the mountain, and the people he loved back home, but he knew how the people felt about him and his family, the way his father had disgraced him and his mother, by the shameful way he carried on, and the way he treated his family. This lonely feeling would come over

Thomas when he thought about his home and the beautiful mountain, but he still stayed away from home.

Thomas would continue to go to the Cannon's house, and although he liked Beth, he wasn't in love with her. He tried dating other girls, but he never tried to get personally involved with them, because his memories of Precious, and the time he was intimate with her, always brought back painful memories, full of the shame he had felt.

Sometimes Thomas would get lonely. Remembering the moonshine that the Williams used to bootleg, and how much he liked the liquor, made him want to visit the little tavern. But this was a different kind of liquor than he was used to. The little bar was always full, and you could meet all of kinds of people, but Thomas was more of a loner, and rarely made friends with these people.

The years went by fast for Thomas. He had been in Lawsonville about seven years, when word reached him that his mother had passed, and his father was in poor health. Thomas was very upset, as he loved his mother very much, and he felt great sorrow within, but he never went home to the mountain.

Thomas would remember the times his mother tried to protect him from the many abuses from his father. He knew his mother was unhappy, and the last years of her life, she just gave up on life, and she existed in a world of her own; her mental breakdown had been caused by her unhappiness over his father.

The painful memories Thomas had of his mother made him unhappy; he decided the liquor eased his pain he suffered so much and would go to the little tavern, and drink until he felt at peace with himself. Remembering the times he would go to Mattie's house, and he would get the jug of moonshine, and ease his pain; he felt that this was the best way to rid himself of guilt and shame he suffered sometimes when he remembered his childhood.

Every town has its brothel house, and Lawsonville was no different. Thomas had heard about this house that had ladies that would make love for a price. After many drinks from this little tavern, Thomas had enough courage to visit this establishment. He was embarrassed to ask for one of the ladies, because he had not touched a woman since he had been with Precious back home, and he was ashamed to even touch a woman now.

But his lonely nights were getting the best of him. He was able to seek the company of a lady of the brothel house, but he could not handle seeing her well-endowed breasts, and her nakedness, and he ran from the house in fright and shame. He could only feel loathing and shame for himself. He remembered Precious' boldness, and this woman was reacting the same way, and he went home too ashamed to think about being lonely at this time.

There were times when Thomas would visit the Cannons, and he always had a good time with the people that helped him get where he was in the business world, but he longed for a woman to ease his loneliness. At these times, Thomas would go the tavern, where he met a woman named Ledia Summers. She was a sweet and lovely woman, and looked as if she didn't belong in this tavern with all of these low class people, but she hung out in this tavern most of the time.

Ledia Summers was a thin, but rather tall, woman. She could see the first time she talked to Thomas that he was scared to get to close to a woman, and she tried to help him get over this fear. Ledia was one person that Thomas was friendly with, and he looked forward to seeing her when he visited the tavern. Ledia was an innocent type of person, and she and Thomas became close. He felt more comfortable with Ledia than any one else. Ledia taught Thomas to relax, gave him lessons in loving a woman, showing him tricks that were unbelievable to Thomas. She gave him lessons in passionate love, and he soon lost his shyness and his fear of women, and he looked forward to bedding with his favorite woman, which was Ledia.

Thomas was fond of Ledia, and he felt that he loved this woman, but knowing that this woman came from the tavern, and not in good standing in this community, he could never think of marrying her for she would not fit into his life, but he wanted to help her start a new life. Thomas approached Ledia and offered to help her start a business, if she would leave the tavern, and start a new life for herself, Ledia had tears in her eyes as she told Thomas she loved him, and would like to marry him. Thomas was seriously thinking of marrying, but he knew she would not fit into his life, especially since he had met the Cannons, and seen the kind of life he would like, rather than where he had come from when he lived in Ovington.

Thomas had been in Lawsonvillle approximately 10 years when one of the residents from Ovington came after Thomas. Willie Monroe was critically ill, and refused to die until he saw his son once again. This was devastating to Thomas because he had hated his father all of these years. But to hear that he was dying shocked Thomas enough that he knew that he loved his father even though they had many differences throughout the years that he was growing up.

Thomas went to see the Cannons, and he explained to James the reason for his leaving Lawsonville for awhile. He asked James if he could borrow two of his horses, so that he could rotate riding them to travel home. One horse would soon get tired from the steep and sharply sloped hills that he had to travel home to the mountain.

The railroad system in Tennessee had many transitions and set-backs in this state before getting the transportation started. The railroad had cleared the thickly wooded area surrounding the mountain and was in the process of laying the tracks near the mountains. Thomas had no trouble going home, because of the cleared pathway, he rode one horse, and led the other one, and then rotated.

Before arriving at his home, he could see a few of the neighbors outside his father's house as he approached. Thomas could hear his father's moans and cries of pain. Entering the house, he could hardly stand the smell. He slowly walked to his father's bedside, and he spoke comforting words to him.

Tears swelled Thomas' eyes as he tried to understand his father's whisper as he tried to talk to him, and he said he wished he had been a better father to him when he was growing up. Willie Monroe told Thomas he loved him, and he had loved his mother. He begged Thomas to bury him   beside his mother, and said that he loved Laura in his own way, but it was too late to amend for what he had done to her. She had ceased to listen to him, and she never believed him when he tried to tell her he loved her, and he wanted to make up for his wrong doing and regain her love.

Willie Monroe had no written will, but he verbally gave all of his possessions and his land to Thomas. At this time, Thomas wanted nothing from his father, but he sat beside his bed, and tried not to think about the past.

Willie Monroe's shallow breathing lasted throughout the night. He would awake for short period of time, and he would tell Thomas that he loved him, and asked him to move back to Ovington. This land belonged to the Ovington family for a long time, and he begged Thomas to come home. Thomas held his father's hand, and he quietly expired.

Willie Monroe was buried beside his wife Laura. Thomas and a few of the neighbors attended Willie Monroe's funeral.

Thomas felt helpless as he went back to his parents' home. He remembered the unhappy times there; he remembered the times his mother taught him to read and write, and told him stories of his forefather, and of the Civil War. Most of all, he remembered the times his mother tried to protect him from his father's abuses.

Some of the neighbors came in to help Thomas clean the house. The house was so different than when his mother was living. Laura had kept an immaculate house, and to look at the uncleanness of this house now, and the terrible smell, was more than Thomas could bear. He sat down in despair. The neighbors, so indifferent to him and his family before he left Ovington, were nice to him now. They offered to do whatever they could to assist him, and they brought food for him, after they had gotten the house back in order.

Thomas asked one of the families that lived on his father's place to oversee the house for him, and to take care of its surrounding land until he decided what he would do with his parents' home. At this time, Thomas wasn't interested in staying in Ovington.

There was a man that lived in Ovington named Frank Carter, with a wife and several children. This man was a womanizer just as Willie Monroe. Frank Carter had a son named Jeffrey, who was about 16 at this time. Jeffrey and his father had many fights, and he showed bruises from the beating he received from his father.

Jeffrey came to Thomas after he had been in Ovington about two weeks, asking if he could help him. Jeffrey wanted to leave home, he wanted no parts of this mountain, he was planning to leave on his own before Thomas came back to town, but he decided to ask Thomas help in leaving, because he knew nothing about any place to settle outside Ovington.

Seeing the bruises over Jeffrey's body made Thomas feel sorry for this young man, and reminded him of the times he was home, and the same bruises would be on his body. Thomas could not promise Jeffrey any hope until he had a talk with his parents. Thomas knew how the people were in Ovington. Regardless of what the parents did to their children, no one interfered.

Jeffrey was a bright young man, although he could not read or write. Thomas was nearing 30, and he was neither married, or was a father to any children. Because he felt Jeffrey was experiencing some of the same abuses he had suffered, he wanted to try to help this young man, and educate him. In spite of his fear of Jeffrey's father, he promise Jeffrey that he would talk to Frank Carter before he left Ovington. If Frank agreed to let him leave home, Thomas would take full responsibility for Jeffrey.

The people in Little Valley had not come up to Willie Monroe's house when he died, although they knew Thomas was home. Thomas decided to visit his friends, since he had not seen them in about ten years. He still loved Mattie, and he would never leave Ovington without going to see her and her family.

The people in Little Valley told Thomas they had been looking for him. The welcome mat was out for him; they were all ready for him as they had food cooked and, of course, they had the jug of moonshine ready and waiting for him. Thomas kissed Mattie, and held her so tightly. She was as robust as ever. The Williams' clan was all there, and they kept trying to hug Thomas, and they were all talking at once.

The Williams' house was always the first house that Thomas would visit, because Mattie was his favorite person. He would go to see her before he visited anyone else, he loved this woman so much; he would never forget her, because she had helped him through some very bad times in his young life. As usual they all greeted Thomas warmly, and they offered their sympathy for the passing of his father.

Mattie was elated to see Thomas all grown, and so handsome and mature. Thomas had the dark hair and piercing blue eyes of the Crawford family, and he had his mother's slimness. Mattie was amazed at how handsome Thomas was, and not even married.

Mattie still kept the jug of moonshine under he kitchen table; she offered Thomas a glass, which she still called her "medicine," and Thomas found out he liked this liquor better than the liquor he was used to drinking at the little tavern in Lawsonville.

Thomas was feeling a little dizzy, but he was determined to visit the other residents of valley. He went throughout the valley to greet many of the people that he used to visit when he was living on this mountain.

The conditions were the same, but Thomas was older, and had been used to better living conditions, so he was shocked to see the deplorable conditions that still existed in Ovington. The housing was so bad, he could see out into the open space in some of them, and he knew the people would be cold when the winter months were here, and the mountain would be covered by the many snowfalls they usually had in the winter.

The winters in the mountain were the worst, because the snow usually fell most of the winter months, and it was hard on the people. Many of these people had problems with respiratory illnesses apparently caused by the conditions in which they live. Many of the children died at an early age; of the many children born in this mountain, some of them were stillborn.

Thomas always loved these people, and they loved him. He was always welcome to those he visited. Thomas decided to visit the Adams, which were Suzette and her husband Roy Adams. They had two children. Suzette was the midwife in Little Valley, since there was no doctor on this mountain at this time. She was the only person that knew how to bring a baby into this world, and take care of the mothers. She was trusted and admired by all of the expectant mothers.

Suzette was as big woman as her mother Mattie. She was very pretty and skilled in her profession. She had learned midwifery from her Aunt Lillian, who was the midwife before her.

After visiting with Suzette and her family, she told Thomas of her mother's illness, which was unknown at this time. This distressed Thomas, but he believed that Mattie looked fine to him, and dismissed this as something minor and not too serious.

Thomas said his good-byes to all that he had seen. He was feeling a little sorry for the people that lived here, but they seemed happy in spite of their hardships.

As Thomas reached the top of the steep hill leading out of the valley, he looked over and could see all of its beauty, and these were beautiful people to him. Thomas was still partial to these people that he loved so much when he was growing up. The only times he was really happy and felt like he would survive the hard times he suffered in his home, was when these people helped him to overcome his unhappy childhood.

There was a small creek that ran throughout the valley. Thomas looked down into the stream. He saw many wild flowers lined upon the bank reflection in the small stream. The tall trees lined above the valley completely hid it and he felt elated that his forefathers had worked so hard to build up into a home atop this mountain.

Thomas deplored the condition these people had to live in. The people in this valley were in need, and Thomas knew he would find a way to help them. Thomas walked home and sat down to try to think of a way that he could do something for the whole community.

The Little Valley atop this mountain was the only flat area around, with all its hills and rocks above this area. The small creek ran around the full length of the mountain, completely down and off this community. The creek always seemed to have plenty of water to supply the whole community. There was a little spring that was rocked around, that provided most of the drinking water in the valley.

The people were very poor, but they survived off the land. There were many wild animals and lots of roots and berries for them to eat. They also knew how to make medicine from many of these roots. Making moonshine had always been a way for these people to make a few dollars, as they made enough to sell sometime, which was against the law, but it was only a small operation, and no threat of anyone being caught and jailed. No records of anything were kept in the valley, so no one really knew what was legal and what was not. Some people weren't sure they were married or not, because there no legal papers were given to them, and some were not sure of the dates of their children's' births. They just assumed everything was legal. There were occasions of violent fights, and someone would be killed, but the murderer, if he was found in the wrong, was outcast, and soon had to leave the community of the valley.

Many of the young ladies were married when they reached early teens, some as young as 13. There were no schools at this time, so the only thing they had to do was to get married, and keep house. Marrying so young, they often had children at a very young age. A few of the young ladies died in childbirth, often leaving a baby that had survived the traumatic labor and birth.

Thomas was the only white man to visit the valley, and being so close to these people when he was growing up, the Hill people came around, but never stayed long or be invited to their gathering as Thomas was always invited to be with them if they were having something special. Thomas was treated as their own, and they loved him. These people would come up the Hill to Ovington only if they needed something, or were bringing something to sell, but went home when business was finished.

There was beautiful singing in the valley when the people got together to celebrate something. They were happy that Thomas was home, and they were thrilled that he had come to see them, and spend some time with them. They had no fine instruments, but the music they made with their hand-made instruments gave a joyful noise, and they really would sing and clap their hands, especially if they had a little moonshine to go with the event.

When Thomas was just sitting in his parents' home, Jeffrey Carter visited him, and begged Thomas to take him with him when he left this mountain. Jeffrey knew that Thomas was leaving soon and he wanted to go with him. He was determined to leave home, and he wanted to go with Thomas. He was frightened of leaving home, but he knew he would be safe if he went with Thomas.

Thomas went to see Jeffrey's father, to ask his permission to take Jeffrey with him to Lawsonville when he left to go home. Frank Carter, a mean, bad-tempered man, was reluctant to let Jeffrey leave home, fearing he was too young. Frank Carter had a hard time feeding his big family, and agreed to Jeffrey leaving home, fearing he would run away one day soon anyway. He felt better knowing Jeffrey would be leaving with Thomas to look out for him in a strange town.

When the residents found out that Thomas was leaving soon, they came to his home to find out if he needed anything. Thomas was amazed at the way they were treating him now compared to the way he was treated when he was growing up in this community. They used to act like they hated him and his family during his childhood.

Thomas had heard that the outrageous Precious had left this mountain, and he was glad she was no longer a part of this community. After the Daniels had passed, she no longer had anyone to care for her. She had gotten tired of Willie Monroe, and refused to have anything else to do with him. She finally left with a man who came to this mountain to visit and she hadn't been seen since. Thomas was glad he didn't have to be reminded of the painful memories of this woman.

Thomas decided to walk around this community before he left to go home. He went up to his retreated area that he loved when he was living in Ovington. He could see over into the areas of this mountain, he could see through the trees down into the valley, and Thomas knew he would try to do the impossible, but his dream would become a reality, he would build his home atop this mountain.

The long walk down the steep hill into the living area of Ovington made Thomas decide to come home. His dreams were to make this community a better place to live. Thomas thought of a school, a big and better school for the children, also one for the valley; he would see that there was a good school built here in Ovington. There were no businesses in this community, and he would see if he could have some stores or something to help the people from traveling miles just shop at a store. This community was a beautiful place, and Thomas wanted the Ovington's name to remain a part of this community. Thomas was the only survivor, and he knew it was left up to him whether or not the name lived on in his community. Thomas left an overseer to look after his family home; he hated this place in his young life, but he would try to honor his father's last request.

Thomas and Jeffrey made the long trip off the mountain. Jeffrey was very tired once they reached Lawsonville. Jeffrey was as elated as Thomas once they reached their destination. He looked wide-eyed in disbelief at this huge farmland. He knew he would be happy in such a beautiful place. Jeffrey made acquaintances with the Cannons. He was invited to stay at their home since he was so young. Beth liked Jeffrey, and James Cannon made him feel right at home, though they knew nothing about this young man, but since Thomas brought him to the farm, they accepted him and made him welcome. Jeffrey was bashful and needed to feel at ease since he was meeting strangers.

Beth took Jeffrey to his room, and invited him to eat something with her after his long trip. Beth agreed to help Jeffrey, and she offered to teach him some schooling since he could neither read nor write, and was a frightened young lad.

The first thing Beth taught Jeffrey was to pronounce his words clearly. Beth being so proper with her words, made Jeffrey say each word until he was almost as proper with words as she was. Jeffrey was tutored by Beth for over a year and a half before he was able to be enrolled in high school; by this time, he was almost 18 years old.

James was very fond of Jeffrey. This young man had nothing but a few personal items when he came to the Cannons, but James promised him he would help him pay for his education, if he wanted to go to a good school for further training after high school.

Jeffrey would do odd jobs around the farm for his room and board, because he wanted to pay his way, and he was trying to make it on his own. Sometime Thomas would give money to Jeffrey for clothes and personal items, but he accepted very little from Thomas and received nothing from his home and family, but he tried hard to make it on the little help from Thomas and the Cannons.

After being back in Lawsonville for a while, Thomas began worrying about his parents' home in Ovington. He knew he had to do something about the property. Thomas had saved only about $3,000 at the bank where he worked, and he had no other assets.

The thought of making a loan was distasteful to Thomas, but he nervously went to James, and asked him for a large loan for $20,000 to purchase land in Ovington. Being a businessman, he had checked for deeds to the land in the valley, and knew there was no legal claim on any of the land. Thomas explained he would like to give the valley people legal papers to their home. These people had no ownership, they had found this land and settled on it years and years ago.

James, loving Thomas as a son, had a contract drawn up for the amount Thomas asked for. The agreement for repaying the loan was to pay five dollars back on each $100 paid back during a year. There was no time limit on paying the money back. James would have given the money to Thomas, he cared that much for him, but Thomas refused. Thomas had learned to make all transactions of business legal, and refused to have it any other way. James deposited the money in Thomas' name at the bank where he worked.

Twenty thousand dollars was an enormous amount of money to owe, and the worry of owing so much money made Thomas visit the tavern he always went to when he was nervous or unhappy. The drinks made him think of Ledia, the one person he could talk to and feel at ease with. He was thinking of Ledia, but he knew that James only let him have so much money, because he expected him to marry his daughter one day.

Thomas liked Beth, but he knew Beth was brought up in a different background than his. She was highly educated, and was used to finer things in life than he was, and she would expect more from him than he thought he would be able to give her. On the other hand, he did not love Ledia enough to marry her because she was no more than a street woman. She only knew the low life, and wasn't used to anything, but he could tell she was friendly, and she got along with everyone. Thomas wanted to help Ledia to change her lifestyle, he decided to set her up in some type of business so she could make a better life for herself.

Checking out the business opportunities in Lawsonville, he decided a ladies boutique would be the best business for a lady to run. After making inquires in this business, he proceeded to invest into this business. Thomas taught Ledia how to run a business, he taught her about material, what to look for, the type of clothes that were stylish, and he set Ledia up in business, unbeknownst to the people of Lawsonville. Thomas did all of this for Ledia for her being a good and loving woman to him.

Ledia was one woman that made Thomas feel at ease, but when he made love to her, he thought of her as a woman who was warm and he always loved to be with her, he was not shameful with her as he felt when he had made love to other women. Ledia was a comfort to him, she thrilled him beyond words, and he loved bedding with her, but he wanted a wife, and he knew he could not give Ledia his name.

James Cannon knew he was sick, but he pretended he was feeling good because of Beth, he still worried about Beth being alone. He was getting so dizzy he could hardly stand up and he made up his mind that he would get his finances together and appoint an executor to handle this estate and his other investments.

James knew this would be a big job trying to get all of his finances in order. He was the owner of a lot of investments, stocks, and bonds in various places. He really had no idea of his total worth.

James hired a lawyer back in New York, and a lawyer was hired in the State of Tennessee. All of his records were compiled and James discovered he was one of the richest men in the upper East Tennessee State. James Cannon's net worth was over a million dollars.

Since Beth Marie was never married, James did not have any grandchildren, and often wished for a grandchild. He prayed that Beth would be married, and have him a grandchild before he died. Wanting to see grandchildren to love and be a part of this farm that he loved so much, he began to try to hurry up a marriage between Thomas and Beth, since Thomas was the one that James wanted to marry Beth Marie. Although James was used to high living and fast cities most of his life, he knew this farm was the ideal place to raise children, and he loved living out his last days on this farm.

Beth Marie had no idea what her father wanted when he called her into his study one day. He told her he would not live long, and asked her to prepare herself for his pending death. Beth, being spoiled all of her life, knew one day she would have to be responsible for herself. Although she was wealthy, she would have to know how to keep her investments growing, and manage the upkeep of her home. Tears flowed from both their eyes as they discussed business matters, and expressed their love for each other.

James asked Thomas to come over at his convenience so he could discuss his affairs with him. Thomas thought of James as a father, knowing that he was responsible for him being able to go as far in the business world as he had, he was able to advance in the last ten years, because of James Cannon, and the way he had made him known and trusted in Lawsonville.

Thomas tried to hold back the tears, but as James discussed his affairs with him, he was very sad, especially when James told him to take care of Beth. Thomas, being a man, made no difference as James asked Thomas to marry Beth, and to take care of his daughter, whom he loved better than life itself. She was all that he had in this world that meant anything to him; his wealth was nothing without her. Thomas promised James he would marry Beth, and assured James that he would always care for Beth, and see that she suffered for nothing. James was satisfied that he could trust Thomas to do as he promised, to take care of Beth Marie. After the tearful discussion between Thomas and James, they got down to the serious business aspects, and of course, this was also painful for both of them.

James wanted to cancel the debt that Thomas owed him, but Thomas would not consent to this. He refused, and insisted the contract remain as arranged. Thomas was named the executor of James Cannon's will, and Beth Marie Cannon was willed all off his possessions, except five thousand dollars that James willed to Jeffrey Carter.

There were discussions about Fred and Anna. James knew that they would always be with Beth. They never left the Cannons house very much, and they didn't want for anything, plus he knew Beth would always see to their needs. Fred and Anna were both getting old, and had lost contact with their families, and they had no one else to care for them.

James sold some of his many beautiful horses, fine milk cows, and various other animals that he really had no use for; they were just to have around the farm. James loved animals, but Beth Marie wasn't too fond of them, so James felt that he should get rid of the animals that were not of use to anyone, only to have as pets.

Thomas began to drink a little too much, and was having trouble trying to sleep. He would think of Beth Marie and Ledia, the two women he loved in a different way. He was hoping that he had taken care of Ledia since he had not attempted to see her since he had set her up in a business. He decided, he should not be sitting in the tavern half of the night just to forget his troubles. Thomas knew he would have to pull his life together, and become a more responsible person.

4

Thomas decided to hire a surveyor because he was unsure of the legal claim to this land, and to determine the legal boundaries of each area of claimed land.

George Wells was one of the best surveyors in this part of Tennessee. Thomas hired him when he found out that he was also a great hunter. He felt that this man would not be fearful of the mountains. George was afraid of the areas that had not been lived on or cleared, because he knew of the danger of the many wild animals and poisonous snakes in that area. However, when he found out the salary he would be making, he agreed to go with Thomas to Ovington.

When Thomas and George made the trip, they were treated warmly. Everyone tried to make George feel right at home. The people really loved Thomas, and were all smiles. They acted like they had never hated him when he was growing up here. He felt like all ill feelings between his family and the residents of Ovington had been forgotten. Thomas was told by the residents of Ovington how they really missed having an Ovington in this Community.

The first thing that Thomas did was to take George to the valley to see the people that lived there. They were thrilled to see Thomas again, and thought Thomas had came to get into some more of their moonshine, so they could raise hell all night, as they typically did. Thomas explained to these people the importance of owning their land. He explained to them that they had no deeds, or any legal documents to prove that they had a right to the land they called home. He tried to explain how their land could be bought and they could be evicted, unless it was surveyed and marked according to the location they claimed, and a sum of money be paid for the land.

There were about 20 families in Little Valley. They trusted Thomas and agreed to let George survey and their land that they claimed. The marking, the walking, and the paperwork was tiring, but Thomas knew one day someone would discover and buy this land, and these people would be evicted. The area that Thomas loved so much was also included in the surveying. Ten men from the valley were asked to go up into the retreated area with George to be his guide so he could survey this area of the mountain. The men scouted the area for any danger as George measured and did the surveying.

The measurements and locations were compiled into records. The job had been a long and tiring one. Thomas asked the local storekeeper to rent him a room in his store for all the records so they could be kept safe.

George was tired and wanted to take it easy for a few days. The job had been a very tiring one, and was strenuous to his body. He had enough of this mountain anyway. George and Thomas were staying in Thomas' parents' home, but Thomas felt lonesome there. He decided to go to Little Valley to see some of his friends without having to deal with all of the legal work.

Mattie's house, as usual, was the first place he always visited. She was sitting in her favorite chair, but Thomas hardly recognized her. She was thinner, but she still had a big smile for Thomas. Thomas had talked to Derrick when they were surveying the land, and he didn't notice Mattie, but now he was speechless as he looked at this once robust woman, almost undernourished. When Mattie hugged Thomas, he was shocked at the weight she had lost, and although he didn't say anything to her, he was immediately concerned. Mattie told Thomas old age was catching up with her, and she shrugged it off as a big joke.

The Williams' clan all came around to greet Thomas. Mattie was slow in getting up, but she was soon on her feet. She brought the moonshine jug out, and the little food she had cooked, and the good-time was ready as always in her little old house that you could see outside in the open, but this house was the one that Thomas loved to visit whenever he came to this mountain.

Thomas and the rest of the Williams stayed up all night, raising a little hell way into the morning, as they joked, told lies, and tried to sing songs that had no tune. These were like old times to Thomas, but he was concerned about Mattie, the woman who used to be the life of the party. She was now was so tired out, she had to be put to bed. The woman who had so much energy before, and would socialize way into the night, was not able to entertain anymore.

After the wild night at the Williams, Thomas was so sick the next morning that he could hardly make it up the steep hill to his home. George was a little displeased with Thomas. He never expected him to stay out all night in the Valley, and be left alone in this strange place, and he wasn't too fond of this mountain, anyway. George was eager to go home, he had worked hard, and he pressured Thomas to finish his business, and leave the mountain.

Thomas worked a couple of days getting the rented rooms completed with files of the land he had surveyed, and he was ready to go back to Lawsonville. He filed one copy in the rented room, and he took the other copies with him to Lawsonville.

When Thomas and George arrived back in Lawsonville, they shook hands, and Thomas thanked him for the great job he had done in Ovington. Thomas hired a lawyer from the Bradley firm, two brothers who practiced law together. In fact they were the ones that James Cannon had hired to do all of his business, so Thomas knew these brothers were good lawyers. Paul and Howard Bradley had a good reputation; they were able to do business transactions as well as practice criminal law.

The Bradleys were glad to get the business, since there was very little business in this small town. The Bradleys were smart, because they had plenty of time to read and keep up to date with the law.

The valley people claimed small areas of land, because they were close, and they wanted to stay close to their families. Thomas gave the Bradleys the copies of the land he wanted to purchase, and the ones he wanted the land to be deeded to. The Bradleys' job was to try to get the best price for the land that Thomas wanted to buy. They were finally able to buy the land from the State of Tennessee, since there were no legal claims on this land. Thomas kept the land his father had given him because he had not decided what to do with the property, even though he felt he would probably not be happy living on his parents' land.

Thomas was excited to be informed by the Bradleys that the State of Tennessee was willing to sell him the 1,000 acres that he had surveyed and requested to buy. The price per acre was five dollars. The contract was drawn up and Thomas paid the State of Tennessee $5,000.

The necessary paperwork was completed, and each title was deeded to the respective person claiming their acreage of land. Thomas was glad all the legal work was completed, and he was the proud owner of the land that he loved so much.

After all of the hard work, Thomas decided he would go to the Cannon's house to see how James was doing. Thomas had not been to the farm since he had come back to Lawsonville. He could see some of the workers around the farm as he approached the house. They were looking at him sadly, and acting very nervous. Thomas immediately knew something was wrong.

Beth Marie met Thomas at the door in tears. She had been waiting for him to get back in town and to come to the farm. She hugged Thomas tightly as she explained to him about her father. Thomas held this small woman in his arms. She didn't want to let him go, but they soon went into James' room to see him together. Beth wasn't making too much sense in what she was saying about James' condition.

One of the workers had found James passed out on the farm. He was miles from home, and no one knew how long he was passed out. It seemed that he was completely paralyzed on the left side. He was also speechless. He could only make slurring sounds as he fixed his eyes on Beth.

After rushing into James' room with Beth, Thomas could only see Fred and Anna tearful, and standing over James' bed. The old Black couple was begging him to speak to them. Thomas tried to console the couple as well as Beth when she started to join them in crying uncontrollable tears. She knew her father wasn't going to make it, and feared he would not last very long. The doctor had given them little hope for James' recovery.

Thomas took Beth into the parlor, the room that was sat apart for the entertainment of visitors, and tried to calm her down so that he could talk to her. Thomas knew that James would never get up from his sick bed. Thomas was as sorrowful as when he lost his own parents, for this man had been was like a father to him. This was his family, too.

Beth clung to Thomas as he put his arms around her tiny waist. She kept on crying; she was so small, and his love for her was greater now as he knew she needed him. For the first time in her life, she really needed someone beside her father, who was unable to help her, and probably would not be around to help her anymore.

Thomas and Beth sat up with James most of the night. There was no response from him at all. The workers would come in at various times to see if they could be of any help, but left quickly when they knew there was no hope for their long-time employer and dear friend.

Jeffrey came as soon as he heard about James Cannon. His love for this man was more a fatherly love than just a friend. James had taken up with Thomas and Jeffrey, and had treated them both like his own family. Jeffrey could not believe that he was losing the one person that was like a father to him these past few years.

The only doctor in Lawsonville was getting old, and he fell asleep during the night. He tried to stay awake with the family and do what he could for James to make him comfortable and to comfort the family, but he knew he could not do anything else for the dying man.

Fred and Anna never ceased crying; the Cannons were their life. The old Black couple held each other as they looked down on the one person they had been with so long, and never thought that he would be leaving them so soon. They had seen James' wife and son pass on, but they always assumed they would have James around. They had not been out on their own since the early years of their life. This devastated time of their lives was taking its toll on them, since they knew James' death would make a difference in their lives.

During the early hours of the morning, James Cannon passed away and Thomas sat with Beth through the night. Beth was grief-stricken, and so was Thomas as the doctor pronounced James' death. He had done all he could for him, but he could not save James Cannon, and he was as sad as the family.

The Cannon's staff of workers gathered in the house as the news of his death reached them. Most of the workers wept; James Cannon had been good to them, and the ones that had been with him for a long time wept openly.

The day that James was put to rest was sad for the Cannon's people that had worked for him and had been a part of this huge farmland for so long. They knew if Beth sold the land they would be out of a job and a place to live.

Beth was grief-stricken and had to be put to bed. She was helpless as far as organizing any business at this time. Anna tried to get Beth to eat something, and to stay up long enough to talk to the many people that came to the house to see her and offer her their sympathy, but she would not see the people. She just stayed in her room and in the bed most of the time.

There were many people in this community coming in and out of the Cannon's house to help out, so Thomas stayed at the farm to try to console Beth, and to do whatever he could to assure the worried workers that things would be the same around this farm.

Jeffrey grieved as much as Beth because James Cannon had been so good to him and had taken him in and made him a part of this family; he was considered a part of the Cannon household. Jeffrey knew he would miss James very much. He joined Thomas as he was meeting the people as they came through to see Beth, but Jeffrey was trying to hide his own grief and hold back his tears as he thought of all the good times he had in this house with the Cannons.

Thomas was finally able to get Beth to dress and come downstairs and talk to the people. A lot of these people he did not know, and he was nervous trying to think of something to talk about with them. Beth tried to hide her puffy eyes that had turned red, and she tried to smile a little when she saw the worried expression on Thomas' face.

Thomas had stayed at the Cannon's farm for about a week after James died. He tried to help Beth with most of the necessary things she had to do getting James' affairs in order. Beth was sad most of the time, but she would not have made it on her own without Thomas help. Fred and Anna were always in the way, never caring about the grief of the others. They stayed under Beth, and they acted like two children as they wiped their eyes and seemed to be heart-broken over losing James Cannon. Beth was busy trying to control her own grief, and to cope with Fred and Anna was almost more than she could bear. Beth was frightened of the transition from being spoiled, waited on, pampered beyond words by her family, to be the head of this enormous farmland and the sole inheritor of her father's wealth.

The Bradleys and Thomas were taking care of the legal work. Beth knew her father left everything arranged so it would be easier on her, but she had come from a family that let the men take care of all of the affairs. She was nervous now that she was expected to handle her own affairs because no woman in her family had to handle what she was going to have to learn to do. She was no businessperson and didn't know where to start trying to take over her father's enormous wealth.

Thomas came to say good-bye to Beth. She immediately began to cry, and she clung to Thomas as he tried to leave. Thomas knew he could not leave Beth in this hysterical state; he held her in his arms and was petting her as her body shook with sobs, and he soon lost control. His passion for this woman began to rise in his body as he lusted for Beth. She responded to his lips, and the thrill of his hands gently exploring her body, though Thomas tried to stop, Beth only begged him to love her. Thomas was aroused to the point that he could not control his feelings as he continued to love Beth as she responded to his body gently pressing into her as she cried out with pain and passion.

Thomas had learned the art of making love from Ledia. He was grateful for her teaching him that love was not shameful, and her patience with Thomas sexually had paid off for him. Even though Ledia was from the low life, she was still one of the best friends Thomas had. She taught him that love was beautiful, and not something to be ashamed of if two people loved one another.

Though Thomas had tried to control his shame and embarrassment after he had made love to Beth, he felt a little ashamed of letting himself take advantage of Beth in her grief. Thomas slowly dressed, he begged Beth to forgive him, but Beth assured him that she loved him and wanted him to love her. Beth felt no shame, or any regrets for giving herself to this man.

Beth knew that Thomas would be leaving soon, but she was sorrowful when he left the Cannon farm, and moved back to his rooming house, where he had lived for ten years. His thoughts now were on his parents' home, and the land he had bought, and moving back to Ovington. Leaving Beth was painful, but he had made up his mind to leave Lawsonville, and he had not told Beth Marie of his decision.

This was a bad time in Thomas' life. He was unsure of which way to turn, but he knew he was going to go back home to Ovington. He would have to give up everything he worked for in Lawsonville, the good job he was able to have for many years, a job he would not have been able to be employed in, if not for this man who took him in when he really needed a friend. He knew he would never forget James Cannon.

5

There was only one little store in Lawsonville, but it sold just about anything you wanted. Thomas bought ten pairs of boots, and several pairs of gloves. As he made his plans, Thomas also hired some men with wagons to go with him as he made his long trip home.

Arriving in Ovington, he was met by some of the residents, and they welcomed him affectionately. Thomas rested for a few days and made notes of the work he was planning to do in this area where he intended to build his home.

Thomas went down into Little Valley, and as customary, he was welcomed by the people who were happy to see him again. He gave them the deeds to their homes, and explained the importance of keeping the deed in a safe place. He went to Mattie's house, and she was unable to get up to greet him. He was devastated to see the unpleasant conditions she was in. Her house was filthy since she was unable to care for herself. He kissed Mattie with tears in his eyes, but she assured him that she was all right.

Mattie's grandson, Thaddeus William, was her favorite grandson, because she felt sorry for him. Thaddeus William had a very bad speech problem, stuttering very badly whenever he tried to talk. The rest of the family thought it was funny when he would try so hard. They would poke fun at him when he struggled to pronounce his words. Thaddeus was about 14 at this time.

Thaddeus was staying with Mattie, and he was doing his best to care for her. Mattie had had six sons, and two daughters; Thaddeus was the son of her third son, James William. Mattie and Derrick were proud parents and they never had any serious problems with their rather large family. Thaddeus was smart and wanted to work, so he asked Thomas for a job. Thomas wanted to help him, but feared he was too young to try to work the clearing of his land, so he asked him to care for his grandmother, and he would pay him a salary. Thomas told Thaddeus if he would take care of his grandmother, Mattie, keep her house clean, and do any other chores that needed to be done for her, he would pay him a salary as if he were working for him doing any other job.

Thomas went throughout Little Valley, and he hired 20 men to go the area where he was planning to build his home. The job of clearing the land was dangerous and a very difficult one to do since it involved many rocks. Thomas hired the most fearless and experienced men that were available.

Thomas gave the first ten men he hired boots to wear because they had to cut down thick wooded area. The next ten came in and cleared the rocks. There were many snakes and other animals they killed as they cleared the land. The small rocks were cleared, chiseled down, cleaned, and stacked neatly in a pile.

Thomas had organized the work process and everything was going smoothly. Thomas felt confident the men could do the work on their own so Thomas decided to visit around Ovington and go over to his parents' home and rest up for a few days.

Walter and Velma Jean Simpson had moved to Ovington with their two children. Walter was a smart man who could build just about anything. Often he carved and built beautiful cabinets and furniture for some of the residents of Ovington and around this surrounding area.

Walter was a disgrace to this community at times. He would go down into Little Valley and get some of the moonshine. He would stay down there until he drank himself into a stupor. He wasn't allowed to come home and drink, and he would stay intoxicated, and unable to function for days at a time. Though Walter was never abusive to his family, they were hurt by his drinking sprees.

Walter's wife, Velma Jean, was against the drinking or anything that was wrong because she was a very religious woman. She asked Thomas to talk to Walter because the family was getting tired of the way Walter would let himself be weak enough to let the drinking ruin his life and his family. Velma Jean would repeatedly tell her husband the devil was going to claim his soul if he didn't straighten up his life and quit his sinful ways.

Thomas was down in Little Valley about a week later, and he saw

Walter. He was just drinking himself into a stupor. Thomas, seeing his condition, followed him as he made his way home. He could hardly walk and stumbled all the way.

There was a man named Paul Benson, who raised the finest milk cows on this mountain. Walter decided to cut through his land on his way home. Paul had a tall fence around this area where he kept his cows. Walter decided to climb the tall fence, and in his intoxicated condition, fell flat to the ground. As he lay on the ground, he looked up and he saw this big black bull with his horns and big eyes staring at him through the light of the moon. Walter screamed hysterically until Thomas ran to him and tried to calm him down.

The next day when Walter had a clearer mind, he told Thomas that he thought he had fallen into hell, and the Devil was waiting for him. Thomas talked to Walter again after he was straight with his thinking, because Walter had made up his mind to change his ways. Thomas believed Walter and hired him to take over the job of overseeing the clearing of his land and to save what he could of the best wood for the building of his house.

Thomas had many things that he needed to do in Ovington, but he decided he should go back to Lawsonville and check on Beth Marie and to complete his necessary business there.

Beth was still grieving for her father. She would never get over losing him, but she had managed to take on the many responsibilities she was expected to do, and to take her place in her father's business enterprises.

Beth really missed Thomas. Even though she knew he had to go home to Ovington, she wanted Thomas to help her. When they saw each other again, she could tell that Thomas was ashamed and embarrassed, because he felt like he had taken advantage of her in her grief.

The workers on the farm were a little nervous having a woman to boss them and some of them left the farm. This disturbed Beth, and she shed tears because she had tried to do things as her father had done, and she paid them good wages. Beth was feeling very low, and needed someone to help her through this rough time. She knew she had to send for Thomas.

Thomas was busy getting caught up at the bank, and whenever Fred called for Thomas, he had tears in his eyes. He begged Thomas to come to the Cannon house, and to see about Miss Beth, because she needed him so much. Thomas assured Fred that he would come to see Beth this evening. Thomas knew that Beth would shed tears whenever she saw him. Thomas knew he must prepare himself for this unpleasant evening.

Thomas was shocked to see that Beth had gotten so thin, and her eyes were swollen a little. Beth was fully dressed, but her clothes were not neat as she always kept herself. Beth ran into Thomas' arms. Wanting him to never let her go, she cried and begged Thomas to come to the farm to live. Thomas only held her and assured her he would never leave her again.

The sadness Thomas felt for Beth was the same that he felt when he lost his parents. He and Beth were alone together, and as he held Beth closer, he confessed that he was lonely, and needed her as much as she needed him. Thomas and Beth sat in the parlor most of the night, just holding hands and onto each other, never wanting to let each other go. Thomas and Beth embraced each other until early morning and they both knew life was lonely without each other.

Thomas made the first move to pull away from Beth, but to try to leave Beth was to hard for Thomas, he kissed her with passion, and held her small body until she cried out with pain. Thomas had never felt this way with any other woman, and all the years of loneliness and unhappiness he suffered throughout his early years of growing up, seemed to disturb Thomas at times. Thomas had promised himself that he would not take advantage of Beth again, but this meant nothing right now, because he could not control himself, as he made love to Beth for the second time.

Thomas and Beth lay close together for hours, and it was daylight before they pulled apart. Thomas asked Beth to marry him. She accepted his proposal and the plans were made for a early wedding, because Beth did not want Thomas to leave the farm, or be away from her again.

The Bradley brothers found a famous architect in North Carolina, named John Smithson, who also owned a huge construction company.

John Smithson was a smart and talented man, famous for designing houses in the mountain, and building very big houses. He agreed to design a house for Thomas, and to build this house for a very big price. Thomas was willing to pay the price, because he wanted his home built on the site that he loved so much as he was growing up on the mountain. Though it was a steep hill that the house would be built on, John assured Thomas he could do the job.

Many plans were drawn up for the house, because Thomas was so hard to please. Thomas was planning on marrying Beth Marie, and he wanted her to be included on the planning and suggestions for the home they would share together, but Beth said very little about the plans of the house he wanted to build.

They finally decided to build the house approximately 4,000 square feet, and designed in a Colonial style with four architectural columns supporting the front entrance of this fine and stately home of Thomas Theodore Ovington. Beth knew Thomas would have his way about the construction of this house that he was building, so she agreed with the plans he liked the best.

Most of the material would be shipped by railroad, and then be pulled by wagons up the steep hill to the construction site. Thomas had made plans to have the material and building supplies stored about twenty miles from his place until he was able to have them transported to his home place.

Thomas knew he would be in financial trouble when his house was completed, but he would not settle for less than he had already contracted the Smithson Company to do.

John Smithson was a hard man to do business with. He loved money, so he tried to bargain highly when he knew he could make the money. But he did beautiful work, in fact, he was rated the best in his state of North Carolina, and the upper Eastern state of Tennessee, and he only hired the best people to work for him.

Smithson spent three months of his time ordering material and making sure all equipment was in top shape for the long and difficult job he was hired to do in Ovington.

Fred and Anna was doing less work now that James Cannon had passed on. They were open with their affection for each other, and they made no secret about their long love affair. Both of them were getting old, and they only had each other to love.

Beth Marie was like their child, because they had been with the Cannons since she was a baby. Fred and Anna wanted to marry and move out of the Cannon house, but Beth became so hysterical when they told her of this idea, that they changed their plans to marry and leave this estate.

Beth finally got her life together, especially since she knew that Thomas was going to marry her. She decided to hire more help for this enormous farmhouse. She was lonely, and needed more people around her, she would need someone around to ward off boredom, and she would have many duties to do in his house.

The first person Beth hired was a man named Clayton Stewart, a young Black man, about 22 years old. Clayton was a bright young man, and most of the people around Lawsonville liked him. But Clayton was different than most of the "colored" people, which is what they were called at that time. He was smart and neat in appearance, and had good manners, but Clayton had trouble getting a job, because he preferred a job that was suitable for him. He worked better inside of the house, than doing outside work. Clayton's family was always worried about him: he was a dreamer, always saying he was going to be famous and wanted to do jobs where he could remain clean and neat in his appearance, which made his family think of him as lazy about keeping a job.

Clayton had very little education, but he could read and write very well, having learned mostly on his own. Clayton went to the Cannon's house looking for a job when he found out that Beth was looking for someone to work in her house. Beth was impressed with this young man, observing how neat he was, and that he talked very nice, and seemed like he wanted to work. Clayton was happy that Beth hired him, and his duties were to be inside the house. He would be taught to see that her meals were served proper, and that the food would be prepared on time.

Beth had to teach Clayton the routine of his duties in her house. He was taught how to set the table, how to serve each course of the meals, although Beth was the only one eating most of the time. He did very little cleaning, but he was taught the way Beth liked things done.

Fred and Anna were happy that someone else had taken over most of their duties, and some of the workload was off them. They loved Clayton, thinking of him as one of the nicest young men they knew, and he had the utmost respect for the two black employees of the Cannon's house.

Clayton soon learned his duties, and he did them well. He was also fascinated with the Cannon's piano. Clayton was able to pick out the notes on the piano whenever he knew Beth was out of the house and unable to hear him practice.

Beth hired a few more of the Lawsonville residents, but they did not live on the Cannon's place. The new people helped with the cleaning of this huge farmhouse, and they would keep the lace curtains that hung throughout the house stiffly starched and then stretched. This house was spotless, since Beth had so many people working to try and keep herself from being so lonely.

Beth missed Thomas, but she knew that he had gone home to Ovington, and would be gone a few days. She waited nervously for him to return. She knew Thomas would marry her when he came back to Lawsonville, and she made plans for her wedding, and was shopping for her wedding dress.

Thomas had been in Ovington about two days, and was looking over the land that had been cleared. He was pleased to see the thick wooded and rocked area cleared to perfection. Walter was with Thomas as he admired the work completed by the men he had hired to do the job, and he thanked Walter for the great job he had done as well.

Thomas had not been down in Little Valley yet, and he was surprised to see Thaddeus running up the hill, calling to him excitedly. Thaddeus was crying and his stuttering was worse than usual. Thomas understood enough to know that there was trouble down in the valley, and he ran with Thaddeus when he heard him say Mattie's name.

As Thomas ran with Thaddeus, he could see the Williams and the Tuckers as he approached Mattie's house. No one spoke as Thomas ran into Mattie's room, pushing his way through the huge crowd of relatives to Mattie's bedside. Thomas was shocked to see this once robust woman, now just skin and bones. Mattie's beautiful face was pale, and her eyes were staring up so big and frightened as she saw Thomas.

There were so many people in the room, but Thomas fell to his knees, as he took Mattie into his arms, begging her to speak to him, and begging her not to die. Thomas cried uncontrollable tears with the rest of the family as he held Mattie. The family watched as Mattie, too weak to speak, smiled weakly at Thomas. She knew Thomas had come to her as her own family, to be with her as she was preparing to leave this world.

The crying was loud now; the matriarch of this family was leaving them. This woman was responsible for two hostile families being united with love for each other, after being so bitter with each other for years. No one would be able to take her place. She was the Rose of this family, and they could not stand to lose her, but she was sinking fast, and they could not save her.

Thomas was remembering how Mattie had helped him through his difficult years as he was growing up, how this woman was willing to share food with others, when she could hardly feed her own family. Thomas thoughts were of Mattie and her jug under the kitchen table, which she called her "medicine," and the "cure for all aliments."

Mattie was breathing very heavy now, she looked very frightened, but Thomas never let her go. He continued to hold her in his arms, and he kissed her cheek when she took her last breath.

The Williams and Tucker families were hysterical, though they had not taken the time to care for Mattie when she was so sick. But to now know that she was gone saddened the families, and they clung to each other for comfort.

The family finally calmed down and Thomas helped the family prepare the funeral and burial for Mattie. Walter was employed by Thomas to make the finest coffin in which lay Mattie to rest.

After the funeral, Thomas went to the Williams' house. Derrick Williams, old and with stooped shoulders, was walking around the house crying softly. Thomas asked Thaddeus to stay with his grandfather, and to care for him as he had did for Mattie.

There was sadness in Little Valley since they had finished the job of clearing Thomas' land. The men were out of work, and getting bored, plus the life of this valley was gone. They really missed Mattie, and the good times they would have with her.

Thomas went to his parents' home, and he tried to control his grief. He thought of Beth, who was the only one he had to love now. He had loved Mattie, and his own family was gone also, so he felt like Beth was the only one close to him left, and he did love her. Thomas decided to marry Beth as soon as he arrived in Lawsonville. The thoughts of living alone any longer only made him sad and miss his own parents.

Thomas looked around the small house, remembering the unhappy childhood he had known here, and decided he would sell this part of his father's land, and never stay in this house again.

6

Beth was happy to see Thomas, she could see something was bothering him. Thomas did not want to talk about Mattie so soon, because he was suffering grief as much as Mattie own family, and he knew Beth did not need to hear any bad news, since she was getting over her fathers death herself.

Beth was excited to see Thomas, and did not know the grief he was suffering. Beth was elated when Thomas asked her to marry him as soon as possible. Thomas felt like his love for Beth would help him through this bad time in his life.

There was to be a small wedding, since Beth knew few people in Lawsonville, she wasn't very popular with the people in this community. Beth had kept to herself most of her stay here in Tennessee, and had not made very many friends in this small southern town, she was thought of as a snob.

Beth had the finest wedding dress made, she had the best food cooked for the event. Beth had taught Clayton the proper use of her finest dishes, silver, and the linens were done up specially for the occasion.

The day of the wedding, most of the guest invited attended, because it was rare to see such a big event as a wedding here in Lawsonville. Most of the young couples were married in the preacher's home or at the local Court House.

Thomas prefer not to make such a big fuss over the wedding. Thomas was still a little shy around a lot of people. Jeffrey Carter was the best man, and he was happy to be in the wedding, because he loved Thomas and Beth so much.

Beth was not close to any of the Women here in Lawsonville, so Jeffrey Carter asked his girlfriend to be Beth bride maid. Reba Brandon was a little shy and wasn't to sociable herself, but this big event was to good to past up, and she agreed to be in the wedding, since Beth had her a dress made for the event also.

The wedding cause quiet a lot of talk here in Lawsonville. There was never anything so big around this part of town, of course, some of the ladies were a little jealous of these two prominent people marrying, Beth with her wealth and Thomas being so handsome.

Some of the ladies in Lawsonville that knew Thomas, since he had been living in this community, the ones that he had personal contact with, were beginning to talk about Thomas, they spread ugly rumors about him, they wasn't able to interest him enough to be asked to marry him. They tried to make remarks that Thomas was only marrying Beth for the Cannon's Wealth, and did not love Beth at all.

Ledia Summer was the only one to be hurt by Thomas marrying Beth, but she knew that Thomas did care for her, or he would never have open this business for her, and taught her to make a decent living for herself. Though it was hurting to see Thomas belong to someone else, she knew that a little piece of her heart would always belong to Thomas, she had taught him what love really was all about, and it was love that would cure all aliments, she was elated that she had known the love and the closeness she shared with Thomas Ovington.

Thomas was wild with fury, as he told Beth about the rumors going around town, Thomas assured Beth that he truly did love her, and wasn't marrying her for her money. Thomas did not want Beth to be hurt by this vicious gossip.

Of course, Beth knew Thomas was upset with the false accusation, and she laughed it off. Beth had already heard the rumors about Thomas marrying her for her money, but she refused to believed this rumor to be true, she knew the love she shared with Thomas was real, and hoped their marriage would always be a loving and lasting one.

The wedding was performed as planned, Thomas and Beth were married at the Cannon's farm house. Beth was radiant, her happiness overflowing now that she was the wife of Thomas Theodore Ovington. Thomas handsome and charming as he clung to Beth, knew this woman was the love he had been searching for.

The wedding guests were excited by the beauty of this house and the excitement of the wedding, they refused to leave until night was nearing, and most of the male guest were getting a little to intoxicated.

Fred and Anna were elated by the beauty of this big event, and to see the many guests in the Cannon's house. They had not seen so much Company in the Cannon's house since they had lived back East, when Mrs. Cannon was living, and she always had big parties and many dinner parties, for James Cannon business associates.

After the wedding party was over, Beth was shooing the household help out of the main house, she was in a hurry to get into her husband arms, she didn't even want any of them to clean the many dishes and linens from the tables, she just wanted the house shut down, and she and Thomas to be alone.

Thomas was as excited as Beth by their marriage. Beth knew she had Thomas in a good mood, she decided to ask him about taking a trip back East to visit her cousins and friends, she had a few relatives that she was really fond of, one of her favorite cousins was Judith Holman. This would be a good time to show off her handsome husband, but she had to talk Thomas into making this long trip back East.

Beth had inherited James Cannon huge stock in the railroad, and could travel to any state first class, and she wanted to take advantage of this privilege.

Thomas wasn't to happy about making this trip back East, but he was wanting to please Beth, thinking it was best to get away for a awhile, he made plans to entrust a overseer to take charge of the Cannon house, and the surrounding area of this big farmland.

Thomas had many interviews with the men for the job of overseeing the Cannon's farm while he and Beth would be gone. Thomas wasn't satisfied with anyone enough to hire them, and he asked Jeffrey Carter if he could handle the job? The many Worker were fond of Jeffrey, so Thomas knew that he could handle the job, though Jeffrey was a little nervous about accepting the position.

The men in this small town knew James Cannon well, and had many business dealing with him, but they were never close to Beth. Seeing this small petite woman marrying Thomas, they were a little envious of him, because they knew Thomas was married to the richest women in the Eastern Tennessee state.

When Beth found out that Thomas was willing to go back East with her, she was elated and started to pack for the trip back home. Thomas made reservation for the finest Coach to travel East, and they were excited as two children taking this trip from this small town to Eastern

New York.

Thomas and Beth were alone, caught up in the excitement of being as one, loving each other passionately, as if there were to be no tomorrow. Thomas wasn't one to travel via railroad, but this was happiness beyond belief. There were many people on the train, but Thomas and Beth saw no one. At times, they even missed the meals prepared in the Dinning Room.

The Ovingtons arrived in New York City. Beth was elated to be in New York again, to see the city after the small town of Lawsonville. This was to a honeymoon, business trip combined, but Thomas and Beth wanted to be by themselves for a few days. Being from a small town, and hardly ever having the chance to leave the Hills of Tennessee, Thomas clung to Beth as he view this city. New York was more excitable than he imagine.

Beth wanted her family to meet her handsome husband, so the family arranged a big Party in honor of the new Bride and Groom. This was a dream come true for Beth, she had one of the finest men in Tennessee, and she knew Thomas would make a good impression on her family.

Beth Marie was well educated and attended the famous LaBelle Charm School, where as, she was taught the strictest rules of being a lady, She also had one of the best backgrounds in education. The years of taking lesson in classical piano from the famous Seam Debois, made her one of the most popular young ladies during her years of growing up in New York.

The Cannon's wealth, and her status among the Biggest business people in this city, was still remember by the high society, and they welcome Beth and her new husband home.

Thomas was a little shy as he met Beth little circle of friends and relatives. The ladies were envious of Beth marrying such a handsome man, and they were amused by his southern accent.

Thomas and Beth were invited to every social event doing the first month of their stay in New York. The parties were a little wild at times, and Thomas began to tire of this big city, the parties lasting until way into the morning, wasn't the kind he was used to, and was quiet different than the ones in the Little Valley when they stayed up half of the night. Thomas wasn't used to the noise, and the city that seem to never go to sleep.

Beth was having a marvelous time, but she soon realize that

Thomas was getting unhappy, he was quiet, and would get moody at times. Beth suspected that he was thinking about his home being build-ed in Ovington.

The Ovingtons decided to rent a small apartment, Thomas found a small one for them to live in as they made plans to shop for the many things they planned to use in their home in Ovington.

Beth Marie had a cousin her age, Judith Elease Holman, they grew up together, sharing the same interest in classical music, often playing in concerts together. Judith was one of Beth favorite cousins, and she loved her like a sister. Judith Holman was married into the Holman fam-ily, one of the wealthy merchants families in New York.

The day that Beth took her husband to meet Judith Holman, she was fascinated with Beth's handsome southern husband, but Thomas was a little leery of this woman, because she was more outgoing than Beth, seem to get to close when she talked to him, and the things that sat her apart from most of Beth family was her thick flocks of red hair.

Edward Charles Holman, Judith's husband, was a man of distin-guished, talked very little and was always well respected among his many business associates.

The Holmans were the parents of four children, three girls, and the oldest one was a boy, named after his father. The children were well behaved and very intelligent, except the youngest, an energetic girl of three, they had named Jane Elizabeth. The other two girls were on the shy side, and seem to be quiet most of the time, now, Jane Elizabeth was more like her mother, she had the same red hair, and could talk up a storm, and just a little girl. This child looked so much like her mother and had the same personally, that she was Beth favorite cousin, and she took this child with her wherever she went in New York.

Beth wanted her husband to enjoy the Theaters that she loved so much, and she would take Thomas with her to see the best plays in this city, of course, these Plays wasn't Thomas ideal of entertainment, he would be much more comfortable in the Little Valley, with his moon-shining friends, and the drinking and the Hell they would raise half of the Night.

After the long and lonely years in Lawsonville, Beth was elated to be with her people and doing some of the things she grew up with and being accepted again in her little circle of friends and Relatives.

Though Thomas and Beth still remained on the Honeymoon, loving one another and holding each other tightly for long periods of times, their interest wasn't always the same.

When Thomas learned his way around New York, he would venture out into the city alone. He would check out the businesses for his own interest, always asking question in the biggest businesses that assumed he was going to buy large amounts of stocks, or for other financial reasons. He was trying to make sure he would protect the Cannon's wealth, and was trying to be careful about the investment he would make, since he was left in charge of James Cannon large estate.

Judith Holman often flirted with Beth new husband, he was different, something about this man fascinated her to the point, she had to touch Thomas at times. Thomas would be embarrass, and he would try to avoid this intimacy with her, it was becoming disturbing to him.

The Ovingtons would write home to Jeffrey Carter often, they would explain the excitement of New York, and the marvelous time they were having, and they wished him well, and assumed he was managing the Cannon's household in a orderly manner.

Sometime Jeffrey wished for Thomas and Beth to come home, because he would get infuriated at Fred and Anna, they refused to do any household duties while the Ovingtons were in New York, and they often talked ugly to Jeffrey about asking them to do anything they didn't want to do.

Clayton tried to do Fred and Anna share of work, but it was getting the best of him, and he went to Jeffrey and asked him about hiring a young woman named Grace. When Jeffrey Carter was fed up with Fred and Anna, and the hard time they would give sometime, he agreed to let Grace take a temporary position in this house until Beth came home, to help Clayton out. Clayton wasted no time bringing this woman to the Cannon's farm to take the job of helping him in the house.

The evenings were lonely around the farm, so Clayton would entertain the workers by playing Beth priceless piano. Clayton had learned to play some mean rhythm on this piano. The worker would have the time of their life as Clayton played sometime till late at night. Of course, Jeffrey did not mind, he loved this music that Clayton played, he would bring his girlfriend Reba, over to the Cannon's farm, and this great music would be enjoyment to both of them.

Grace was taught by Clayton to do everything that Beth had taught him. Grace was quiet, and didn't fit in with the household staff very well, she did her work well, she was always neat, and only talked to Clayton. When the day ended, and the worker gather around together, Grace preferred to go to her room alone, and she rarely stayed to listen to Clayton entertaining the farm workers.

Jeffrey had given Grace a room next to Clayton. Jeffrey was told by Clayton that Grace was his distance cousin, he never did tell Jeffrey her last name, or where she came from. The two rarely talked or acted as if they really liked one another, but Grace did everything that Clayton told her to do. Grace learned the routine of the household duties very well.

The letter arrived that the Ovingtons were ready to come home. Jeffrey made sure all work was up to par. Jeffrey drove the worker hard, especially the household staff to make sure everything was in order as Beth had left her home.

There were a few gripes among the workers as they tried to get everything in order, but the work was completed. Anna knew that Thomas was a little different than James Cannon or Beth, she knew he wasn't going to spoil her or Fred and let them have their way as the Cannon's had all of these years.

As the Ovingtons planned to leave New York, the marvelous time Beth was having, wasn't the same with Thomas. Beth would catch him getting moody at times, and seem in a hurry to come home, she suspected he was thinking about his place he was having builded in his home town.

Thomas and Beth had seen just about everything there was to see in New York City, and attended many social events during the year they were living in this city. Beth knew her stay had to end, but she wanted to stay here with her family and friends, but knowing Thomas, this was only wishful thinking.

Beth had shopped in the biggest Stores in New York, she brought bolt of the finest brocade material for decorating. They shopped for the best furniture to be shipped to their home, there were many other rare and valuable pieces that they purchase to decorate their new home. Thomas paid for all of the things that were brought in New York, he refused to spend any of the Cannon's money.

The Ovingtons were packed and ready to come home to Tennessee. Beth wanted to have one last party for her friends and the few distance cousin, especially Judith Holman. Beth feared this would be the last time she would be able to see them for a long time, because they would never make the trip to Tennessee to see her and Thomas, though they had promise many times they would come to visit, they never did when James Cannon was living, but now they had promise they would come to Tennessee when she moved to their new home.

The trip home was less thrilling to Thomas and Beth, than when they made the trip to New York. The Ovingtons were able to see many places and admire the beautiful country they missed on their trip to New York. The train stopped in the little sleepy town of Lawsonville, this town was much different than the big city they had been used to for the last year. Beth feeling depressed coming home to the Cannon's farm, clung to Thomas for comfort.

Jeffrey Carter greeted them and the Cannon's staff welcome them home. Jeffrey had manage to run the farm and the household staff as well, there were a few problems, but no one seemed unhappy by the arrangement of the work orders he had each of them to do while the Ovingtons were away from this farm.

Fred and Anna were glad to see Beth, she was like their child, they both loved her and was happy that she was happy, and so in love with her new husband, but they were a little leery of Thomas, he was different, his background was different, he did not have the same love for his workers as the Cannon's. Anna especially seem to be less fond of Thomas than Fred, she felt like Thomas married Beth only for the wealth and the upper class position he had inherited by marrying her.

Thomas had no comments when Jeffrey told him he had hired Grace to help with the household duties. Though, Thomas knew there was enough help in this house to keep the house up to par. Beth seem pleased with Jeffrey ability to run this huge farm while she and Thomas were in New York.

Clayton bent backward to please Beth, he wanted her to like Grace, and to let her stay on in this house, and to keep her job. Grace was quiet and never refused to do anything she was asked to do. Her long starch dresses were always neat, but she rarely had anything to say, and Beth didn't press her to talk, because she always kept a distance from everyone, she was a very private person.

As the Cannon's people got used to Beth and her having a new husband now, they began to relax more. Thomas was eager to go home to Ovington, he didn't exactly feel comfortable in the Cannon's house himself. Thomas would think of James Cannon and the love he had for him as a father, and he would feel sadness by missing him, and the way he respected his advise all the years he knew him.

Thomas immediately made arrangement to go home to see John Smithson. He was anxious to see how far along the Building of his house was before moving to Ovington. Beth wanted to go with Thomas, but he felt it was best for her not to travel the rough mountain until her home was completed, and she could move into her new home that he had built for her.

Beth was never happy at this farm that her father loved so much, but she didn't want to move away from the home she had shared with her father all of these years in Tennessee. She knew Thomas would not live on this farm again after making up his mind to move back to his home in Ovington.

The tears would swell Beth's eyes whenever she would think about leaving behind the best of her memories of her family. This move to Ovington would be a traumatic time in her life, but love won, because Thomas was her life now, knowing he was away from her made the loneliness unbearable.

Anna was making Beth's life hell by her grips about leaving this farm, she could not understand why Thomas could not stay here at the Cannon's home place, since he once lived here too. Trying to cope with all the things she had to leave behind, Beth only wished Anna had some of the quietness about her that Grace had.

Clayton still played piano whenever he had the chance. Beth never suspected that he had mastered her piano, the music he could play was unbelievable to those that were lucky enough to hear him play, because he still had to be discreet whenever he played this pride and joy of Beth, since he knew she loved this piano so much.

Grace seemed to be happy especially if Clayton was around close by as she did her duties. They did not communicate very much, she didn't seem to like his music as the others in the Cannon's house, but there was a closeness between them that no one noticed. Clayton's room was next to Grace's room, he was supposed to be looking out for his cousin, so no one notice anything wrong with the sleeping arrangement.

Sometimes Anna seemed a little jealous of Grace because Beth was becoming very fond of Grace, she had no trouble communicating with her, she did whatever she was told to do, Beth did not have to go through the back talk she had to hear from Anna. Anna was like a second mother to Beth, since Mrs. Cannon was so caught up in her social affairs and the Cannon's businesses, she had very little time with the spoiled child that was quiet a headache at times. Over the years, Anna still thought she had the right to treat Beth as she treated her when she was a child. Anna had spent most of her adult years looking after and caring for Beth Marie.

The loneliness was getting to Beth, with all the hard work and the desires she had for her husband, she had gotten used to having Thomas close to her this past year, the passion and the fulfillment of the love they shared together, made her wish for his return home.

Jeffrey and his girlfriend had stayed together at the Cannon farm while the Ovingtons were in New York. Reba Brandon was there as a guest, and they never slept together, but Jeffrey missed Reba so much since she had went home, he had asked her to marry him. This was no surprise to anyone, since they could see the two were in love.

Beth was elated to hear the good news from Jeffrey Carter, since she loved him so much, and Reba was her bridesmaid when she married Thomas. Beth remember she had no one else to stand by her side, and this was special for her to see Jeffrey and Reba married, and she wished Jeffrey happiness.

After Beth had been home a couple of weeks, there was a business associate of James Cannon that came to see her. He was making Beth a offer to buy this huge farm. Beth had no use for this farm since she would be moving miles from this site, and probably would not be coming to this farm to often, but this was her father love, the place he found peace, and was very happy in his last year of his life. Beth knew she would not sell at any price, this was one thing that Thomas had not mention to her about selling or renting this farm.

Clayton loved the Cannon's house, he had learned the many duties Beth had taught him, he had worked very hard helping Beth with the wrapping and packing the priceless glass ware carefully, but he had rhythm in his body, and he found that his love for music was greater, he was lonely for the night life he had while the Ovingtons were away by his entertaining the worker in the evening, the way they enjoyed his music, and the thrill he would feel by seeing their bodies swing to his creations he had learned on Beth's piano. There were no pianos among the black people in their homes, just the old beat up one in the small church that served this community, and half the time, the piano wasn't in tune, but the people that sung in the church would not notice, they would be singing much louder than hearing the tune of the piano. Clayton wanted to be where the music was that he liked, not the classical music that Beth would play as she would entertain the people, or for her own enjoyment.

Clayton had planned to move to Ovington with the rest of the household staff, but he was getting restless, and was not satisfied with this job, the way he was when Beth hired him.

Anna made one last plead to convince Beth not to move to Ovington. Everyday was Hell for Beth, listening to Anna worrying her about leaving this farm, and the loneliness of not having no friends in Lawsonville, made her life unbearable at times. Sometime Beth wished for her cousin Judith Holman, the good times they would have together, the theater that they enjoyed in New York, Beth knew these people in Lawsonville would never accept this great entertainment here in this small town. The only social Beth had ever been invited to was the church picnic, which was dull to Beth, and she rarely attended.

Jeffrey and Reba were married, there was no elaborate wedding, the kind Thomas and Beth had when they were married, but there was just as much joy since, Beth was elated and acted as if Jeffrey was her own child. Thomas was in Ovington, but Beth wished he was in Lawsonville to see these two beautiful couple married.

There were no plans for the farm at this time, but Beth knew Thomas would take care of the arrangements and decisions to be made concerning James Cannon estate. There was a lot for Thomas to do in Ovington, and Beth knew he would be gone for awhile, there were many things to do after the completion of their home. Beth knew Thomas would see that everything would be taken care before he returned, so she tried to do as much as possible before he returned to Lawsonville.

There was a couple that lived in Lawsonville, the Davis's, Richard and Geneva, they worked for the Cannon's from time to time to help them when they were in a bind. Beth sent for the couple to help them when Jeffrey was married. Geneva could really sew, and she prepared and sewed some of the beautiful material that Beth had purchase in New York. This was a married couple that always worked side by side, they were always together. Poor Richard was a quiet person, but a little silly at times, he told a lot of jokes, and had the people laughing at him all the time, the man wasn't a go-getter, he preferred to hang around Geneva and see what she was always doing.

Geneva had sewed for some of the best people around this small town, so she knew how to stitch the finest material, she spent a few weeks at the Cannon farm making some of the beautiful items that Beth was taking from the farm.

With all the people working and helping Beth with the packing, she still fell into bed exhausted, she wasn't able to sleep, thinking of Thomas and missing him, and the warmth of his body, but everyone was exhausted, and the tempers flew hot at times.

Anna jealously of Grace turned to fondness of her, the shy Grace who was like a shadow around you, because she was so quiet. Anna almost felt sorry for Grace, she was a loner, and never seem to enjoy being around the rest of the household worker. Sometimes she even seem a little ill, and she didn't eat very much.

Anna tried to think up ways to cheer up Grace or make her more comfortable around them, but Grace just became more withdrawn. When Clayton was question about Grace shyness, he only commented that she was just a shy person, she had always been that way. Clayton wasn't to happy being question about Grace, Beth had tried several times to question him about her background.

There was many hours spent preparing to leave Lawsonville to move to Ovington, there was cooperation between the many workers and friends of Beth. Jeffrey Carter and his new wife would often help out, but this was like living in paradise, they were enjoying their new marriage, and hardly realize they were working. Beth hated to ask the Carter's to work so hard, knowing they wanted to be alone together, but Jeffrey seeing Beth so tired all the time, offered to do as much as he could to take some of the pressure off Beth.

When Beth heard from Thomas, after a long period of time, she knew that he was coming home soon, she was elated to know that she would see her husband soon. Beth wasn't in a hurry to move to Ovington, but at least she would be able to see her husband.

Beth knew that Thomas would be in Lawsonville soon, and she felt like she was going to a church picnic, everyone was caught up with the excitement as Beth, except Anna, the tearful Anna felt so sad, she went to her room and cried. The Cannon's big farm had been home to her for many years, she felt like this farm was part of her life, and she was getting to old to try and change to another home so far away. Of course, Anna unhappiness caused Fred to be unhappy too.

Beth was tired of talking to Anna and trying to cheer her up, she knew how stubborn Anna could be. Beth tried to keep it a secret from Thomas, the way Anna felt about moving to Ovington, the new home he had taken so much pain to be perfect for her and her servants, he had said they would be welcome to move to Ovington with her, and she hoped they would be happy to go with her, she would miss not having her own people to be with her.

7

While the Ovingtons had been in New York, John Smithson had wasted no time in starting the construction of the Ovington estate. He broke the ground for the house that Thomas had given permission for him to build. Construction was started, but not without trouble from the start. The men became unhappy from the hard work because this was one of the hardest jobs they had ever done. The hard work and the lonely nights seemed to never end.

The men had to cart most of the building materials up the steep hill to the construction site. Although there were few injuries, tempers flew hot. Of course, the danger was always a problem with the mountain, but Smithson was a smart man, and he soon had most of the problems solved.

Smithson had hired many skilled men that knew how to do rock work, and he had the best carpenters this side of the mountain. In this crew of skilled workers, there were many black men that he hired to work this job. These black men were called "Colored folks," or "Negroes." The colored men were the strongest to do this type of work; they had the strength to lift, dig, and could stand the mountain's unpredictable weather.

Smithson never did a job without a man named Daniel Johnson, who was about six feet tall. Daniel was a smart man, but he was quick to anger. He was very dark skinned; in fact, his skin was so black, they called him "Blue" as a nick name. This man wasn't afraid of anything, and he would go about his work, when others were ready to quit. Daniel or Blue, as he was called, wasn't afraid of the mountain. Some of the men were so afraid of this mountain that they left. Either that, or they got tired of this isolated place. When the workers heard about Little

Valley, and the moonshine you could get there, they soon visited them. They were afraid at first, because the workers didn't know how to approach the people, and didn't know if they would accept strangers. But the people were friendly with the workers, and they would let them have jugs of their moonshine. They would drink the moonshine, and relax, but the nights were still lonely to them.

Blue was one to mix with people, and he was lonely enough to get real friendly with the people in the Valley. Blue would play his harmonica for the people. They were fascinated with this instrument that he could make talk. Blue and some of the workers had other instruments, and they would play some of the low down blues numbers they knew, and would sing some soulful songs, that the people never heard before. They were only used to the hill people singing these hillbilly songs. The music the workers made, and drinking a little moonshine, put the people in a mood they never experienced before.

Sometimes the lonely nights and moonshine was just too much for Blue, and he would get a change of personality when he had been drinking. Most of the workers were afraid of him. Although some of the men complained about Blue and his meanness, John merely spoke to Blue about the complaints. He refused to do anything about Blue's abusiveness, because Blue was one of the best men this side of Tennessee to do any kind of rock work. He was fast, and he was skilled with his job. After weeks of going into the valley and getting to know the people, the men began dating the women. The men were lonely, and hated to leave this job, since Smithson paid them fair wages. Times were hard, and they needed money to survive. The men in the valley weren't too happy with the colored men taking to their women, but the women seemed to be happy, and continued to date the colored men. This created problems between the workers and the men in the valley, and sometimes there were fights among them. Smithson had a time trying to keep peace among the workers and the men in the valley.

John hired more men after the foundation was completed and the building took on a new look. John hired six men from the valley to help with the lumber as the tall building was being elevated.

Walter was employed to do the cabinet work, once the interior was completed enough to start the tedious job of building the many spacious bookcases, china cabinets, and storage cabinets that were to be built throughout the house. Thomas had specified that no one but

Walter build these cabinets and bookcases.

Blue, as they called Daniel, continued to drink the moonshine and raise hell half of the night in the valley, but by daylight, he was on the job, and he never tired or slowed down as his hands quickly mixed mortar to brick the building's exterior. Blue's lean body remained steady as he did his job with the greatest of ease.

Blue began to teach the men in the valley about his card games, which was a form of gambling, showing them how to gamble with money. At first he let them win, but once they were interested in the game, he began to win and take their money. This made the men upset, and they began to get into fights over the card games. The fights were just slaps at first, but once it became violent, Blue proved that he was as quick with a knife as he was with the tools he worked with. Blue made a lot of enemies, and the men were afraid of him.

Blue began to date one of Mattie's granddaughters, Vera Williams. The beautiful Vera was the darling of the Williams family, and she fell for Blue hard. She loved this tall black man that everyone considered a little dangerous. Blue was as mean as a snake to everyone else, but he worshipped the ground that Vera walked on, and he was nicer to her than anyone else he was around.

John Smithson continued to hear complaints about Blue, but he never fired him and said very little to him about all the complaining, because he didn't want to make Blue angry himself, fearing he would leave the job. He depended on Blue too much.

Blue was always trying to find something to amuse himself, since he would get so bored at times. When he met Thaddeus, he was amused at the young man's attempts to talk. He would stutter so bad, he just had to stop talking sometimes, because he was so confused with his words. Blue would poke fun at Thaddeus, and laughed his head off when he was trying to talk. Tears would swell in Thaddeus' eyes as he would listen to Blue repeatedly poke fun at him.

Thaddeus tried to avoid Blue as much as possible, and would go out of his way to avoid him, but Blue just loved to pick on Thaddeus. He would often go to Mattie's house where Thaddeus was staying and called him out. Derrick Williams, old and feeble, was unable to take care of himself, and could only watch as Blue would ridicule the young man.

The irate residents of the valley soon realized Blue was only trouble to them and their neighbors. They called Blue the skunk he really was, and they began to wish him deader than one. The worst was that Vera was so in love with Blue, she up and married him before he could be run out of the valley. The marriage between Daniel Johnson and Vera Williams established Blue as a resident of this community.

8

When Thomas arrived in Ovington from New York, he was elated to see his house being raised in the beauty surrounding this small community. Thomas told John of his joy and gratitude for the great work he was doing. He saw the many workers, was proud of all of them.

Thomas greeted the men he knew, and thanked them for doing a great job. He saw Blue working atop this tall building and noticed his professional skill. Blue looked at Thomas – no smile, no greeting, only a blank stare. Blue had heard of Thomas and his love he had for these people in the valley. Blue knew that Thomas was going to hear the stories that had started about him, and he felt like Thomas was a threat to him, but he turned his back and kept working.

Walter was anxious to show Thomas the beautiful work he had completed, including the many designs and beautiful carvings he had done. Thomas beamed with joy to see his dream becoming a reality.

Thomas went to his rented room in the little store, where he decided to put in an office since the space was so large. Thomas knew he had a lot of work to do before returning to Lawsonville.

The Ovington house was well kept and there was no untidiness. Thomas was well pleased that everything seemed to be neat and orderly. Thomas decided to stay in his parents' home until he finished his business in Ovington.

Thomas went down into the valley to see his friends, and be with the people he loved. Mattie's house was the first house he always went to, although it was sad, now that Mattie was gone.

Thaddeus met Thomas at the door. He hugged him and tried to say a few words, stuttering as usual whenever he was excited about something. Derrick Williams was a pitiful man to see since Mattie was gone.

He only rocked in his chair, as if he was waiting to join his wife. He was glad to see Thomas, and tried to get up to greet him, but stumbled as he tried to shake Thomas' hand.

Thomas could see that there was some tension with some of the people here. Times were better since most of the men who were the head of families were finding work. The housing was better, they had learned to do repairs on their homes, and the living conditions were getting better, so Thomas expected everyone to be happy, or at least be in a better mood than when he left.

Thomas went to Suzette Adams' house, with whom he had communicated since he had lost Mattie. Suzette was the midwife in the valley, and she had a concern for the many babies born in the valley. She asked Thomas about getting a school built for the children to attend. Thomas agreed to be responsible for seeing that a school would be built and a teacher would be employed.

There were several more families that Thomas went to see before returning to his parents' home. He felt sad as he left Little Valley. Thomas could see the lifestyle of these people was changing. The people were living better, but he could tell there was more hostility among the people, and families were not as close.

Thomas missed Beth, and he knew she would be expecting him to come home soon. The completion of his house was near, and he needed to go to Lawsonville and make arrangements for the long and complicated transition to Ovington.

Beth had been busy with the house and the farm since Thomas had been in Ovington. There were many changes in the year that she had been in New York. New help was hired, and she was happy that Jeffrey had hired Grace. Beth was really fond of this woman, though she seemed sad and lonely at times. But she did her work well and she was dependable, and she never refused to do anything she was asked to do.

Beth was nervous and irritable trying to keep the house in order, and organizing the separation of family heirlooms to be packed and shipped to Ovington. There were many items that Beth would not part with, but most of the furniture was to be left at the Cannon's farm.

Beth was so used to Anna and having to beg her to do things for her at times, she was so glad to have Grace at this time, since she had so much more to do. Clayton and Grace were close, even though they did not favor in looks as cousins. Grace was polite as Clayton, and did whatever he asked her to do.

Clayton still played the piano whenever he assumed Beth was out of hearing distance of the music. He had mastered the piano on his own, and he could play by ear. He entertained the workers when he could, but now that Beth was home, he rarely had the chance to play very much. No one had told Beth that Clayton could play her piano so well. Jeffrey did not mind that Clayton played the piano so much when the Ovingtons were in New York, because he loved to hear Clayton play himself.

While Beth went shopping was a chance for Clayton to practice on the piano. Beth came home sooner than usual when she went shopping in Lawsonville. Beth heard the beautiful music, much different than the classical arrangements she was used to playing. She was surprised to hear this music, but she knew it was coming from her house, and from her own piano.

Clayton was so preoccupied with the thrill of playing that he didn't hear Beth come into the house. He was surprised and ashamed at being caught. He jumped up and tried to explain his way out of playing her piano without her permission.

Everyone knew the piano was Beth's pride and joy. Beth scolded Clayton, telling him that she was surprised that he was so talented with music, but that he should have asked her permission to play her piano. Clayton knew Beth was angry at him, and it saddened him to think that he would never be able to play his music he loved to play on the piano.

Seeing Clayton so unhappy, Grace tried to cheer him up. He was more quiet than usual, and withdrawn, but he did his work as usual, but once his work was completed, he went to his room, and stayed there until the next morning.

Fred and Anna were still doing as little as possible, and sometimes Beth would get irritable with them. If she didn't have Grace, she would have had a hard time trying to get everything done. Beth told the two that their new home would be in the mountain, and would be in an isolated area. This frightened them, and they again begged Beth not to move to someplace that seemed so dangerous to them.

Beth tried to get Fred and Anna and the rest of the household staff to work a little harder to help her since she expected Thomas any day now. Beth set out the best linens, and had special food prepared for his welcome home dinner.

Grace came to Beth crying on the day that Thomas was expected home. Clayton was nowhere to be found; his clothes were gone, and there was no sign of him anywhere. Grace swore she did not know where he was, or that he was leaving because he never told her he was leaving the farm. Beth was devastated. To lose Clayton was hurting to her and she started to cry as she hugged Grace.

The day that Thomas came home was to be a happy occasion, but Beth was worn out from packing and Clayton's leaving left her very unpleasant. Beth ran to Thomas, threw herself in his arms, and starting crying. Beth was ashamed, but Thomas assured her everything would be alright.

Fred and Anna were shocked by Clayton's leaving, and began to help with more duties around the house. They were afraid of Thomas, being used to only the Cannons and having their way, they knew Thomas would not give in to their laziness and refusal to work at times.

Beth felt better as Thomas told her about the beauty of their house in Ovington. Thomas excitedly described each room. Beth was still reluctant to move to the mountain, but was eager to see her new home.

Grace was more withdrawn since Clayton had left. She would go to her small room when the day was ended. Beth noticed Grace putting on weight; she was rather plump, wore long dresses, and a apron over the dress, but she seemed to spread out from the hips. Grace seemed to grieve very hard for Clayton. Beth asked her about other family members, but she never got a answer from her.

Fred and Anna would cry each time that Beth mentioned the move to Ovington. They were getting old, and didn't like changes, and weren't too fond of Thomas. They were more happy at the farm since they had lived there so long. Fred missed James Cannon; he was like a shadow behind James Cannon when he was younger, traveling with him, and enjoying the benefits of associating with James Cannon.

Anna had always taken care of Beth, the spoiled and pampered child that no one liked, because James Cannon let her have her way, and she had ruled the Cannon house when she was small. Beth Marie turned Anna's hair grey as she tried to please her and keep her happy as a child.

9

Thomas and Beth discussed the farm, and the conditions of letting Jeffrey Carter have the job of overseeing this huge farmland. Beth wanted Jeffrey to stay at the farm just to be in charge, but Thomas had a contract drawn up. There was to be an agreement on the profits from the farm that Beth be paid twenty-five percent of all profits. Jeffrey didn't have to buy any equipment, and the farm had a lot of stock already here. Beth loved Jeffrey, and wanted him to have a good start in life. Beth knew she did not need any money.

The first phase of the Ovington house was completed in 1912. This was the year that Thomas moved Beth Marie to their home. The month was June when the weather would be nice enough to travel.

Thomas experienced one of the hardest tasks in his life trying to move Beth's priceless heirlooms and other valuables to the Ovington's new home. These valuables were packed in wagons, and secured by thick quilts around them to prevent breakage. They were driven by the finest Cannon horses. Thomas knew Beth had a lot of items that were dear to her, but he knew she had no use for some of the many dishes that were packed.

Grace had agreed to move to Ovington with Beth. Grace knew she would be a long way from home, but since Clayton was gone, she didn't mind leaving Lawsonville.

Fred and Anna were unhappy as usual as they packed. This was the second time for them to leave home. With tears in their eyes, they went to the many workers and told them good-bye, because they felt like they would never see them again.

Beth went to her father's grave, this was the second time she would leave a loved one behind. Beth stood over James Cannon's grave, and cried uncontrollable tears as she said good-bye to her father.

Remembering how unhappy she had been in Lawsonville, she was more sorrowful to leave her only family behind. Beth whispered his name, and wet his grave with her tears. Thomas came to get his wife because she was so weak from her grief. She hated to leave her father's grave. Thomas led her back to the Cannon house as the servants looked on.

Thomas tried to make everyone comfortable. The drivers of the wagons were standing attentive until Thomas assigned them to their wagon to be driven the long way to his home. There were two Phaeton's on the farm; one was Beth's, and one had been for James' comfort, when he decided to ride around the community. Thomas had the two carriages hitched to the best horses on Cannon farm, and made sure they would be comfortable to take the long trip to Ovington. Thomas and Beth rode in the first one; the second one was to carry Richard and Geneva, the couple Beth had asked to go with her, since they often worked for the Cannons and were well liked by the family. There was also a big carriage on the farm, and this one he had Fred, Anna, and Grace to ride in. Thomas wasn't planning on taking so many people, but Beth liked the Davises, so Thomas employed them to go with Beth, and they were to stay at the Ovington house. All of them were eager to see the new house, except Anna. She never gave up; to the last minute she still tried to get Beth to stay at the farm.

The trip was long and hard with the heavy loads. All the bumps and rough gravel they had to drive over were tiring. They slept for short periods of time, and spent little time eating.

Thomas and Beth were like two children as they traveled to Ovington. Thomas would steal a kiss from Beth, and he loved to squeeze her small knee as he would whisper his love to her, and assured her they would be together and happy for the rest of their lives.

Everyone was quiet as they came close to the mountain. The hill was so steep, and the horses, already tired, were difficult to handle. The drivers were tired themselves, and they cussed and lashed the whip at the horses when they tried to make the trip up to the mountain.

Fred and Anna seemed more frightened as they neared the Ovington house. Grace was sick most of the trip. She had to stop sometimes because of her sickness. Beth was getting worried about her; she knew Grace never complained. Grace was looking pale, and seemed in pain. Thomas assured Beth that only the trip was making her sick.

Richard and Geneva were happy during the long trip. They rode in their own Phaeton, which was luxury to them, and they enjoyed the country as they traveled. They worried about Grace, but for Thomas to let them ride in this Phaeton was thrilling to them.

They were a few miles from Ovington when Grace began to have severe stomach cramps. Thomas stopped the Phaeton, and had Grace to lie on the ground for a while as they bathed her face with cool water. This lasted for a couple of hours, and Grace seemed to be alright. Thomas made Grace a pallet in one of the wagons, and had her head elevated, and Grace seemed to be better as they continued the trip.

Some of the residents in Ovington had seen the wagons and Phaetons, all in a neat formation as they tailgated to the Ovington's house. This was a joyful sight as they knew an Ovington would be living in this community once again.

The neighbors gathered around to welcome Thomas and his new wife. They had prepared food and more than 25 people had come to help them with unloading the wagons and unpacking the many items for their new home.

Beth expressed her joy at the beautiful work John Smithson had done building the enormous house. The greatest joy was over the beautiful porcelain oil lamps hanging from the ceiling in each room. Thomas let the neighbors take a tour of his house.

Fred and Anna were calm as they looked throughout the house. The tears were gone, and they seemed happy as they looked at all the beauty of this house. Thomas showed the workers their rooms. They were as large as the rest of the rooms in the house, and although there was only a bed in each room, the flooring and walls were as nice as the other rooms. Of course, Thomas would have it no other way. He would not have any room built in his house that wasn't the best.

Grace was still sick, and she went to her room and laid down. Beth told her to stay in bed and rest from the long trip. Anna took food to her room, and stayed with her until she felt better.

Richard and Geneva Davis' room was the largest one of all the workers' rooms. Beth felt that since they were married, she should give them a larger room than the single workers. Although they had only a bed in the room, they had brought a small chest, and a sewing machine, given to Geneva by her mother when she had married Richard.

The neighbors that had come to help Thomas stayed into the night, they were enjoying the company and this beautiful house. They were elated when Thomas lit the porcelain oil lamps throughout the house, they stared in disbelief. Thomas thanked each one, and invited them to come back to visit, and promised he would have dinner for each one who had helped him when he really needed help.

The Ovingtons had been in their new home about five days. The house wasn't in order yet, there were many things that needed to be done, but they were still tired from the long trip, and everyone wasn't up to doing very much.

Thomas and Beth renewed their love for each other as they clung to each other, sometimes going to their bedroom in the middle of the day, refusing to answer the door when anyone called or knocked on their door. Thomas hands explored Beth's small body. As she trembled with passion, he kissed her lips until they were bruised. Beth's breasts become sore from the bites, as he was unable to control himself, and he taught Beth many tricks of love as he thrilled his wife until she was drained of all her strength.

The household finally settled down after a couple of weeks, as each person did his duties. Grace would do her work and go straight to her room. Everyone would worry about her, but she assured them that she was fine. The third week, Grace seemed to be in pain, and sometimes Anna would see her crying, but Grace would only say that she missed Clayton.

The house was in order, and everyone seemed to be more relaxed and happy. Each one cooperated and duties were being performed as assigned. Each one of the women that worked for Beth was allowed to make curtains for their room with some of the many bolts of material that Beth had brought from New York.

One night after approximately a month, the house was quiet, and all were asleep, when each member of the household was awakened by screams in rapid sound as if they were being cut off. The Davises, and Fred and Anna, knew it was coming from Grace's room. Thomas and Beth awakened confused; they jumped out of their bed, and ran to the servant's quarters. Thomas pushed open Grace's door, shocked speechless as the other looked on. They could see Grace as she clawed at the sheet, still screaming as she pulled up her shirt, and tried to hold her stomach.

All of the Ovington household people were standing over Grace as she cried out with excruciating pain. They finally realized that Grace was in labor, and was about to give birth. They continued to stand over Grace, she was screaming so loudly, but she didn't say anything between pains. Thomas finally woke up enough to know that he had to go into the valley to go to Suzette Adams house to bring her to help Grace.

He quickly dressed, and found his lantern, knowing that he would have to walk to her house. It was dangerous at night if you rode a horse, because the horses would be spooked by the many sounds in the black night and they would throw you if something spooked them when it was dark.

Thomas knew the mountain, but he was scared sometimes to travel this mountain himself. He walked alone, seeing only a short distant in front of him with his lantern. He was very nervous, but thinking about how sick Grace was, he hurried on to Suzette Adam's house.

Suzette jumped out of the bed at the sound of loud knocking on her door. She knew something awful had happened, and when she saw Thomas at the door, she feared the worst. Explaining that he needed her, she quickly dressed, and followed him to the Ovington house.

Thomas explained to Suzette about Grace being in labor. Suzette stared into the black night speechless. She didn't like this at all; she always went to the mother's house before they would get into hard labor, and stayed until the baby was born. Thomas explained that they never knew that Grace was with child, or in labor until tonight.

Grace screamed between periods of unconsciousness, never saying a word. She was perspiring badly. The women bathed her face, and tried to wet her parched lips. They became frightened as Grace became pale, her hands became white and she soon was too weak to scream.

After Thomas explained Grace's condition, Suzette was worried, for she knew this would be a difficult birth.

They finally approached the house, there was no sound, only the stillness of the black night. Suzette's heart was pounding as she tried to keep up with Thomas. They rushed into Grace's room. When Suzette saw Grace, she knew that Grace was beyond help. This was a breech birth; Suzette saw the tiny foot as she examined Grace. Her shadow breathing was visible. Suzette worked frantically as Thomas tried to help free the tiny baby girl from her mother's body as Grace drew her last breath.

The house was in a uproar as Beth, Anna and Geneva began to cry hysterically. Even Richard looked at Grace's still body, shook his head and wiped tears from his eyes. Poor Fred was as bad as Anna as they held each other crying.

Suzette was real nervous as she tried to get the bruised and tiny baby to breathe, who was almost dead herself. Suzette wrapped the baby in a small cloth, and spanked her bottom as she tried to get her to breathe. The baby's faint cry was so weak, but Suzette continued to try to help her as best as she could.

The hysterical state of the women was annoying to Thomas, and he asked them to leave the room, knowing that there was nothing they could do for Grace, and they were making him nervous. Suzette asked the women to boil water to clean the baby, and to make her a little sugar water to feed the baby if she continued to live.

Suzette had some of the ladies in the valley to come up to the Ovington house and bathe and dress Grace for burial. There was no embalming, so the bodies were usually buried within a couple of days, but they kept Grace in a cave by the little spring where it was cool, thinking the baby would die, and they would bury the baby with her mother.

Beth allowed Anna to care for the tiny baby. Anna named her Sarah Anna Jackson, giving her the name of herself, except Sarah, because they did not know Grace's last name. She had never told anyone, and she avoided questions about herself. Anna gave the baby sugar water, and a mint tea that she was able to force down the tiny baby.

After five days, seeing that little Sarah was still alive, they buried Grace in the Little Valley. Thomas, Richard and Geneva were the only ones present besides the men Thomas hired to dig the Grave, and lower Grace into her final resting place. Geneva cried uncontrollable tears, as Richard held her in his arms. Even Thomas wiped tears from his eyes, as he turned to go home to Beth, who had to be put to bed.

Beth blamed herself for not suspecting Grace was pregnant. Grace was supposed to be Clayton's cousin, but Beth was sure cousin or not, she believed Clayton to be the father of Sarah. Clayton had run off in the middle of the night, fearing the truth would come out.

Sarah began to get stronger with Anna's tender loving care. The baby began to fill out, her hair was long and curly, and the baby had a beautiful color. By this time she was a month old.

Thomas knew he had to find a family to take care of Sarah. There were no Black families for miles around. These people were more Indian, except Blue, and Thomas would not ask Blue to take a child, because he considered him to be too abusive. Thomas asked Suzette to take Sarah, and to care for her until he could find a home for her. Suzette agreed to keep her temporarily, because she had two children of her own, and kept very busy delivering babies in the Little Valley.

Anna became hysterical when Thomas came for Sarah. She begged Thomas to give her the baby, and let her raise Sarah. Thomas, believing Anna too old, only shook his head as he wrapped the baby, and carried her and the few belongings to Suzette's house.

Beth would only cry and hugged Anna, as she tried not to show her grief of losing the baby. Anna cried and wrung her hands as she was in a hysteric state. As usual, Fred would only try to comfort Anna as she broke loose and ran to her room.

Beth, remembering the happiness of moving to her new home and all the household staff being excited, was now clouded by death. Beth could not understand why Grace did not tell them of her condition, so that they could have helped her.

Beth rearranged the household duties, since Grace was gone. The work would be harder on Anna and Geneva. Of course, Geneva wasn't as smart as Grace, but she assured Beth that she would try to learn her way of doing the duties as Grace had.

Thomas was worried about his finances. The completion of the first phase of the Ovington's house had cost him nearly $10,000, and he was nearly broke. Thomas went to his office, and went through all his records. He decided to sell all of his parents' land. He would have the land surveyed and marked off in sections, because he did not want one person to buy all of the land.

Beth realized her husband was nearly broke. Looking around, she saw the beauty of this house, and knew Thomas had built this home just for her. Though she wasn't too happy living in this isolated area, but to be with Thomas, she would have moved to any location. Beth decided to put her husband on a sort of salary, to take care of her father's businesses. She wasn't one to take over a business, and she knew her father would want Thomas to take care of his estate, rather than anyone else. She had more than enough money to take care of herself, and to live comfortably the rest of her life, but she knew her husband was poor, and had only been able to build this home because of the loan from her father.

Thomas decided to hire the same team of men to clear his parents' land that he had hired before to clear his section of land. He wanted the land cleared so that he could section each track of land, no more than 50 acres of land to each section. This land was to extend backward into the woods surrounding the property. Thomas would sell enough to each person or family, hoping they would start building some type of business in this community.

Everyone within miles knew the well-respected family name, Ovington. Willie Monroe was the only one of the Ovingtons to disgrace this community. The residents began to respect Thomas, and considered him a leader in the same way as his forefather, Joseph Clyde Ovington.

Thomas was always lean, and was noted for his natty attire, wearing only the trousers and vest of a full suit. He seldom wore a hat, rarely left his house without his boots on, and never walked this mountain without his shot-gun by his side.

Walking around the community, as Thomas usually did, he noticed someone living in the Daniels' old house. He was curious because the Daniels were deceased, and no one knew where Rose Ann was. Walking past the house a couple of times, he noticed the house was so run down, it was about to fall in.

Knocking on the door, Thomas waited for a few minutes before someone finally came to the door. Thomas stared speechless, the woman was hardly recognizable, but he knew this woman was Rose Ann, his heart skipped a beat as he stared at her.

Rose Ann tried to smile as she looked at Thomas, he was trying to recover from the shock. The once beautiful Rose Ann, that everyone called Precious, was beyond being the darling of Ovington now, she was much different than when Thomas last saw her.

Rose Ann's once beautiful skin was now wrinkled. Her big round eyes showed dark circles; her parted lips revealed stained and bad teeth. Rose Ann told Thomas she was sick, as he stared at her body crippled by rheumatism. Her once beautiful black hair was grey and needed combing. She asked Thomas to help her, because she was sick and needed food, and money to live on.

The past had come back to haunt Thomas. He thought about the pain Rose Ann had caused his mother. What was worse, he thought about the memories of when she had seduced him on the mountain when he was vulnerable. He remembered how she took him when he was a helpless young man, and feeling unloved. He was still a virgin and didn't know anything about women. She taught him about women and the art of making love. In fact, she knew so much about lovemaking that she was able to passionately satisfy herself. Thomas remembered how he had never forgiven this woman for causing him shame.

Thomas stepped back in shock, as he wondered how this woman had the nerve to come back home after all the pain she had cause him and his mother. She was the most disgraced woman to live on this mountain because of the way she had behaved. Thomas was feeling guilty as he went home to Beth.

Beth knew something was wrong with Thomas; he wasn't good at hiding hurt or sadness in his life. He asked Beth to send food to Rose Ann's house. He gave Richard directions, and told him to tell her that the food was from Thomas.

10

The people in Little Valley were going through many hardships, suffering financial troubles because of the lack of work. There was grief when they found Derrick Williams dead in his own bed, who had gone to sleep and never woke up. Thaddeus was still living with his grandfather, but he hardly ever went out of the house because he was still afraid of Blue, who had continued to harass this young man.

Blue was still the devil. He had the people believing he could make them lots of money and that they could make a fortune by selling their moonshine liquor to the Colored people in a small, isolated community about ten miles off the mountain called Spalding. The Colored people were known to buy the moonshine from the few people that made it. They had money because some worked on public jobs, which were few, but they lived a little better than most of the Black race.

Blue was the head of this dangerous scheme to take the moonshine off the mountain. The Tuckers and Williams began to talk of going into business big time, as Blue laid out the plans of getting the liquor off the mountain.

They got together and began to build more stills for their operation. Thomas was disturbed when he heard the rumors about Blue's persuading the people to bootleg moonshine.

Blue loved Vera, but she refused to leave her family and the valley she had lived in all of her life, so Blue had refused to leave the valley with John Smithson when he had finished his job in Ovington. Blue was getting bored and was always causing some kind of trouble. These people lived as a close-knit family, but Blue tried to make trouble between them whenever he had the chance. Thaddeus was afraid of Blue and avoided him whenever possible, going out of his way if he saw him coming to keep from getting anywhere near him.

Blue knew that Thaddeus was trying to stay out of his way, so he hid in the outhouse near Thaddeus' house. He waited until he passed, and jumped out on the frightened young man. Blue began to push him, slap his body, and even knocked him down, as he laughed at Thaddeus crying and pleading with him to let him alone. Thomas was walking through the valley, as he did almost everyday, and he saw this cruel prank. He was so infuriated that he raised his shotgun and shot the outhouse door to smithereens. Thomas reloaded the gun, and ran to where Blue was standing, calling him names beyond repeating, and aimed the gun at Blue's body as Thaddeus pleaded to Thomas not to shoot.

Blue, too frightened to move, only pleaded with Thomas not to shoot him. Blue was quick with a knife, but he was afraid of a gun. Thomas verbally lashed out at Blue, warning him never to abuse or pick on Thaddeus again, or he would be shot dead wherever he was standing. Thomas comforted Thaddeus as he took him home. Seeing the way this young man was living, he asked him to pack his clothes, and whatever few belongings he had, and he would let him live in one of the servants' rooms in his house.

Thaddeus went with Thomas to Suzette's house to see Sarah. The baby had grown to four years old, and seemed to be free of sickness. Thaddeus was ecstatic as he told Suzette he was going to live in the Ovington's house, and he would be paid a salary for the job Thomas was giving him.

Beth was having her own troubles with Anna. She was unhappy, never left the house, and she talked about Sarah all the time. She had never forgiven Thomas for not letting her keep Sarah. Anna loved Sarah and wanted this child, since she had never had a child herself.

Beth and her servants were afraid to leave the house because they could not get used to the many animals that frightened them. When they were told of bull snakes that were as big around as a big tree, and sounded like a bull, they just about fainted. The most frightening things were the screams in the night as animals cried for their life, as the vicious animal would catch them, and kill them as they roamed the mountain.

Beth asked Thomas to have the outside grounds of their house landscaped, so that they would be able to enjoy the outside, and not have to stay in the house so much.

Thomas gave Thaddeus what had been Grace's room, and asked Beth to find a job for Thaddeus to do. Thaddeus was thrilled to be a part of the Ovington's household staff, though he was rather clumsy inside the house.

Everyone was beginning to settle down again. Beth was getting worried about Thomas. She knew he was in debt, and refused to use her money, and was trying to sell off his parents' land to help him out financially.

Geneva was the only one to sew, and did such beautiful work, she was always busy sewing the many items that Beth wanted her to sew for the house. In her spare time, from the scraps she had left over, she would sew little dresses for Sarah.

Everyone seemed to be happy again, trying not to think of Grace, and losing her. Thaddeus was trying his best to do the duties he was asked to do, but he only got in the way. Thomas let him work outside more to help get him out of Beth's way. Richard was in charge of keeping the horses and stables in tip-top shape, as well as most of the outside buildings. Sometimes Fred would help, but Thomas was beginning to let Thaddeus help Richard more outside. This new arrangement helped Beth since she wasn't too happy with Thaddeus in the house.

Beth decided to build around the Ovington's house, believing Thomas to be in too much debt already. Beth asked Walter to get her a good carpenter. The main purpose for the additional buildings was for cottages for the servants to live in.

Thomas employed men to clear the land he was selling, and told them to start clearing the left side of the land. Since his parents house sat near the south end of Ovington, the land cleared as far down the mountain as he owned.

The next three years were busy around the Ovington's estate as the land was cleared, and building was in progress. Walter had found a man that could build anything you asked him to, and he was very good.

Beth also sent for Blue, and she asked him to help with the garden, which she wanted to be rocked, since Thomas refused to even talk to this man. Blue agreed to work for Beth as long as she needed him. Beth had the backyard close to the house landscaped. Beautiful flowers were planted to show off the beautiful rock garden that Beth had hired Blue to build. This was a real show place, and Beth was proud of this work done by the men.

Thomas was real busy these days, selling his land that he had decided to sell. It was slow to sell at first. He was careful who he sold his land to. He never talked to anyone that could not pay the price, and he took no mortgages on the land.

Sarah was shifted from one home to another. Suzette was too busy delivering babies to care for her. She was a healthy child, in spite of her traumatic birth. The families in Little Valley cared for her as best they could, but weren't able to keep her for long periods of time.

The people in this community were so racially mixed, you didn't know what they really were. He was as mean as ever, but knowing both of Sarah's parents had been really black, Blue began to teach Sarah some of the low down mean blues songs that he knew. These were the songs that these Colored people were singing, and Sarah could really belt out these songs, to everyone's surprise.

Suzette never let Thomas rest until he got busy and started to see about getting a school built for the children in the valley to attend. The residents of the valley finally decided to build the school on the property of Derrick and Mattie Williams. This was a good location because there was plenty of ground for the children to play, and it was next to the little rocked spring.

Thaddeus loved to follow Thomas whenever he could, as he walked different areas everyday. Beth was glad that Thaddeus was out of the house; he was forever making her nervous with his clumsiness. He was eager to make her happy by doing as much for Beth as he could, but she preferred that he just stay out of her house.

Sarah never stayed with Blue and Vera, but Blue always went to the house where Sarah was staying and played with her, or would get her to sing some of the songs that he taught her to sing. Of course, Sarah enjoyed singing and was happy to put on a show for anyone that would listen to her sing.

Blue and Vera were having babies of their own. They had had a baby each year they were married, and this was enough work for Vera, so she never took Sarah into her home. But some of the other residents did try to keep Sarah for short periods of time.

Blue was out of work again after completing the job Beth had hired him to do. He had time on his hands, and he began to help with the stills. He was always doing something that wasn't right anyway. At night he would go to the house where Sarah was staying, and asked her to sing. Most of the songs she sang were the ones that he had taught her. Sometimes he would take her on his knees and sing along with her. This would be so much fun for Sarah because Blue was the only one who seemed to enjoy these low down blues songs.

Blue went to Spalding and talked to the people there about this good moonshine that was made in the valley. Blue assured these people that he could supply them with this fine liquor if enough of them would buy from him. They were a little afraid of Blue because his reputation had gotten around even in this little isolated community. Big John Patton, as they called John Patton, agreed to trust Blue, and purchased gallons of the moonshine if they would deliver it to them. The men in Little Valley hauled the moonshine down the steep mountain in wagons. Most of the moonshine was made by the Tuckers or the Williams; they were the two biggest moon-shiners in Little Valley.

Thomas was getting unhappy with them making so much moonshine. He was afraid of the kind of people that this business attracted. Thomas knew Blue was a dangerous man, and had influenced these people into doing something that could get them hurt. This could be dangerous, but the men were happy with the money they were making.

Beth could tell Thomas was worried by the look on his face. The lines were visible as he worried about the people in this valley. Thomas hated Blue but since he was a part of Mattie's family, he tried to tolerate him.

The Colored people in Spalding became very friendly with the moonshiners. They learned where Little Valley was located, and started to visit these people after they had been invited. They were skeptical of these people at first, but the Colored men, seeing so many beautiful women, lost their fear. They knew how Blue was welcome in this valley, so they just made themselves at home.

Blue was having the time of his life as he started up the card games again. Blue was the best card player among the men. That Blue never lost a game, of course, made the men angry, but they loved to play cards with him, even though they knew he was going to take their money.

Thomas went to Vera and asked her to talk to Blue about taking the men's money playing cards, because they needed their money for their families. Vera could see that Thomas was angry and worried about Blue taking advantage of these people. She tried to assure Thomas that Blue loved her family and would not do anything to hurt them, or cause them to get in trouble with the men from Spalding that came to visit. Thomas knew better, but seeing Vera wasn't going to believe him, he decided not to worry about Blue and his card game.

The big money the men made with their bootleg moonshine helped them to live a little better. The homes were repaired, and living conditions were much better, plus money was collected among the families to build a school for their children.

The valley was really a beautiful place, and Thomas loved these people as his own. He wanted only the best for the families there. He wanted no shame or corruption to come to this tiny community, but he was afraid of Blue's talking these people into doing something to get them into trouble. He could make them think they were doing no wrong.

The men from Spalding became regular visitors to this valley. They were involved in love affairs with some of the women there, and there were pregnancies among the women, and a new generation of mixed races began.

Beth tried to cheer up Thomas, as he seemed to be distressed over the change in the people of valley. Beth tried to be affectionate around him. She wanted to love him as passionately as when they first married. Thomas' mind was so occupied with so many worries that he wasn't paying too much attention to Beth as a wife. He was hurting Beth's feelings, making her feel that he put these people before her.

Beth began to shed tears as she begged Thomas to forget the things that the people were doing in Little Valley, and try to be happy. She wanted Thomas to help her with the house, and the buildings she was having added around their estate.

Beth was still having problems with Anna. The poor Black woman was so unhappy. She hated this place, and often asked Beth why she brought her here. Anna was really too old to work, and she began to just sit and rock in her chair most of the day, as if she was just waiting on death. Fred was no better. If Anna was unhappy, he was unhappy. Beth was sorry she had brought them away from the farm.

Thomas was getting more financially stable as he sold off his parents' land. Thomas would request that he be paid cash, rather than making a mortgage on the lots. He needed the cash more than tying up the land with a mortgage. Of course, he was happy with the profit he collected from each sale.

Rose Ann still lived in the old Daniels house. Thomas finally got enough nerve to visit Rose Ann and asked her if she needed anything. Rose Ann's condition was pathetic–she was almost bedridden and crippled, but she only asked Thomas to bring her some food. Seeing Rose Ann's condition, and the way she looked, he assured her he would see that she had the things she needed.

Thomas was ashamed of the way that he hated this woman, blaming her for all of his childhood unhappiness. But seeing the condition she was living in now, the bad feelings he had for this woman were gone. He agreed to take care of her and would try to find her brothers to make sure someone would be with her all of the time.

Beth saw Thomas coming, and could see that he was in a good mood. She ran to him and clung to her husband. As he picked her up, he asked Beth to forgive him for being so cold to her. Beth was elated to be loved by Thomas again. This was a lonely place to be, with only the servants to comfort her when Thomas was absent, which was often. Without Thomas' love, she never would have moved to this isolated place. The household staff observed the joy between Thomas and Beth. Thomas went to each of them, and asked them to visit Rose Ann each day and to take her food and try to help her until he found her brothers to come for her. Since she was unable to care for herself, he wanted one or two of them to visit her each day to help share this responsibility he had taken on.

Beth Marie knew Thomas was in a good mood now, so she felt this was a good time to ask him a few favors of her own. Thomas was holding her as if he would never let her go, and kissing her passionately, thrilling her to the point she could hardly speak. But she took this opportunity to ask him to bring her piano to Ovington. Beth missed playing the piano she enjoyed so much, which was relaxing to her. Thomas agreed to bring her piano to Ovington.

Beth knew Anna was getting too old to take care of herself, but she didn't know what to do about Anna, and the way she was acting these days. She did very little work these days, and she was just a burden to the Ovingtons, and she kept poor Fred upset all the time. Thomas asked Fred to talk to Anna, and try to cheer her up. Thomas knew Anna missed Grace, and that she worried about Sarah. But most of all, she was unhappy because he didn't let her keep Sarah and raise the child as her own. She was grieving more than just being unhappy with this new home.

Richard and Geneva had moved into one of the small cottages that Beth had constructed for the servants. As soon as they finished their work every day, they would go to their small home, and rarely came back to the Ovington's house until the next morning.

Beth asked Thomas to take Thaddeus with him when he left for Lawsonville. Thaddeus wanted to be helpful, but he only stayed in Beth's way most of the time. She hated to hurt his feeling by refusing to let him do some of the duties in the house, and thought the trip to Lawsonville with Thomas would do him some good.

11

The years of World War I, 1914 through 1918, were to make a drastic change in the Ovington community. The young men went off to the war, some never to return. Of those that lived, some refused to come back home to this isolated place that had no future for them after the war. Some of the young men had girlfriends that they were planning to marry. They came back for their girlfriends, married, and then left this community to seek a better place to live.

The passing of Paul Benson, who owned a big farm, and the takeover of his brother Carl, was devastating to the people in Little Valley. This man was nothing like his brother Paul, who was a kind and likeable man around this part of the community. Carl Benson proved to be the worst yet to move to this mountain. Carl Benson's abhorrent behavior to the residents in the valley started from the beginning when he set his foot on the mountain.

Carl Benson was a short, potbellied, tobacco-spitting man. He moved to this community with his loud mouth, and in his voice you could hear that he detested the people down in valley. He made no secret about his hatred of anybody that looked black. He was a die-hard racist, and a genuine son-of-a-bitch.

The long creek that ran through Little Valley routed through Carl Benson's farm, and on down the mountain. The Little Valley people had made a path the length of the creek, and this was their way of getting out into the community. This was also the wagon route to deliver their moonshine, or to go places to shop, or haul their supplies to their homes.

The first thing that Carl Benson did was to put a stop to these people coming through his property. When Carl found out that these people would be coming on his land, his meanness came out real fast. He put up a sign, and he stood guard with his shotgun to assure them he would shoot, if they come through his land.

The men, bewildered and very frightened of this man, decided to wait for Thomas to come back from Lawsonville. Blue was even reluctant to cross this man's path. The first time he and some of the men passed through Benson's place, Benson had used some of the worst obscene language, and told them that "he hated all niggers," and ordered them off his land. This was the worst behavior they had seen out of anybody that ever lived in this community.

Paul Benson had always been nice to the people in Little Valley. He would send them milk, meat or whatever he had plenty of to families that needed help at times. But his brother Carl was much different, and had a meaner personality.

During this period, there were other changes with the clearing and selling of Thomas' land. Other people came to the mountain with blueprints of new homes that they would build here in this community. These people were more of a prominent type of people. Thomas refused to sell to anyone that wasn't capable of changing Ovington, because he wanted this community to build up into a profitable place with businesses.

There was also going to be trouble for Little Valley, with the drive for national prohibition, as the 18th amendment was being adopted. Prohibition was inevitable, and it was sure to be signed into law.

There was also a school being built for the children in Little Valley. The building was constructed of three rooms in a straight, long ranch type of building, approximately 4000 square feet. There were six long tables built by Walter, and tiny chairs for the children at each table. Blue rocked the fireplace in the center of the building.

On Thomas' trip to Lawsonville, he had made arrangements to bring Beth's piano back to Ovington. This was a long and treacherous job for Thomas, as he had to hire several men to help him. If Thomas had known the trouble he would have had in moving this piano, he would have left it in Lawsonville. However, he loved Beth enough to try to do whatever made her happy.

Arriving in Ovington, Thomas was happy to be home with Beth. He had missed her, and he had managed to bring her piano home, to her joy and delight. Thomas also had planned to find Rose Ann's brothers while he was away, and this was a success, because he was able to find them. They made Thomas a promise to come to Ovington and take her back home with them. When Rose Ann's brothers came to take her home, Thomas went to their house and offered to buy the Daniels' property. Rose Ann was glad to sell the land, since she would never be able to take care of the house. She wasn't able to support herself, the times were hard, and she needed the money.

Thomas went to Suzette's home to talk to her about the school. Together they went to each family with children to enroll them in the new school. There was no teacher, so Thomas agreed to teach the children himself until a teacher could be found.

Carl Benson was still acting mean and refused to let the residents of Little Valley come through his land. Thomas was told about this man's refusal to let the people come through his land. This was disturbing to everyone, because as long as anyone could remember, they had cut through the Benson's farm. Thomas was also told of this man's hatred of the black race of people. This was distressing to Thomas, but he told them not to worry about this man; he would make another route for them to travel.

The clearing of the land down the mountain was visible for miles around. The large estate of Thomas Theodore Ovington could be seen clearly down the mountain. This attracted transients looking for work, although some of them were bums who never stayed in one place for long. They began to make their way up the mountain looking for food and work if any were available.

Construction for the new homes were under way. This meant strangers were in this small community. Most of the men would always find their way to Little Valley, and what it had to offer, which was the moonshine. They always seemed to hear the news about the bootlegging, and they found their way to the place where they could find something to keep them company while they were there.

Blue always loved to see new faces, so he could try and work his con game on them. He was making a lot of money with the card games, and moonshine he was getting orders for.

Thomas had given the men permission to cut a road up the hill to his land in front of his estate directly in front of his house. The ground was cleared, and small rocks from the mountain were spread to keep the mud off the road. This took many weeks even though the men worked hard and long hours to finish the road. They were anxious to finish it because of their long delay getting their moonshine off the mountain.

There was always the troublemaker Carl Benson watching these people. He approached Thomas shortly after the road was built, and asked him why he was so fond of these people in the valley. Carl claimed these people were a disgrace to this community. Thomas tried to ignore this man, seeing him only as trouble, and asked him to please mind his own business.

Thomas always went into the valley each morning to meet the children for classes. This was a different experience for the children, and some were frightened at first. Most of the children knew Thomas, but had never left home without their parents. Of course, they soon realized this was different, and found the classes very interesting and loved for Thomas to teach them. Even though he was strict with them, after several weeks they began to enjoy this new experience called "school."

Sarah was enrolled in school, and was excited to be in school with all of the other children. Having lived in most of these children's homes at different times, being together with all of them at the same time in school made her happy each day. Sarah was smart, and she could sing the songs that Blue taught her. Thomas was moved by this child's talent. Sarah was big for her age, seemed to be a very strong girl, and never seemed to be unhappy by the way she was shifted from one residence to another.

Thomas told Beth about Sarah's talent of singing a song and sometimes acting more grown up than a child her age. Beth asked Thomas to bring Sarah to the Ovington's house so she could hear Sarah sing. She believed this would also make Anna happy to hear this child sing.

Anna was still sitting and rocking in her chair that she occupied most of the days. Geneva would try to talk to Anna every day. Worried about the old woman, and her withdrawal from reality, she feared Anna was going to die. Fred would try to get Anna to work or get more interested in something around the house, but he never scolded her or tried to make her do anything she didn't want to do.

Thomas brought Sarah up to the Ovington's house to let Beth, Anna, and Geneva hear her sing. Beth was moved to tears to hear this child sing in such a beautiful tone of voice. Anna, seeing Sarah, and hearing her sing so beautifully, brightened her face. When Sarah finished singing, Anna got up and hugged Sarah, and began to cry, repeating over and over, "my baby, my baby." Thomas looked speechless, as Beth, Geneva and Anna all began to cry together. Thomas just picked up Sarah, not understanding all the fuss with the women. Sarah began to cry also as Thomas carried her home to Little Valley.

12

The workload was heavy for Thomas as he tried to go into the valley to teach the children. He would go to his office to try to attend to his own business, but the biggest headache was listening to the gripes of Carl Benson. He never seemed to stop finding fault with the people Thomas loved in the Little Valley. Carl knew he would upset Thomas whenever he talked harshly about these people, so he made it his business to annoy Thomas every chance he got.

There was heavy construction going on as the new homes were being built. The new homes were beautiful, but none of them was as stately as the Ovington's house. This community was becoming totally different, and this made Thomas stand back, and look with pride, knowing his name proudly built this community.

Many new faces were seen among the residents as the work was being completed. The saddest were the workers at Carl Benson's farm. Carl only hired the white race of people when he first took over his brother's farm, but by word of mouth, the news got around that he was an evil man to work for, and the white people stopped working for him, including all of his brothers' old help that he had working for him for years.

Carl Benson started hiring some of the Colored men that wandered up the mountain looking for work. Some were bums or hobos, who had gotten off the trains, where they usually rode anytime they could sneak a ride. None of these men came with a family. Carl Benson hired about ten of these men. He worked them hard, and gave them very little to eat. The poor men slept in the barn. Carl Benson knew from the first day he hired them that he wasn't going to treat them right. He made them think he was going to pay them good wages until the day came for them to be paid.

These colored men had worked for Carl Benson for about a month without wages, and they began to wonder when they would be paid. The men went to Carl, and told him to give them their pay for the time they had already worked. Carl Benson, spitting his tobacco, turning red in the face as he fumed, told them he owed them nothing. He began counting up the food he had given them, and a place to stay, which he considered good pay for their keep. He told the men he considered this to be equal wages for the little work they had done, and ordered them off his land with his shotgun.

The men were devastated by this evil man's temper, and the way he treated them. They went to Thomas, and begged him for work, or money to leave this community. Some were pitiful as they told Thomas of Carl Benson's abhorrent behavior. This news was mind-blowing to Thomas, and with the last of his patience gone with this man's cruelty, he decided to visit Carl Benson, and have a little talk with him.

Thomas walked up to Carl Benson's house. Only seeing Thomas when he turned around, Carl was surprised and fearful of him; from the look in Thomas' eyes, he could tell Thomas wasn't here on a friendly visit. Thomas tried to be calm when he told Carl Benson if he hired anyone in his community to work, they should be paid or, he should do the work himself. Carl recovered from his fear of Thomas to spit at him, and he threatened Thomas with bodily harm, but he was slammed in the mouth with the butt of Thomas' shotgun, got a few teeth knocked out, and a bloody nose, when he called Thomas a son-of-a-bitch, and was nothing but a fool for taking sides with the bums that were good for nothing, and would steal you blind. Thomas left this man lying on the ground as he stormed away from Carl's property.

Thomas was very angry and he walked down to the little creek, and he went to Suzette's house to calm himself before he went home. He wasn't used to seeing people act like Carl Benson, and he didn't know how to handle this sort of problem. This was a bad time to have to deal with this man, and he wished Paul Benson had left his farm to someone else.

Suzette could see that Thomas was upset, and she tried to comfort him, but she knew that she would not be able to comfort and calm Thomas like her mother, Mattie Williams, but she did her best to calm the infuriated Thomas down.

The moon shiners were really having a big operation with the boot-legging in this valley. Thomas went to each moon shiner that he knew, and he told them if they did not shut down their stills, they would have a lot of trouble because Prohibition was about to be signed into law, and they would have the law on their backs, Carl Benson would surely see to that. Of course, these people did not know the meaning of Prohibition, and could not have cared less, because they had more money and living conditions were good for them. They didn't realize the trouble they would be subjected to if they were caught making illegal liquor.

Blue was still encouraging these men to produce as much moonshine liquor as possible, because big John Patton was stocking up the liquor, believing Prohibition would be signed into law.

Thomas was still walking around in a rage when he heard Thaddeus calling him, all excited as usual when he had something interesting to tell Thomas. There was a rumor out that Carl Benson was talking about doing bodily harm to Thomas because of the fight between them. Beth had heard this rumor, and she was in a rage, thinking that this man would harm her husband, and she had sent Thaddeus to find Thomas to warm him of this man. She was fearful that Carl Benson would do something drastic to Thomas.

When Thomas came home, Beth ran to him and hugged him. She could smell some of the moonshine on his breath, he said he had gotten some of the liquor at Suzette's house, as she tried to calm him down. Beth was disappointed with Thomas because she hated for him to drink this terrible moonshine they were cooking up down in the valley. She didn't want her husband to drink this liquor that she feared wasn't good for anyone to drink. Thomas assured Beth that she should not worry about Carl Benson hurting him, because he was only a headache to him and this whole community, and wasn't a man to be feared.

Beth had two worries: about Thomas being hurt, and Anna, who was getting to be one a real problem. She was always begging Beth to leave Ovington, she wanted to go back to the farm, saying she did not want to die here on this isolated mountain. Richard and Geneva were happy, and tried to do everything they could to cheer up and please Anna, but they could see how Anna was getting on Beth's nerves. Of course, Fred was no better. If Anna wasn't happy, Fred seemed to be in a depressed state of mind himself.

Beth was getting worried about the welfare of her two black employees. In her desperate attempt to please Anna and make her happy, she asked Thomas to bring Sarah up to the Ovington's house to live and be with Anna. Thomas, still feeling angry from his fight with Carl Benson, answered Beth sharply that it wasn't a good idea and assured her Anna would be all right.

The worry that Thomas had over Carl Benson's violent behavior made him want to run this man out of the community, but he was left this farm by his brother Paul, who had been very fond of all of the people around the mountain. All of the people loved Paul Benson, but his brother, who no one knew before he moved here, was the worst yet to live in this community, and he was a danger to some of the people.

The Benson's farm was very large, as far as you could see, over from the Ovington's estate. There were many fine milk cows, and you could see some of the other animals that were on the Benson farm that Paul had before he died. When Carl Benson arrived in this community, he brought nothing but his mean temper and big mouth.

Paul and his wife had no children, so Carl was left the estate by his brother, since he had no other relatives to leave this farm to. Paul's wife died long before he did. Thomas wanted to be friends with Carl as he was with Paul, but they were different in personality, and it was bad for the people of Ovington that the one with the bad personality lived the longest.

Carl and his wife Mable, moved to the Benson's farm with nothing, because Carl had no money, or owned anything before he inherited his brother's estate. Mable was rarely seen, and she was scared of her husband. He treated her no better than anyone else, all mean and lowdown like he treated most of the people he knew.

Mable wanted to know her neighbors. She had seen Thomas a few times. She liked him right away, since he seemed friendly, and he was so good-looking. Mable would see Thomas walking around by the creek, and she would smile at him, considering him to be a respectable man. But she was afraid to be too friendly, since she knew Thomas and Carl weren't on good terms. She also knew that it was Carl's fault, knowing how her husband was at times.

Mable was very lonely, and wanted to get someone to help her in this enormous farm house. Since she had only lived in one-bedroom shacks, she didn't know how to keep up a house this large and nice. But she was afraid of the people that Carl sent in to help her out, because they were of the same low class of people as he was, and she wasn't comfortable with them in the same house with her.

The bums Carl hired to work this farm were no better than the men he hung out with before they moved to Ovington. He hated the black race of people, and was always bragging to his wife and anyone else that would listen to him, how he would kick a "nigger's ass," and dared them to fight back. Mable wasn't prejudiced or brought up with this hatred toward any black race of people, nor was his brother Paul, this was just some of the meanness he had in him on his own. Mable never said a word when Carl talked so ugly, because she was afraid of crossing her husband, and she knew he would certainly do this same type of harm to her also. Mable wanted to tell her husband of her disagreement with his cruelty toward these people, but she felt it best to just let him have his way, and hoped he never harmed anyone real bad or killed someone, and be jailed for this crime.

The people she would see over into Little Valley, looked harmless, and seemed to be nice people; she wanted to speak to them and be friendly, but she was afraid of the trouble Carl would cause these people. She was afraid he would do harm to one of them and there would be an outbreak of violence.

Thomas knew there was little he could do about Carl Benson because he had been legally left this farm by his brother. Thomas would think about how nice Paul Benson had been to all of the people, and he wondered how his brother could be so mean. Thomas was trying to deal with this unwanted person in the community for now, hoping he could think of some way to deal with this man later on.

13

Prohibition was signed into law in 1920. Thomas knew that the people were in trouble in Little Valley, if they didn't shut down their stills and let up on making the moonshine liquor. Thomas went into the valley and warned each of the moon shiners of the danger of getting into trouble with the law.

There were many people just hanging out in the valley; Thomas knew this was trouble, and they were getting the people that lived there in a low moral frame of mind. They would listen to anything that sounded like a quick scheme to make money. There were many fights with the drinking crowd and Blue was the ringleader with his cards. No one knew a card like Blue and he was forever pulling some con game with the people with his cards.

Sarah was known all over Little Valley. When there was a crowd together they always went to get Sarah to sing some of these songs that Blue had taught her. She never forgot the words and she loved to sing loud, and the blues type of singing would get the drunken crowd into a sensuous mood. Though Sarah was a child, her adult-sounding voice made a few of the men forget that she was a child, and they tried to hug her in a passionate way as she sang. Of course, they would only be thrown out of the crowd, and and told they would not be invited anymore.

When Suzette heard of Blue teaching Sarah to sing all of these blues songs and having her to sing to these low class of people that were hanging out in the crowd, Suzette feared one of them would harm Sarah. She went to Sarah and asked her to come back to her house to live with her and her family again.

Blue was annoyed with Suzette when he asked for Sarah to sing for the crowd again, and Suzette refused to let her sing for the people that hung out with him. Blue knew the men would spend more money when he could get Sarah to sing these blues songs, and they were in a different mood, and easy for him to con out of everything they had.

Carl was still keeping a close watch at the little creek near Little Valley. He knew they were still drinking and making moonshine in their community. He wanted to get something on these people, because he hated them with a passion. He wanted to harm some of them just for old time's sake, but he was still afraid to do anything because he knew they had the support of Thomas Ovington. Carl Benson would catch one by themselves and he would abuse them verbally, and make racial slurs to them, even calling their children bastards. Carl Benson's atrocious treatment to these people was deplorable to the people in this community.

With the completion of the new homes, five new families moved to Ovington. The surrounding grounds were beautifully landscaped, and the area took on a new astonishing look and Thomas was proud of his little community. Thomas hated his parents' home, but he was elated to see his home place built up into such an enormous and beautiful home after the small and unattractive home that was once built on this site.

Thomas went to each of the new residents when they moved to his community, taking Thaddeus with him, to see if they could assist them with the moving into their new homes. Thaddeus was excited to be introduced to the domestic help as each family moved to this community. Most of them were friendly and did not seem to mind his stuttering as most people did whenever they first met him. Thaddeus was sure most of them would be bored since they were strangers here, so he invited them to come into the valley to meet his family.

Beth was elated by the new residents moving to Ovington, and assured Thomas that she would give a dinner party for the new residents to get acquainted with each other. Beth was hoping this community would be more sociable and she would be able to entertain more and ease the loneliness she felt sometimes.

The five new families who moved to Ovington were: William and Louise Harrison; Alfred and Jane Nelson; Fred and Ada Sullivan; Frank and Elaine Grant; and Albert and Joyce Green. All of the men were businessmen and they were taking a chance moving so far away from the main town, but this was a good place to relocate. They took the chance since they knew Thomas and trusted him enough to invest in some business for the growth of this community.

Thomas along with Thaddeus went to each family to invite each of them to the Ovington's house for a dinner and to get acquainted with each other. Of course Carl Benson, nor his wife, Mable, was invited though he was considered to be a part of this community now. He did have a big business, owning one of the biggest tracts of land around here, plus the finest farm animals.

Thomas had Beth prepare for the big occasion. Of course, Beth could only depend on Richard and Geneva because Anna was beyond work. Thaddeus was trying to help, but he was clumsy as usual. He did manage to help prepare some of the food. Fred was busy trying to take care of Anna and did very little himself.

The five couples were welcomed by Thomas and Beth. All went well with the dinner, though Beth was completely worn out. Their main discussion was mostly about business, but William Harrison questioned Thomas about the bootlegging in Little Valley; he had already heard about the moonshine being made on this mountain. Thomas, feeling uneasy, tried to avoid the question, but he knew trouble was on its way for the moonshiners.

Thomas was so busy these days trying to take care of his business and going into the valley each day to teach the children. Albert and Joyce Green's domestic help, Faye Kennedy, had a sister who was a certified teacher. When Faye told Thomas about Ester, and that she was certified to teach, Thomas gave Ester the position.

Ovington was a very busy place these days. Thomas was trying to help the new residents with the completion of their homes, and the many other things that they had to do. He was going from house to house to see if he was needed, and sometimes he would see Carl Benson, who would have a smirk on his face and refused to speak to Thomas; but he always made sure Thomas saw him. Thomas just tried to pretend that he wasn't seeing him at all. He just ignored him, but Thomas felt that Carl was a threat to him and he needed to watch himself, because he knew Carl was capable of doing some kind of harm to him.

Beth and Thaddeus were trying to run the house, although Beth wasn't too happy with Thaddeus as a house worker at all. Beth knew that Thomas was fond of Thaddeus and he wanted to help him in any way that he could. Thaddeus wanted to learn to do things as Beth had taken her time to teach him, but she seemed to be annoyed whenever Thaddeus would always mess up something and would get on her nerves so bad.

Beth met Thomas at the door one day, crying so hard that she could hardly talk. She told Thomas to find a place for Thaddeus to stay and work outside of the house because he only got in her way and she was always afraid he would break some of her precious heirlooms since he was so clumsy, and besides Thaddeus was making her so nervous.

Thaddeus was sort of pitiful when he found out that Beth did not want him to stay at the Ovington house anymore. Thomas wondered what to do with Thaddeus, he still wanted him to work, but he wanted to please Beth, too. He knew that Beth would have her way, and Thaddeus wasn't cut out to be a house man. Thomas always paid him to help out in the house, and remembering the way he took care his grandmother Mattie, and his grandfather Derrick, he hated to send him back to his people in the valley. Thomas he knew he would have to find him a place soon.

14

Sarah was about eleven when Suzette developed a serious illness. Suzette had been sick for many days when Thomas heard about her illness. He went to visit her and Sarah, as he did, occasionally. Thomas normally tried to keep up with how Sarah was getting along, so that he could keep Beth, and the household staff informed. He would acquaint them with her learning, social, and physical development. He kept Beth informed on the type of things that Sarah was learning, now that she was getting older.

Sarah was a fully developed girl and had the body of a woman. She wiggled her high behind as she walked; her large nipples on her huge breast showed through her print dresses that Geneva always made for her, and as Sarah grew, these dresses were getting too tight. Sarah had the smoothest skin on her medium brown complexion. Her hair was still long, but rather kinky. Suzette always kept Sarah's hair braided. Thomas stared at Sarah and thought, this child that he once carried in his arms was now a woman. He felt uneasy looking at her, not as a child, but as a woman.

After Thomas got over his shock, he realized that Sarah was a very smart girl. She was already out of grade school which, was unusual for someone her age who went to school in the valley. Since, Sarah had completed school all their was left for her to do was assist Suzette, especially now that she was sick. Sarah had become a big help to her, and Suzette really enjoyed her company.

Thomas asked Beth of her opinion concerning Sarah returning to the estate. He realized that neither of them never felt good about her leaving their home in the first place. He wanted to offer Sarah a job at the estate, since she was no longer in school. He recognized that Suzette was so sick that she really couldn't take care of her now. Of course, Beth agreed to the arrangements, and she was happy that Thomas finally decided to let Sarah live in the house with Anna again. Thomas and Thaddeus went to Little Valley to let Suzette know of his plans for Sarah. Thomas thought that this would be a good opportunity for Thaddeus to see his family again, and he could get a few of Sarah's clothes to bring back to the estate.

Beth told Anna about Sarah moving back to the Ovington house to live. She thought maybe this would brighten up her depressed mood. Of course, there was little, or no response from Anna. She was still unhappy, and wanted to leave the estate, anyway. At the present time, Anna was unconcerned about Sarah moving to this house. She was too self-absorbed in her own misery.

Suzette knew that Thomas had come for Sarah when he returned with Thaddeus. She could tell by the looks on their face when they came through the door, and their faces filled with excitement. Thomas told Suzette he had come for Sarah, and she started to cry. Suzette had grown to love Sarah, and she did not want her to leave. She knew that Sarah had thought of her house, as her home, and of her, as a mother. Nevertheless, she recognized that this was best for Sarah. Suzette had taken care of Sarah most of her life, and she felt as though Sarah was her own child. It upset her, but she helped them to pack what few belongings Sarah had. Suzette knew that she didn't have any authority to stop them from moving Sarah into the Ovington's house.

Thomas and Thaddeus were walking Sarah up to the Ovington's house, and they met Blue on the way. Sarah stopped to talk to Blue, explaining she was going to live in the big house, as some people still called the Ovington's house. Blue furiously stared at Thomas, he was unhappy knowing that Thomas was taking this young child to do his housework. This distressed Blue, but he walked on with his head down. He never understood that Thomas was doing what he thought was best for Sarah. Beth was waiting for Thomas and Sarah at the door. She was so excited to see Sarah, and how she had grown. She still had hopes that Sarah's presence in the house would restore Anna back to her old self, and make her happy again.

Thomas had already moved Thaddeus out of the house, and into another area closer to him. He decided to move Thaddeus into the little building where he had his office, and fix him up a room where he could sleep. Thaddeus was always happy about anything Thomas did for him. He didn't complain about moving into the smaller room where he would live. Beth put Sarah into the little room that Thaddeus moved out of. In fact, this was the room where Sarah was born.

Beth began to train Sarah as she had done with her mother and father. She realized that Sarah had the same neatness as they did. She was a strong girl and quick to catch on to whatever was taught to her. When Beth told her something to do, she never had to tell her again. She knew that she would enjoy Sarah being at the estate.

Sarah was always in a cheerful mood, and she had such a beautiful smile. Sometimes, Beth would hear her singing the songs that Blue had taught her. She did have a beautiful voice, and she could sing like an angel. Beth decided to teach Sarah the scales on the piano out of curiosity, and she soon discovered that Sarah had inherited her father's musical talents. Beth allowed Sarah to practice on the piano in the evenings. She even taught her some of her favorite classical arrangements.

When Beth would bring Anna into the room to hear Sarah play the piano and sing, Anna would only stare at Sarah with love in her eyes. Nevertheless, she never said a word about her musical talents. Beth was hoping this would make Anna joyful enough to engage in a conversation with Sarah, but she said very little.

Thomas was in and out of the house, since he stayed busy trying to work with other people concerning business. He was hoping his own finances would get better, and he always studied the investment markets since he was in charge of the Cannon's wealth. He tried to be careful with the chances he took, whenever he invested Beth's money.

Thaddeus stuttered as badly as ever, whenever he tried to talk with Sarah. He was beginning to watch Sarah, and Thomas noticed how he was hanging around her a lot. Thomas knew that Thaddeus was a man now, but Sarah was still a child. Thomas talked to Thaddeus, and he told him to stay away from Sarah because she was too young, and to wait until she was older before trying to date her.

Geneva still made clothes for Sarah, but she was getting to be a big girl now. It took more material than the scraps she had been using to make her a dresses with. Geneva loved Sarah, and she wanted her to have some knowledge about the world. She began to talk to Sarah about her body, and being a woman. She feared with Sarah being beautiful, alone, and without any parents that some man might try to take advantage of her.

Sarah's first thought, like the other girls her age on the mountain, was of being married early in their lives. But Sarah seemed to be happy. She still loved to go to Little Valley, and she loved going to see Suzette and her friends. Sometimes she would spend the night with Suzette and her family, and would occasionally follow Suzette as she carried out her profession of delivering babies around the community.

Every once in a while Thomas would see some strange men walking around the Benson's farm. He was curious, but he wasn't surprised about anything that happened there. He noticed that these men were always looking over into Little Valley, as though they were looking for something. His instincts told him that they were up to no good. Every time Thomas seen these men at Carl's place, he had a strange feeling about them. He knew they were up to something, but he didn't know what.

The new residents, and the domestic workers were always going down into Little Valley. They often brought moonshine, and would return to where they worked, or lived with huge jugs of it. Most of the time their employers would drink some of this liquor, and they loved it. Normally, anyone who was use to drinking, that tasted it, loved it. Drinking and making moonshine was acceptable to most people in Ovington, the only people who disliked it was the outsiders.

The new residents of Ovington were aware that Carl Benson was one of the troublesome people that they didn't want to have any dealings with, and they refused to have anything to do with him. Of course, Carl blamed Thomas for this as always; he blamed Thomas for anything bad that happened to him. The new residents could see that Carl Benson was not like the rest of the people in Ovington, and they didn't invite him or his wife to any of the social events. They excluded his family from anything of importance going on in this community, which outraged Carl.

Sarah was popular with the people in Ovington that knew her well, and she was still popular with the people in the valley. Most of the people knew she could sing, and they often asked her to sing for them. She was also asked to play the piano at the Ovington's house when someone came to the estate, and wanted to hear her sing and play the piano for entertainment. Sarah loved to sing and she loved the attention she received.

Anna appeared to be a little happier after Sarah was back at the Ovington estate for a while. However, she still talked very little to Sarah, or the other employees. Whenever, Anna had something to say it was about home. She kept begging Beth Marie to take her back home to the farm. She told Beth that she didn't want to die on this mountain. Anna annoyed Thomas by her comments all the time about not liking this home he had provided for her and Fred, and the rest of the domestic help he employed here. Anna never felt comfortable here on the mountain. She was used to the Cannon's farm, and she referred to this house as Thomas' house. Ever since, Anne came to Ovington she never felt like this was home to her.

Beth felt happy since Sarah moved here. She had been very fond of Sarah's mother and father, and she could see some of both of her parents in Sarah. She loved her as she had loved Clayton and Grace. Sarah was a cheerful girl, and her singing kept everyone in high spirits. Even Fred was more alert as he listened to the songs that Sarah pleasingly singed. He was an old man, but he could see that Sarah had been blessed with a lot of different talents.

Thomas decided to build another extension onto the Ovington's house. He wanted to move his office into his home. The building where he rented was getting too small for his business, and countless records. He wanted to be closer to his house, too. He was becoming concerned about the drifters that started coming to his house. Thomas knew that his house looked like a place where there was food, and work for the new comers, so many of them came to his place. He was more worried about the women not having any protection if someone came along, who had evil intentions. Fred was getting too old, and Richard was outside most of the time. Thomas thought that neither of them would be of any help if trouble came along. The only other person that could protect the women was Thaddeus, who was always running behind him, so he wouldn't be any help for them. His fear for the women in the Ovington house was always making him nervous, so he decided to move closer to them. This was the only thing he could do to keep someone from harming them, and to alleviate his anxiety.

Beth began to teach Sarah the household tasks that Thaddeus used to do. He didn't do very much, so these were just small chores that even a child could handle. Beth was so glad that she didn't have to be bothered with Thaddeus in the house, and his clumsy ways. For reasons unknown, Beth Marie never cared for Thaddeus, and would rather he worked outside of the house. On the other hand, Thomas was very partial to him. Beth didn't try to make any excuses for not wanting him around her.

Anna was still a big pain in the neck, and Thomas was getting more annoyed with her. Thomas mentioned to Beth that he would take Anna and Fred back to the farm. However, he would not take one without the other. Beth was horrified by this unspeakable suggestion from Thomas, and she voiced her firm belief that she would never hear such a thing.

This discussion about Fred and Anna going back to the farm made trouble between Thomas, and Beth Marie. Thomas stormed out of the house disgusted by the way that Beth pampered Anna all of the time, and letting her worry her the way that she did. Of course, Fred was no better, and Thomas wondered why Beth put up with it. Thomas made up his mind that he would try to make arrangements for them to be transported back to the farm.

The changes in this community were unbelievable. The town of Ovington was beginning to be a place that anyone would want to live. Sometimes Thomas would look proudly around this community, and could not believe that this was the town he grew up in, where he had spent so many unhappy years. Though Thomas was no elected official, he was always consulted before any new changes were made or something new was added to this community.

Beth Marie was respected as well, because of her husband's popularity, but she wasn't very popular here in Ovington, no more than when she lived in Lawsonville. The new residents of Ovington always included her in some of the social gatherings, but she was never put in charge of anything. They more of less tolerated her, because of her husband. Beth always tried to be friendly, but the way she talked and the things that she was used to doing seemed to be out of place here. She just wasn't up to the ways of the South, especially the hills of Tennessee. Beth loved Thomas with all of her heart, and she was willing to put up with anything to be with him.

15

Thomas made arrangements with John Smithson to build an extension onto the left side his house, and the construction crew came to Ovington for the second time. John Smithson wasted no time hiring Blue, believing no one could do a good rock job like Blue.

John Smithson was also contracted to build a new county-seat. There was no correctional facility in Ovington, but he was to build a small room on the back of the building for the purpose of housing one or two people if there were ever a need for one to house a prisoner. When all of these buildings were being completed, there was also a small bank, and a little dry-goods store, which the ladies were thrilled about, since many items were sold in this store, and the ladies enjoyed shopping.

The addition onto Thomas's house was the last building to be constructed, and it was as stately as the first phase of the Ovington's house. There was four more big rooms built: the main front part was his office, and the other two rooms were for Beth to put her things in that were dear to her. She would separate her mother's and father's favorite things that were dear to them, and these things were secured enough to keep them from breaking; this was her special room to remember her parents.

Blue was busy the next couple of years that it took for the big construction jobs to be completed in Ovington. The bootlegging was no more interest to him now, but he still edged the moon shiners on to keep the stills fired up. Blue was making a lot of money, and his family lived better than the rest of the families. Blue worked hard on the Ovington house, even though he knew that Thomas still didn't like him, so Blue was trying to please Thomas. He also had a chance to see Sarah from time to time.

Sarah was still singing and playing the piano beautifully. Beth gave her permission to play the piano as long as she had the household duties completed. Sarah would always play the piano when Blue was working on the Ovington house, because he enjoyed hearing her music more than anyone else that she would sing to and play the piano to in this community.

Blue began to try to see Sarah when he worked on the Ovington house. He was seeing her now as a woman, and he began to lust after this child, who had the body of a woman. Sarah trusted Blue and idolized this man that she had known as long as she could remember. Sarah knew Blue had taught her to sing, and she always went to him to sing, since he just got all bent over listening to her belt out her songs to him.

The construction job was good for Blue. He was able to do a lot of things for his family, and he would give Sarah money often to help her out, though she rarely spent anything on herself. Most of the time she would give the money to Geneva to keep for her, or to make her a new dress.

Blue was beginning to realize that he was in love with this child, though he never thought of her as a child now; he was beginning to think of her as a woman. Blue went around in a sort of dazed condition, but no one realized that Blue was in love with Sarah. He became obsessed with his thought of love for her. Seeing Sarah made Blue ashamed by his evil thought, and he knew he must never touch Sarah.

Carl Benson was still walking around this community trying to stir up trouble. He knew that Thomas disliked him, and he never did anything good for this community, but the biggest thrill he would have was when he knew he was getting on the nerves of Thomas Ovington.

When all the construction was finished, Thomas started planning the trip to Lawsonville. He had many things to do there , but his main reason was that he was going to do something about Anna and Fred. He was tired of Anna complaining, and she never did any work; she wasn't in any shape to do anything. The thought of having to go through this same routine almost everyday, of her constant whining about wanting to go back to the farm, was just too much for Thomas, and he planned to do something about it.

Thomas had to check on his investments in Lawsonville. He had invested some money in the railroads, and in the Eastern Tennessee coal mines. He wasn't making a lot of money from this stock. Beth was still a wealthy woman, and the Cannon's farm was profitable. Jeffrey Carter had made her farm into one of the best around this part of the state. Jeffrey had worked very hard on this farm, and he was proud of the progress he had made with the growth on this farm. He wanted Beth to be proud of him, since she trusted him to take care of her father's pride and joy that he had of this farm.

Jeffrey Carter was glad to see Thomas, whose visits were very rare now since he was so busy in Ovington. Thomas wasted no time as he asked Jeffery for a favor before he lost his nerves. Thomas asked Jeffrey to prepare a place for Fred and Anna on the farm. Jeffrey was shocked, and he thought that Thomas was kidding him about bringing Fred and Anna back to this farm to live, and without Beth. Jeffrey was saddened by this favor Thomas was asking him to do, but of course, he knew that Thomas could count on him to do whatever he could for him and Beth. He questioned Thomas, wanting to know what Beth thought of this decision to send her two long time employees back to this farm. Thomas knew that Jeffrey would be shocked and disappointed by his decision to bring Fred and Anna back to the farm, and this would be a burden on him and his family, but he had made up his mind and this is what he intended to do.

After Jeffrey Carter was over the shock, he assured Thomas that Fred and Anna would be welcome to come home to this farm, the place where they had been so happy. Their memories of James Cannon would be good for them. They had never wanted to leave this farm in the first place, but Beth thought that she must take them to Ovington with her. She had been so used to Fred and Anna, plus they had always been around her. James Cannon had trusted Beth Marie to look after them since they had no one else; their families were dead or they had lost touch with them. Jeffrey shook hands with Thomas as he was getting ready to go home to Ovington, and he promised him that the old Black couple would be taken care of whenever he was ready to bring them back to the farm.

Thomas knew that Beth would never forgive him for what he was planning to do, but he felt that it was best for Anna, who was forever begging Beth to bring her back to the farm before she died. This was a good time to tell Beth before he lost his nerves, but Thomas knew he would never be able to take James Cannon's place in Anna's and Fred's lives. He must do something before Anna became too sick to travel to the farm, and he would have to send Fred back also to take care of Anna.

The trip home to Ovington took longer because Thomas was dreading to talk to Beth about Fred and Anna. As he neared his home, Thomas was seeing many strangers. The men were friendly and talked real nice to Thomas, but something about these men made Thomas uneasy, unlike the many transients or plain bums that came up the mountain; there was something different about these men.

Blue was at the Ovington estate when Thomas approached his home. Blue was working on something that was a last minute thing that he had to do, but Thomas spoke to him politely for a change, telling him he had done a beautiful job on his house. Blue thanked him, but he was still a little nervous around Thomas, knowing this man had a bad temper at times.

Beth ran to Thomas as she did whenever he was away from her, and Thomas held on to her tightly, but he wasted no time when he told her of his decision to take Fred and Anna back to the farm. Thomas spoke bluntly and didn't back off as Beth became furious and was trying to get away from Thomas. He held on to her tightly as she tried to run away from him, holding her until he thought she understood. These were such cruel and hurting words to her that she kept shaking her head that she would never do such a thing.

Thomas went to Fred and Anna, and he asked them to collect their belongings, the things they loved the best, and all that been given to them by the Cannons, and to pack them together. Thomas told Fred he would go back to the farm to take care of Anna. Fred looked shocked, and tears immediately swelled his eyes. Fred had considered this to be his home, and he didn't want to leave Beth. He did love his home in the mountain; he had gotten used to this beautiful place and he loved to work in Beth lovely rocked garden, but he never said a word to Thomas. Anna seemed to understand what Thomas was telling her, but she showed no expression, she only stared at Thomas.

Beth cried for days as she continued to beg Thomas to let Fred and Anna stay here at the estate. Thomas was very busy doing the many things that he had to do, and he never gave in to her pleadings. Thomas was being cold toward Beth, and she began to understand that her pleading with him was useless.

Blue made every excuse he could to stay at the Ovington's house to find some little odd job he needed to finish, just so he could be close to Sarah. Blue heard Beth crying inside the house, and he knew something was going on. He would look for Sarah every chance he could, but Sarah didn't understand what was happening either, but she was afraid to come out to sing for Blue, because of so much tension in the house.

Thomas, along with Thaddeus, went down into Little Valley to each of his friends and told them to tear down their stills. He was seeing so many strangers in the community that it made Thomas fear something was wrong, and begged them to stop making illegal liquor. Thomas went to Suzette, who was getting weaker from age and her sickness sometimes, and she wanted her relatives to quit making the moonshine, but she told Thomas it was useless to try to talk to them.

Suzette asked about Sarah, and asked Thomas to bring her to see her sometimes, but Thomas told Suzette that he was taking Fred and Anna back to the farm, and Sarah would stay at the house with Richard and Geneva until he returned. Suzette was a little shocked, but she tried not to show her feelings.

The little schoolhouse was one of the places that Thomas always went to in the valley. He would watch the children and this was his love, knowing he was the first person responsible for this school being built for the children. He was the first one teaching them before he became so busy in his own business, but he still missed teaching the children. Thomas was sure Ester Kennedy was doing a good job teaching the valley children.

After Beth was over her shock of Thomas asking her to send Fred and Anna back to the Cannon farm, she was obedient to her husband. She loved Thomas too much and usually did whatever he asked her to do, within reason, but she did make plans to take Fred and Anna back to the farm. Beth was heart-broken as she helped them pack. Anna was hardly aware of anything in recent months, she just lived day by day, hardly paying any attention to Fred, the one person she had loved as a husband.

When Thomas saw Beth, he felt a little sorry for her. He knew she was having a hard time coping with his decision to take her two favorite employees away from his house. But he had made up his mind, and had made arrangements for them to be taken care of at the Cannon's farm, and he attended to follow through with the plan.

Beth worked for about three weeks helping Fred and Anna clean and pack their clothes. She was making sure they had everything they needed for the trip to Lawsonville. Thomas wanted Thaddeus and Richard to help him take Fred and Anna back to the farm, but Beth Marie put her foot down. She made it clear to Thomas that she would be the one to see that Fred and Anna were made comfortable back in their old home and would see that they would have their old bedrooms to sleep in. She would not leave the Cannon farm until she was satisfied that they would be taken care of by Jeffrey Carter and his family.

Sarah was a little nervous by all the tension in the Ovington house. She was still a child and she only did what she was asked to do. She would see Fred wiping his eyes and also Beth with tears in her eyes. Even Geneva was looking sad, and whispering to Richard something that she didn't want Sarah to hear.

The day that the trip to Lawsonville was planned was one of the saddest days to remember in the Ovington house, except when Grace died. There were so many tears. Fred was a pitiful broken man as he stepped into the carriage to take him from this mountain. He knew he would never see Beth Marie again after she left him at the farm. Beth was no better as she helped Anna to sit beside Fred. The tears were heavy on her cheeks, and she continued to plead with Thomas to reconsider, and leave Fred and Anna at this house until they passed. They weren't going to live much longer, but Thomas only shook his head, and finished loading their things onto the wagons.

Richard and Geneva were devastated by this seemly terrible thing the Ovington's were doing to Fred and Anna, who had been employed for the Cannon's family for so long. Although Anna was forever begging to leave this mountain, Fred was happy here and wanted to stay, but he would never stay without Anna. He would follow her if he was asked to stay, and Thomas knew this, and that is why he made Fred go with Anna.

When Thomas was ready to leave, he went to Richard and Geneva and asked them to stay at the Ovington house all the time he and Beth would be gone to watch after Sarah, and to run the house while they were in Lawsonville. Geneva cried and held on to Richard, as they both promised to be sure and take care of Sarah, and to make sure that the house would be taken care of too.

The good-byes were long and Geneva kissed Fred and Anna as she cried softly. Sarah who loved the two employees of the Ovington house since her childhood, went to Anna and hugged and kissed her. This was the first reaction from Anna; she was crying as she held Sarah, this child she had wanted for her own, and she was leaving her. But she soon let Sarah go, and acted anxious to leave this house, and be gone from this mountain.

News traveled fast in this small community, and everyone knew that Thomas and Beth were taking their two old Black employees back to the Cannon farm. Most of the residents were disturbed since most of them knew Fred, since he worked all around the Ovington house. They had gotten used to him, but few knew Anna, because she hardly moved out of her chair during the day.

The Ovingtons had been gone for about a week, and the finishing touches were being completed on the Ovington's addition to their house. This community was beautiful and admired by all who saw the changes with the new homes and the new businesses. The new residents were proud to be a part of this community, and were glad that they had invested in its growth, believing Ovington was the best little community to live in.

Then all hell broke loose atop this mountain.

16

John Smithson's work was always admired by all that saw the beautiful building he could do. He never left a job until he was completely satisfied that everything was done as contracted, and never left a job unfinished. John knew that Thomas was eager to move into his new office, and Beth was excited as Thomas, since she wanted to have rooms for her favorite things too, and the new addition was beautiful. John Smithson was always glad to build in Ovington, because he could see that his work built this town up from nothing but a lot of hills and wilderness to the beautiful community that it was now.

Blue was still doing some work at the Ovington's estate, or he was just hanging around since the Ovington's had left. Blue had seen the Ovingtons as they left for Lawsonville, saw Fred and Anna all packed, and when they were put in the carriage, he could see Fred with tears in his eyes, and this had haunted Blue for the past few days. Blue had felt sorry for Fred, who wanted to be with Anna, but he also wanted to stay at the Ovington's with Beth.

Blue knew he would be finished with the Ovington's house before they would return. John Smithson had trusted Blue to finish his job, but he had no desire to work any longer on this house. Blue could hear Sarah singing in the house as he worked, but she never came out of the house as she usually did. Blue had seen Sarah crying as the Ovington's left with Fred and Anna.

Richard and Geneva were to move into the Ovington's house until Thomas and Beth returned from Lawsonville. Sarah was doing most of the work in the house, so Richard and Geneva decided to come to the Ovington's house to stay with Sarah at night. Sarah was alone in the house in the daytime to do the work, and cook for herself. Richard and Geneva were staying in their servant's quarters, and sort of had a little honeymoon of their own.

Blue knew he had to finish this job. He had only a day's work left. He could hear Sarah singing loudly in the house. Blue wanted Sarah to sing him one last song before he left the Ovington's house, and he called Sarah to the door. Though she was warned not to let anyone in the house, she invited Blue into the Ovington's house.

Blue asked Sarah to sing him one last song before he left to go home. Sarah went to the piano to play one of her favorite songs she learned to play on her own. The words were of love; being almost 15 now, she dreamed of love and a family.

Blue was speechless as Sarah belted out the song she had created on her own. He felt joyful as she put all she had into this song. Blue just closed his eyes as he felt the thrill of the music; he had not felt so good in a long time. As Sarah neared the end of her song, Blue put his arms around Sarah, and hugged and kissed her as he thanked her for singing so good to him.

Sarah stood up as Blue stared at her. This was a woman, and Blue became aroused. No child had a body like Sarah. Blue put his arms around her again, and felt her large breasts. He kissed Sarah in a passionate way as she stood trembling. She did not know what to do and did not know what was happening to her.

Blue led Sarah to her little room and she followed him obediently. She was still trembling from his kisses, and the way she was caressed by Blue. He told Sarah to undress, and even though she knew this was wrong, she continued to do as Blue asked her to do; she was unable to stop herself. She only tried to make Blue stop as she cried from the pain Blue was causing by the rough way he eagerly made love to her.

Sarah was crying in a childlike voice, and this shocked Blue back to reality. He jumped up, and tried to apologize to Sarah. Blue was staring at Sarah as she was crying, and all he could do was to run from this house in disgust for himself.

Richard was outside and he saw Blue running from the Ovington's house, he was curious since Blue didn't have his tools with him. He had never seen Blue run so fast. Richard went into the house. He could hear Sarah crying, and went into her room where she was still undressed. Richard knew that Blue had taken advantage of Sarah, and he ran to get Geneva.

Geneva ran into Sarah room, and tried to comfort her as she asked

Sarah the details of what really happened to her. Richard was angry, and hated Blue. He ran out of the door with one of Thomas' shotguns, and was half way into Little Valley, when he was shocked back to reality as he saw the big white man standing with a gun, loudly asking Richard his destination with the shotgun. Richard was afraid of Blue anyway, and he began to have second thoughts about getting into a fight with the likes of Blue.

Richard ran nervously back to the Ovington's house, he was afraid of this tough white man he saw, and he was really afraid of Blue. Geneva was still trying to comfort Sarah, explaining that she would get over the shock of her first coitus with a man, and the pain would go away, and the next time she would not hurt so much. She was scared that she and Richard were in for big trouble if the Ovington's found out this terrible thing that happened to Sarah while they were in Lawsonville. It would be even worse since the man had been Blue. Geneva begged Sarah not to tell anyone of this experience she had with Blue, and never let the Ovingtons find out, or they would be in big trouble. Thomas had asked Richard and Geneva to stay in the house day and night to watch over Sarah. The three of them swore to secrecy about Blue, and the way he had taken advantage of this young girl.

Blue felt terrible about the way that he had treated Sarah, this child that he had held on his knees and taught to sing. He had always loved Sarah, and had felt sorry for her. The way she was shifted from family to family, and the worst was the way she was put to work in the Ovington's house at age eleven. Blue was hurting real bad; the worst thing to happen to Sarah in her short life was what he had done to her. Blue felt he of all people should have protected Sarah from the likes of himself. This was unspeakable for him to force himself on this innocent virgin child, and take advantage of her. This was the worst thing he could have done, just to satisfy his own shameful lust.

Blue was hurting, but he could not force himself to go the Ovington's house one last time to complete last minute things he needed to do. Blue would sit at home and look sad; no one knew what was the matter with him, but he wanted to destroy himself. After about a week, when John Smithson checked the completion of his job, and could see that Blue needed to finish his last job at the Ovington's house, he sent for Blue, and asked him to please come and finish his job so he could go on with the other jobs he had to do.

Richard and Geneva were still nervous about Blue and the way he had treated Sarah. Geneva was so scared that the Ovingtons would find out about Blue and Sarah, and they knew violence would rock this mountain. Blue had finally gotten his nerves together, and was on his way to the Ovington's house when all hell broke loose and violence did indeed rock this mountain.

Blue was coming up the hill from Little Valley when he saw many men, none he knew. They had many chains, axes, and many other weapons, including shotguns. Blue was very frightened as they were coming toward him, and they were using the most abusive language. He knew he was in trouble, but did not understand as they grabbed him, and chained him up, also beat him about the body as he screamed for mercy, and he tried to ask them questions about the way they were treating him, but they just kept on abusing him. These men were big and tough, and Blue looked behind them and saw the devil himself, Carl Benson.

The strange men on the mountain were law enforcement officers, they called them revenuerers. They were sent to this mountain in search of illegal bootleg liquor operations in Little Valley. Blue saw so many men, they also had wagons as they went into the valley. The residents in the valley saw them coming, and were about to welcome them, as they did most strangers that came into their little community, but they found out too late, that these men were only trouble to them.

The team of alcohol revenue agents had the location pinpointed because they had been watching this operation for weeks; they knew who the moonshiners were. The worst was yet to come as they took their axes and destroyed the stills, busting each still to smithereens. The revenuers arrested the men they knew were responsible for these stills, or at least they thought they did. The families were torn apart because most of the families were affected.

The revenue agents and the team of law officers that came with the revenuers shackled the men at the ankles as they marched them throughout Little Valley. Most of the Williams and Tucker men were arrested, the old as well as the young. Those who protested were beaten on the spot.

The wives of these men were devastated by the atrocious treatment of their husbands by the revenuers. The wives pleaded for their husbands' release, as the children cried hysterically for their fathers. The men were dragged from their homes and taken by the revenuers. Carl Benson was walking around Little Valley with the law officers with a smirk on his face as these people cried uncontrollable tears.

The people in Little Valley had seen hard times, and had suffered many hardships, but they had never experienced trouble like this raid in their little community. They knew too late that Thomas had warned them to shut down their still, but making moonshine had been their means of making money. They could see no wrong in making money in the only trade they knew.

John Smithson heard of the raid in the valley and that they had Blue among the men. He was outraged at this brutality from the revenuers, and he went to the head of the revenuers making the raid. He demanded that they release Blue because he worked for him and was not a part of this bootlegging operation. John Smithson was a rich and powerful man, well known for miles around the eastern state of Tennessee. The revenuers decided to let Blue go free because they did not have anything on him. They had not seen him operating the stills, but Carl Benson tried his best to persuade the revenuers to arrest Blue along with the others.

Thaddeus heard the news about the raid and he ran to his father who was among the men arrested. Thaddeus pleaded for his father's release, stuttering so badly they felt sorry for him. They could not let him go, but Thaddeus promised with tears in his eyes that he would get Thomas to come for him and he would be home in no time. Thaddeus knew he would have to wait for the return of the Ovingtons because he had never been to Lawsonville and had no idea how to get in touch with Thomas.

The county seat had no jail big enough to hold all of the men, so they were hauled off the mountain in wagons. The revenuers had hidden the wagons on the Benson farm. The men were taken to a place about ten miles off the mountain provided for this purpose when they had decided to raid Little Valley. The revenuers also went to Spalding and arrested big John Patton. They had found out about John Patton buying up the moonshine for the people in Spalding, and they arrested him for the same purpose that the men in the valley were arrested.

Blue was out of his mind with worry because he felt responsible for this raid. He had encouraged these people to go into bootlegging business big time, and once they began to make money they didn't listen to the warning of bad trouble for them. Blue had encouraged these people to produce more moonshine because of the enormous amount of money that could be made.

Sarah was still upset by Blue persuading her to engage in coitus with him. She was old enough to know it was wrong, but she had a love for Blue. He was old enough to he her father and she had a father type of love for him, but felt ashamed to know that she had given in to him. Sarah saw Blue approaching the Ovington's house; she went to her room as tears swelled her eyes. She felt as though she was as guilty as Blue.

As Blue knocked on the Ovington's door he looked as if he had not slept in days. Geneva answered the door and was about to slam the door in his face when Blue pleaded with her to talk to him. Blue asked Geneva to forgive him for the way he had let himself get out of control and attack Sarah in such a brutal way, but he confessed he was in love with Sarah and wanted to ask her forgiveness. Geneva refused to let Blue see Sarah but she assured him they would not tell the Ovingtons if he did not bother Sarah again.

Blue finished the job on the Ovington house, and he was glad to leave this house because he was feeling so guilty. Blue felt like so much had happened to make him hate himself. He only wanted to go home to Vera and his family. John Smithson looked over all the work he had completed and he was ready to leave this mountain. So much had happened these past few days, he was still in shock by the atrocious treatment he had seen out of Carl Benson and the revenuers to the people of this community.

Blue saw Thaddeus as he was walking home. He was a pitiful sight to see. He cried for his father and uncles, and most of the men arrested and hauled off the mountain were related to him. He was saying over and over he had to go to Lawsonville to find Thomas to help him bring his father home. Blue looked at this young man and felt sorry for him. The same boy he used to tease and taunt now Blue was trying to comfort.

The news of the big raid in Little Valley reached Lawsonville. Thomas heard it and was devastated to know this was going on in his community. He was trying to hurry to get home to see what the trouble was all about, but he knew it had to do with the bootlegging in the valley. Of course, Thomas knew who was making the moonshine and therefore knew it was his friends who were being affected by this raid.

Thomas went to his lawyers, Paul and Howard Bradley, explaining that he needed their help. He wanted them to go with him to the location where the moonshiners were being incarcerated and asked for their help in getting the men released so they could go home to their families. Paul and Howard Bradley were well known lawyers. They worked for big businesses and were famous for winning big cases, but they wasted no time telling Thomas that they refused to help, explaining it would hurt their business defending these common colored men and no amount of money would change their minds.

Thomas was horrified by these lawyers' refusal to help his friends in the valley. As Thomas stormed out of the lawyers' office he knew he must leave Lawsonville and go home to Ovington as soon as possible. Thomas knew he was in for a sad time because he would have to leave Fred and Anna behind. He would have an unhappy wife on the way to Ovington.

The Carters were used to Fred and Anna because of the year that they spent with them while the Ovingtons were in New York. But at this time, they were not too happy to be responsible for this old black couple. Beth had put Fred and Anna in their old rooms; they would be off from the living quarters of the Carters and should not be any trouble. Anna was beyond working so Fred would have to do his best to try to care for her as long as he would be able. Beth Marie knew she had done her best for Fred and Anna. They had no one else to care for them. Beth trusted the Carters to do their best and the money was no problem because Beth had provided for their care for the rest of their lives.

Beth was calm as Thomas picked her up at the Cannon farm. Beth knew this was goodbye to her two servants that she had known all of her life. Their housing was the best she could offer them. Beth was looking at Fred and Anna's bewildered reaction as she prepared to leave. Jeffrey Carter asked Beth to trust him to see that the needs of Fred and Anna would be taken care of. In tears, Beth clung to Fred and Anna, believing that she would never see them again. Fred was crying so hard, but Anna just stared at Beth, motionless, and at Thomas with hatred in her eyes. Beth ran to the Phaeton and never looked back as Thomas drove away from the farm. Thomas was having his own troubles. He was angry with the Bradley brothers and couldn't wait to get home to Ovington to see what he could do for the arrested men and to bail them out if he could.

Beth knew nothing of the raid in Little Valley, and it was just as well, because she cared nothing for the moon shiners. She hated for Thomas to drink any of the horrible mash they were always cooking in their stills. Beth would wipe her eyes as the tears fell on her cheeks. She kept a cool attitude toward Thomas as he drove the horses hard, in a hurry to get home. Thomas hardly noticed Beth's behavior as his mind was on Little Valley and the terrible raid on the people he loved there.

The Ovingtons were worn out when they reached their home. Thomas helped Beth into the house, but he left quickly to be with the families in the valley, knowing there would be sadness among the families the raid had affected.

Thaddeus saw Thomas and ran to him crying as he tried to tell about the terrible raid, but his stuttering was so bad Thomas had trouble understanding. Thomas went to each of the busted stills and looked with sadness, and then we went to each of the families affected by the raid. He wanted to know what he could do to help, to see what they needed, and to comfort them as best he could. The whole valley was devastated and so was Thomas, but he assured them that he would do everything in his power to get the men home. Thaddeus was feeling better now that he knew Thomas was going to see about getting his father and the rest of the men home again.

Beth Marie was having a hard time coping with the Ovington house without Fred and Anna, though they had not contributed much to the household duties. She could not remember when they were not around her or a part of her household. Fred and Anna had always been loved by her family and were an important part of the Cannon household when they were younger.

Richard and Geneva wasted no time telling Beth about the raid in Little Valley. Beth then knew why Thomas took off so fast when they reached Ovington – he must have heard about the raid before he reached home. Beth was sad but decided not to worry about the busted stills since she never liked them anyway. She never wanted her husband hanging around the moon shiners and drinking samples that they always gave him.

Sarah was still walking around a little hurt from being too weak to stop Blue from taking advantage of her when she was unable to know how to handle a man like Blue. Richard and Geneva were still nervous about Sarah. They were afraid that the Ovingtons would find out about Blue and the terrible way he had taken advantage of this innocent child. They knew that Thomas asked them to watch the house while they had gone to Lawsonville, to be sure and keep an eye on Sarah. If Blue had impregnated Sarah, violence would rock this mountain.

Blue watched Thomas as he walked throughout Little Valley. He could see the despair in his face and made no attempt to say anything for fear he would be blamed for all the trouble that had happened. Blue decided he would stay out of Thomas' way because he knew this man had a bad temper and he didn't feel like dealing with him now after all the suffering he was having.

Thomas went to Suzette's house, and seeing her so tearful broke his heart. She asked about Sarah, and she cried even harder as she asked about Fred and Anna, and their move back to Lawsonville. Thomas assured her not to worry about Fred and Anna. Their housing was the best and their needs would be taken care of. Suzette was the one Thomas talked to about any business in the valley, and he was annoyed to hear anything about Fred and Anna because he had done what he felt was the best for them at this time.

The town council, which really wasn't too stable yet, had elected William Harrison to be the constable. Thomas went to his office to talk about the release of the men in the valley. William Harrison was nervous as he sat down to talk to Thomas, assuring him that there was nothing he could have done to prevent the raid because they were turned in by Carl Benson. He felt like Thomas blamed him for the beating of the men, and that he should have stopped the revenuer from harming the men when they couldn't help themselves. Thomas tried to be calm as he talked to William Harrison, feeling anger when he repeated the stories he had heard from the residents about how Carl Benson had treated the moonshiners, and how he had tried to get the revenuer to arrest the innocent along with the guilty.

Thomas was horrified to hear how the revenuer, along with all the law officers, had the men marched to the wagons with chains on their legs, and they shackled these men as they traveled through the community. This had been most disturbing to them. Carl Benson was the worst, joining the revenuer in marching these men through the town, some bleeding, and some crying, but all of them were a pitiful sight to see.

William Harrison promised Thomas he would do everything he could to try and get the arrested men released. He knew a few of the men in the town since they had been incarcerated before.

Thomas went home feeling better, believing that William Harrison would be able to help the arrested men. He went home to Beth since he had left her alone as soon as they arrived in Ovington. The petite Beth Marie looked so small and unhappy. Thomas took her in his arms and stroked her hair. Thomas knew he had put his wife through hell and now he was getting ready to leave her again.

William Harrison had asked Thomas to go with him. He hated to tell Beth, but Beth made no fuss about Thomas' decision to travel with William Harrison to make arrangements for the release of the arrested men. She had learned long ago to accept Thomas' love for the people in Little Valley, and she assured him that she wanted him to do everything he could to help these people.

Carl Benson was still being a big jackass, always looking into the valley to see if anything was happening now that the stills were busted. He wanted to get something on these people so badly, he wanted to run them out of this town, but he wasn't that powerful around this community. The bums he had hanging around his farm were afraid to mess around these people too much. Benson was still angry because Blue wasn't arrested along with the other men. He knew that Blue was into everything illegal as the others, but John Smithson saved him. Blue would catch Carl Benson watching him, but he never backed off from him, and this made Carl nervous. Blue carried only hatred for this man since he had treated his family so badly. Carl was used to doing harm to anyone black, and they let him get away with it, but Blue was trying to think of a way to slice this man up.

Blue was having his own private hell within himself, blaming himself for the men being incarcerated, since he taught them to go into bootlegging big time. He was also having nightmares about Sarah. Even though she had a woman's body, she was still a child, and he could not help loving her. Blue knew he wanted Sarah, but if the Ovingtons found out about him and Sarah he believed that he would surely lose his life.

Beth made herself settle down into the same routine. Sarah was a smart girl, doing most of the household duties as she was told. Since Richard and Geneva were a carbon copy of Fred and Anna, Beth paid little attention to them, as her attention was on Sarah. She began to cling more to her, now that she had lost Fred and Anna.

Beth sent for Walter, hiring him to complete the addition for their home. Walter was employed to build the cabinets and bookshelves for Thomas' office. Thomas was so worried about the welfare of the incarcerated men from the valley he had not made arrangements for Walter to complete the new rooms with the beautiful work he was noted for.

Thomas and William Harrison went to the place where the men from the valley were incarcerated. As punishment, the men were put to work the nearby rock quarry. The conditions were deplorable to Thomas. He saw these men working the quarry excavating rocks, looking like they were mesmerized state of fear with chains to their ankles as they were forced to work.

Thomas was speechless as he looked at his friends, and they looked as if they didn't know Thomas and William Harrison. This was mindblowing to Thomas. William Harrison tried to talk to the law officers when he saw how upset Thomas was. He tried to get the law officers to release the men, and they paid a fine for them, since there were about 20 men. William Harrison was told that the men had to stay at least six months or longer for punishment for breaking the law.

Thomas and William Harrison said very little to each other as they traveled home to Ovington. William knew that Thomas was suffering within himself as he looked so unhappy. He stared ahead and did not mention anything about the arrested men, or the conditions he had just witnessed that the men were subjected to.

The times were hard on the families of the arrested men in the valley, and Thomas knew that the wives had no means of supporting themselves. Thomas would have the domestic help cook extra kettles of food, and he would send the food down to the school in the valley to feed the children. Blue was also feeling the pinch of financial problems because without the bootlegging and John Smithson completing his work here in Ovington, there was no money to be made. Without the moonshine liquor, no men came to this valley, and he wasn't able to have his infamous card games.

Blue really began to be hard to deal with. He was still thinking about Sarah, still wanted her, and was dying to see her again. He missed her singing to him so much. Blue got into a mean mood one day and walked up to the Ovington's house. Richard almost dropped dead as he saw Blue coming up the hill. He knew Blue was up to no good. Beth liked Blue, she always talked to him and invited him into the garden to see the many flowers and the beautiful landscape of the rock garden he had built for her.

Blue made excuses that he was looking for work, that his family was suffering since he was out of work. Beth felt sorry for him, and knowing that he did have a family to support, she hired Blue to help in the garden with Richard. Blue acted real elated when Beth gave him the work to do, and he knew he would be able to see Sarah again.

Thomas came home to see Blue still in the garden talking to Beth. When she told Thomas that she had hired Blue, Thomas was furious that Beth had hired Blue without his permission. Richard and Geneva were real frightened for they knew Blue only wanted the job so that he would be close to Sarah and they feared the worst would soon happen.

Thomas closed his office in the rented room and moved his office to his own addition that he had built for this purpose. Thaddeus was out of a place to stay so Thomas moved him back to his home in one of the servants' rooms. Beth was furious because she knew Thaddeus would be a part of the household staff again and she could not cope with Thaddeus being so clumsy.

Richard and Geneva were still nervous with Blue working around the Ovington estate. Sarah stayed indoors most of the day, but Beth wanted all the domestic help to eat lunch together. Though she and Thomas were always around, Blue still watched Sarah while they were eating, but the shy Thaddeus was also trying to talk to Sarah, and when Blue noticed this, it made him furious. He had to be careful not to show his feelings. Geneva tried her best to talk to Blue, but he was beyond listening to anyone.

As he tried to get Sarah's attention, Sarah tried to pretend that she knew Blue only as a friend and never let on that Blue was after her because of the intimacy she had shared with him. Sarah was driving Blue crazy with desire for her and Geneva was about to have a nervous breakdown because she was afraid someone would finally catch on to what was happening to Blue.

Thomas would take Thaddeus into the valley to see if any of the wives of the absent husbands needed anything done, asking if they wanted Thaddeus to help them do anything around the house.

The prohibition-dry valley was different now and most of the busted stills were cleaned up. There was little left to do since there was no moonshine liquor flowing. Most of the filled jugs had been poured out when the revenuer came through. The residents that were lucky enough to save some that was hidden away were afraid to let any of the liquor be seen.

Suzette wanted Sarah to come back to the valley. She was getting feeble and she needed to train someone to take her place. She remembered how she took Sarah with her to deliver babies and she was always a help to her and she knew Sarah would be a good midwife if she was trained for this profession. Suzette believed Sarah was smart enough and had the patience to wait the length of labor with the mothers.

Suzette knew the Ovingtons would never give Sarah up and she feared there would be no one to take care of the labor and delivery of the babies born in Little Valley. Thomas told Suzette that Sarah was too young to be a midwife, that the responsibilities were too much for such a young girl and to try to find an older woman to train, and to take over some of her mothers that were expecting.

Thomas made sure that no family suffered while the arrested moonshiners were incarcerated. Thomas took Thaddeus to the valley to stay while he asked him to help his family and to be the man they needed in the absence of their husbands and fathers.

17

The community of Ovington was beautiful, Thomas had made big money buying large areas of isolated land, clearing it, and then sell the land at a profit. One of the tracts of land that he bought was connected to the Benson's farm. Thomas cleared the front of this land, and left the back which was a thick wooded area because the land was so close to Carl Benson's place. The front of this land was directly in front of his estate.

The arrested moonshiners had been incarcerated close to eight months. William Harrison told Thomas that he had information they would be released and would be coming home soon. This news pleased Thomas; he had worried so much about his friends knowing they were suffering these past few months. But the news that they would be released soon elated Thomas and he wasted no time getting the news to their families.

When Thomas saw Thaddeus, he sent him to the valley immediately to tell the families the good news. There was always a big celebration when there was good news or anything that was a big event. Of course, Thomas and Beth Marie were always invited, but Beth never accepted the invitation to visit the valley. Thomas wasted no time making the arrangements for the men's release. William Harrison helped Thomas with all of the arrangements, and the transportation to get the men home.

Carl Benson had hired many of the transient men to work the farm, since no one close to this community would work for him. These bums still made their way up the mountain; they had heard they could get work among the prominent residents. These men worked cheaper than the permanent residents.

The community could do without the transients because some of them were dangerous criminals running from the law, but Carl Benson was just as dangerous as the bums. In fact, he was more dangerous than an angry jackass locked up in a glass room. Most of the residents of this community were just as afraid of him as they were the bums.

The residents of Little Valley were excited about their relatives coming home. There were many tears of relief. Just knowing the nightmare was over made them know that things were going to get better for them. Thomas had sent food to the little schoolhouse each day, so at least the children had something to eat every day.

Beth refused to worry about the people in the valley. When Thomas asked Beth if she wanted to attend the big celebration for the men coming home to their families, she was horrified to think Thomas would ask her to go down into the valley that she didn't particularly like and she refused to talk to Thomas about it when he pleaded with her to accompany him.

Sarah had been asked to sing some of her songs for the people in the valley at the big week of fun and celebrating the homecoming of the husband and fathers. The women cooked; they caught and dressed the meat that was used for the celebration, and baked their best desserts.

The men that came home were very thin and their wives wanted to make sure they regained their weight and the strength of their bodies that they always had.

Thomas took Sarah and Richard to the big celebration in Little Valley, leaving Geneva to stay with Beth. Thomas never left her alone because she was still afraid of the mountain. Some of the colored domestic help was also invited. The big celebration was at the schoolhouse. Thomas met the families at the place that he loved the most, the old home place of Mattie and Derrick Williams where the school had been built. The food was stored at the rock spring to keep it cool. There were coal oil bottles strung along lines to be lit at dusk since the celebration would last way into the night.

The families all come together outside of the building of the little schoolhouse. The children were having the most fun of all because there were many treats for them as the food was passed around. There were many hugs and kisses among the families. Sarah was considered one of them since she grew up among the families, and Thomas was their family too, since he had always been a part of this valley for as long as anyone could remember. They knew that Mattie had loved him just like she did everybody in this valley.

The crowd became bigger, and there was so much fun, then some-one asked Sarah to sing for the people. This was always the best time for Sarah, she never was too shy to sing, no matter how large the crowd was or who was watching her. She stood up and belted out her songs, some of them were the low-down blues that Blue taught her and some were more mellow type of singing. She was more into this type of singing since she lived at the Ovington's estate and Beth had taught her to appreciate the better type of music. Blue, sitting in the crowd, never took his eyes off this beautiful woman. Sarah knew that Blue was watch-ing her, but she tried to look the other way; of course, Blue had no good thoughts on his mind, but he was a little ashamed of his feelings of Sarah.

Richard was having a good time, although he kept an eye on Blue also. He never said a word to Blue, but he wanted to beat this man with his fist, but he was still afraid of Blue, and Blue knew he was. Richard and Geneva would never tell the Ovingtons about him being with Sarah and the terrible things he did to her.

Thomas was elated as the rest of the crowd, though they had no moonshine liquor, Thomas had manage to get some homemade wine that he had purchased for this special occasion. The crowd was loud, Sarah was singing, and her songs had put them into a romantic mood, even Thomas was thinking about Beth, he wanted to love his wife in his own passionate way – something he had failed to do in weeks.

Everyone seemed to be happy since the families were back togeth-er. Thomas was having the time of his life. He felt a little high, and the thrill of Sarah singing had him moving his hips as the others. But Thomas never took his eyes off Blue, and he could see this man was lusting after this child. The way Blue looked at Sarah was shocking to Thomas; it seemed like he was in a trance as he looked at Sarah's body. Thomas decided that Blue would not be employed on the Ovington estate again since he could see that Blue was lusting for Sarah, and he never trusted Blue anyway. He was always up to something no good.

The crowd was having the time of their lives, there was so many hugs and kisses as the families were thankful to be together again, and tried to forget the horrible experience they knew the men of this valley had been through these last months. The coal oil lamps were lit as the beauty of this event was at its peak. There was no hint of trouble, nor were they prepared for the next tragedy to take place in this valley.

The fun was cut short as the crowd was frozen in shocked reaction. About half a mile away, they saw flames shooting upward in the air, a raving inferno. The fire had lit up this whole valley. Thomas stood as the rest of the families in total shock.

Everyone ran toward the flames, Thomas along with the others, and was devastated to see the house of Thaddeus Williams' father and his family home was burning to the ground. The families of this valley were distraught as they looked at the ruins of this house. This had to be an act of arson. The people of this valley could smell the flammable liquid that had been poured around the house. The tears were wild as they knew this had to be the evil act of Carl Benson, and the bums he kept on his farm.

Thomas tried to comfort the Williams and the crying Thaddeus. Thomas felt beaten down himself as he wondered what this man would think of to do next. Thomas stayed until the early hours of the morning with the families trying to help them solve this terrible problem. Thomas and Richard took Sarah home, and he promised the Williams that he would come back the next day to see about rebuilding their home. This was one more nightmare for these people, and Thomas felt their anguish.

Beth was still asleep when Thomas came home and he went to Beth's bed and awakened her. Thomas was feeling so hurt, he wanted to be comforted by his wife, the small body was held tightly by Thomas as he felt relief to have someone that loved him dearly to get him through this sadness he was feeling at this time. Beth Marie was a little surprised by this affection from Thomas, since he had not touched her in weeks. She embraced him eagerly, wanting him to love her, this was the moment she had been waiting for. Beth had felt neglected and feared Thomas wasn't in love with her anymore.

Beth awoke the next morning feeling like it was a dream that she had the night before, but she could still feel the arms of Thomas as he held her so tight and the thrill of his lips as he kissed her for long periods of times. His heart was beating so fast, she knew her husband went through a lot of pain for these people in the valley and she wished she could understand the way he took on their problems to make him suffer so much. Beth dressed and decided to make breakfast for her husband instead of one of the servants. She knew that Thomas had only slept a couple of hours, but she quickly made his breakfast and awakened him to serve his breakfast in bed.

Thomas could see a change in Beth, he was glad he had loved his wife, he had needed her. Thomas had many friends, but Beth had only him; she wasn't close to anyone else except the household staff. Beth wasn't likeable in Lawsonville, and she wasn't too popular here in Ovington either.

When this little closeness between Thomas and Beth was over he dressed and went to William Harrison, who had already heard the news. This was one of the days that his job seemed real hard. William Harrison was very angry, but he had no proof that it was Carl Benson and his bums that had set the fire, and since he had no proof, he could not arrest anyone.

Thomas felt beaten down by this cruel act out of Carl Benson. He wondered how anyone could hate so much. The people in Little Valley bothered no one and they stayed in their own little homes, and whatever they did, hurt no one outside of their own little circle of people, and they didn't deserve the bad treatment Carl Benson had been responsible for these few months.

Thomas sent for Thaddeus and he told him to stay with his own people for awhile and help out wherever he was needed. Thomas decided he would stay with Beth, he would spend all of his time with her, because he had noticed that his wife was unhappy, and he wanted to try and make up his neglect to her.

After the men were settled and the building of the William's house was rebuilt, the men went back to being trappers to make a living. For generations, this was the trademark of the men in the valley. These men were skilled in this trade and they could make money when they caught and dressed the animals that would bring the most money.

The children always played along the creek bank, where the water hardly ever came over the bank, so the children were allowed to play at the creek as long as they stayed on their side of the creek, especially since Carl Benson had moved to this community. One of Thaddeus' cousins, Kenneth William, who everyone called Kenny, loved to wander off by himself. One day he was hanging around the creek by himself, when two of the bums from Carl Benson's farm caught him and they held him and covered his mouth so he could not scream, and one of the men had a big stick, and whipped him on his back and legs real bad.

Kenny body was bruised real bad, and when he could stand up, he ran home in shock. All of the family stood around him in total disbelief seeing him in this condition.

This last act of violence infuriated the families in the valley so much they decided to deal with Carl Benson and his bums in their own way. They decided not to tell Thomas or William Harrison and they sort of decided to take the law into their own hands.

Beth and Thomas became closer than when they first married. Thomas would have the phaeton hitched by two of his finest horses, he rode Beth around Ovington visiting the neighbors and trying to be more sociable. Beth seemed to enjoy this time with her husband, though the neighbors still seemed a little distant toward her.

Beth still clung to Sarah, trusting Sarah to do things as she was told. Geneva was always there when Beth needed her. She loved to sew, and did beautiful handwork, so Beth let her do all of her sewing. When she had the time, or had enough material, she would make cute dresses for Sarah, she knew that Sarah was beginning to be conscious of her appearance, and she loved to dress and was always neat.

Thaddeus would come up to the Ovington's house everyday to see Thomas, sometimes he would run errands for them, or do chores that needed to be done around the house. Thaddeus also had a crush on Sarah, he would look at her, and though he was very shy, he would try to talk to her. Of course, he never stopped the stuttering, and it was hard for Sarah to understand him, but she never tried to make fun of him, or make him feel uncomfortable.

William Harrison came to the Ovington's house all excited and white as a sheet, he was so nervous he could only whisper his words. A man from Carl Benson's place had been found dead, cut up from his head to his feet. This had happened about a couple of weeks from the time of the whipping of Kenny Williams. William Harrison wanted Thomas to go into the valley to investigate the murder. Carl Benson had come to him, and he told William about one of his men's murder, and he knew some of the men in the valley had committed this terrible crime, because the victim had been trapped in some sort of a trap, and then murdered. Carl knew no one knew how to set this sort of trap except the men in the valley. Thomas listened to William Harrison, and he was concerned, but Thomas refused to go with him when he found out the victim was one of the bums from Carl Benson's place. Thomas knew how evil these men were, and the man had no business on those people's land.

Carl Benson had made a big fuss, and he did a lot of talking, but he was a little frightened because he wanted to make these people afraid of him. He tried to frighten the darker race of people, but he knew by this act of violence that these people could be dangerous. He had no idea that they would defend themselves, but these men could set a trap so neatly, you would never know it was there, and to mistreat one of these people was detrimental to the person responsible. Most of these bums that were so evil soon left Carl Benson's farm; they were only doing what Carl asked them to do, but when they saw how one of their co-workers was trapped and killed, this atrocious murder frightened them, especially after they threw him back across the creek to Carl Benson.

Thomas worried about this behavior from the people in the valley. He had always believed them to be peaceful and loving people, and he was ashamed to know they had stooped so low. Thomas refused to worry about this incident since he had other worries to cloud his mind. There was trouble coming for all of the residents of Ovington, those who had invested in various stocks, the crash of the stock market.

18

The late twenties was a dark period for the Ovington's and the resident of Ovington. The crash of the Stock market threw a panic throughout the community. All of the residents weren't involved, but the ones that did, and depended on the profit of these various stock, were in trouble. Thomas was always careful about the management of the Cannon's money that he was trusted to manage for Beth, she never question him about any of the business he conducted for her.

Thomas and Beth had been close these past couple of years, they were inseparable as they loved one another. Beth always loved the evening so that she could play some of her classical arrangement for Thomas, though he wasn't fond of her classical music, he would listen to the music to please Beth, this was her favorite time of the evening that they would have together.

Thaddeus had moved back to the Ovington's estate, he could not stay away from Thomas, Thaddeus would stutter so bad that people made fun of him. Blue hearing that Thaddeus had a crush on Sarah, began his old habit of picking on Thaddeus, Thomas knew this, and he moved him back to his old job and in his house, he knew Beth wasn't happy about this decision by him, but he moved Thaddeus back to the servant quarters, he knew that he loved to be around him, and follow him when he walked this mountain, as he did daily.

The times were hard on most of the families, the depression had hit hard on some of the people, though the Ovingtons never suffer that much, some of the people were having bad financial problems.

Thomas had asked the men who were the best trappers in the valley, or the best hunter that did hunting for their food, to bring some of their meat to Ovington to sell to the resident, or if they had more than they could use, he would buy their meat to help those that needed something to help them out. Most of the new residents were afraid to go into the most remote parts to hunt, they were not used to these mountain, and were still a little afraid. Thomas had the men to cut down trees in different parts of the mountain for heating and cooking. This community survived the most difficult years, because of the men working hard and helping each other to survive the hard times during these years. Thomas never hunted or was one to kill animals for sport, but he wasn't afraid of going anywhere on this Mountain.

Sarah was in her late teens now, she still lived with the Ovington's, and she was still smart, as she did most of the work in the Ovington's house, though there were always other people employed on this estate. Everyone seem to like Sarah, she was a likeable person, she depended on Geneva, as she would a mother, and sometimes she would get lonely for Suzette, since she kept her when she was small. Sarah would ask Geneva question about her mother at times, since she knew Grace for a short time, but Geneva could not tell Sarah very much about her mother or father, because Grace talked very little about herself, and Geneva wasn't around Clayton, he was already gone from the Cannon's house when Richard and Geneva came to work regular for Beth Marie after she married Thomas.

Suzette was sorry that she let Sarah leave her home to live on the Ovington's estate, she always asked Thomas to let Sarah come back to the valley and live with her since she was getting old now. Thomas was annoyed by Suzette forever asking him this same question, and he always refused her with one word, no.

Sarah was being pursued by most of the young men in Little Valley, they loved this black woman, with her smooth skin, and her rather wide mouth, she was noted for her smile, as her rather big eyes sparkle, she would drive the guys wild, and Blue could not get over this young girl, he knew there was nothing he could do for Sarah, since he was married and had a family, but he could not get over Sarah, although he tried. Thomas had asked Beth not to have Blue around the estate doing odd jobs, since he didn't trust him, he had a feeling that Blue had a crush on Sarah, and he knew how low down Blue was, and decided he wasn't to be trusted around Sarah.

Beth had voiced her fear to Thomas about Sarah, she would see the restless young woman, her body fully developed, the way she would walk around the Ovington's estate, Beth could see all the sign of a woman wanting to belong to a man, and this was to be loved. Beth was afraid that Sarah would bed down with one of the young men that was trying to date her, Beth didn't want to go through the same thing with Sarah getting pregnant, Beth was remembering the nightmare of Grace, when they found out to late she was with child, and she died before they could get help for her. Thomas was worried about Sarah getting involved with the wrong man, and he began to think about a husband for Sarah.

The times got worse before they got better, there was penny pinching everywhere. Beth wasn't hit to hard by the depression, but thanks to Jeffrey Carter, and his hard work on the Cannon's farm in Lawsonville, he made some money by his family all working together, and Beth still received her share of the profit. With Thomas it was different, he was still in debt to the Cannon's estate, he remained broke most of the time as he struggle to survive as the rest of the residents of this community, but he was still making loans from Beth to bail him out of financial trouble. Sometime he would feel bad that he could not support his wife as he would like to without borrowing from her all of the time, but he always put the money back in her accounts whenever he made money on his own, which was rare in these days.

The hard times brought more bums or transients people to Ovington than ever before. Most of these people were riding the trains, and they could see up the mountain, or had heard stories of the Ovington's estate, and they would come to this place looking for work or something to eat and a place to stay. Sometimes the men had a woman with them, and they would work for someone in the community to make a few dollars, and then they would leave, but none of them came with children.

The biggest surprise was the time when a black man came to the Ovington's estate riding a horse, he was a very neat man, and seem to have more intelligent than most of the people that came to the Ovington's estate. He told Thomas his name was Roscoe Floyd Bennett, and he was a Baptist preacher, this shook up Thomas, because he wasn't prepared to meet a preacher. Roscoe wasn't looking for work, he had traveled from Alabama through Tennessee, and he had made his way up the mountain looking for the men that lived in the valley. Rev. Bennett had heard about these men when they were incarcerated for their illegal bootlegging liquor. Rev. Bennett had heard about these men when he was preaching in the town where they were held, and he was curious about these men, because there were so many of them jailed together.

Thomas was surprised to see a preacher in this community, but he agreed to take him to Little Valley to see the people, because if he sent him, the people would be suspicious of him since they didn't know him, and were afraid of strangers at times, and they were not religious people.

The people in the valley were glad to see Thomas, and they welcome the preacher that had come to their community. Roscoe Bennett was made acquainted with the residents of this valley, those that Thomas thought would be interested in meeting with this man. Roscoe Bennett was about twenty-eight years of age, a very mature looking man, and he seem to be as religious as he claimed, at least, that is what Thomas was thinking.

Roscoe Bennett told Thomas he was called by the Lord to preach when he was working the cotton fields of Alabama as he picked cotton. He ran up and down the rolls of cotton, and praising the Lord. The other workers thought that the hot sun had gotten to him, but Roscoe Bennett knew the hands of the Lord had touched him, and wanted him to reach the people with his words, so he had began traveling the state holding religious meetings, but he never stayed in one place for long, he was more of a evangelist, and felt like this is what the Lord had in mind when he called him to preach and convert the people interesting in living for him.

Thomas had gotten a place for the Roscoe Bennett to stay while he was teaching the Bible to the people, most of the residents of the valley seem interesting in what he had to say, and was real nice to him. As the people seem faithful attending the meeting, even Blue was interesting in this man, he wasn't to big with religious meeting, but he went along with the other residents, since there wasn't much excitement in the valley now, and this was a way for the people to get together.

Thomas began to watch Sarah as Beth had asked him to, he was seeing her as a woman, and sometimes she seemed real restless, and at times she seem unhappy, as if she wanted to leave the estate. Sarah was the youngest person to work, and to live at the Ovington house, therefore, she was alone most of the time. The Ovington's wanted Sarah to be happy, since she had no relatives, or at least none that they knew of.

Thaddeus was shy around Sarah, and he did little talking, Sarah would try to talk to him, but he stutter so bad, he was ashamed to say very much.

Carl Benson, as the other resident of Ovington was hit hard by the depression. Carl was humble enough to try and make amends to these people of the Ovington community for the hurt and embarrassment he had causeed this community. Carl Benson even had the audacity to go to Thomas and try to make amends for the way he had treated his friends. Thomas wasn't about to trust this man, he felt like Carl was only acting soft, because of the hard times he was feeling, as well as the other residents of this community. The residents started to purchase the dairy produces from Carl Benson, since they were traveling a good distance off the mountain to buy the dairy produces.

The times were getting happy in Little Valley, as the Roscoe Bennett met the people at the little school house, where they were holding the meeting. Roscoe was really stirring up the people with his fire and brimstone preaching of the gospel. Blue was always there with the rest of the people, he enjoyed excitement, and he was enjoying Roscoe Bennett, and the way he was moving the people, but most of all he could see Sarah, Thomas always brought her to hear the dynamic Roscoe Bennett. Roscoe could sing the gospel hymns so touching, tears would swell the people eyes, the residents were really moved by his beautiful songs, and the way he would speak to the people, made them feel like the holy spirit was within you.

Sarah loved the way that Roscoe Bennett sung the gospel songs, she began to try to sing these songs herself, she only knew the blues type of songs that Blue had taught her to sing, but whenever she learned the songs, and she stood up with Roscoe Bennett to sing these songs, they almost brought the little school house down. Sarah loved to sing along with Roscoe, and the way they excited the people, brought a thrill to her, and she felt better singing these songs, and loved them better than the blues type of singing she was taught by Blue. Of course, Blue felt proud of Sarah, and he loved her more and more as he realize that she could belt out these gospel songs as she could the blues.

Thomas was glad that Roscoe Bennett had come to Little Valley, he would clap his hands and pat his feet as the others at the meeting. Thomas loved to hear Sarah sing, although Thomas wasn't a religious man, he began to enjoy hearing Roscoe Bennett preach, he believed this man to be truthful when he said that he was called to preach to the people. Thomas asked Roscoe to stay longer in the valley to bring the people together and teach them the true words of the Bible. Roscoe was in no hurry to leave, he was enjoying the people, he could see these people were peace loving people, and he wanted to reach as many of the residents as he could.

The domestic help of Ovington started to come to the valley to hear Roscoe Bennett and his preaching of the gospel, they looked forward to the teaching of the gospel, since the bootlegging had been cut off, this was getting to be a dull place to live. Blue was itching to get his card game going, since there were so many people gathering together again, but he was a little afraid to start up some of his con games, knowing this was a different kind of meeting of the people, and they would not want nothing else bad in their lives now.

The men were kept busy by their hunting and trapping food for the community. Little Kenny Williams was always wondering around this mountain, it seemed like he had not learned his lesson since he was whipped so bad by some of Carl Benson's bums. Kenny's father and some of his uncles was taking him out to learn the trapping business. They had taught Kenny how to use a gun, and on one of their hunting trips, he ran ahead, he was wanting to please his father, he spotted a furry tail, going down in the ground, and he ran to the hole, shot in the hole in the ground. Of course, what he saw was a skunk and he had shot in their den, because he saw several skunks running, and they were spraying the worse stink at the men, and believe me, Kenny was lashed with some pretty nasty words also.

Thomas would feel sorry for Beth when he knew that he was neglecting her, and he began to spend more time with her in the evening, and they would sit in the rocked garden she loved so much. Beth wasn't very sociable as the other prominent ladies in this community. Beth started to sit in her rocked garden in the evening instead of playing her piano as she usually did. Beth would ask Sarah to play the piano for her sometimes. Thomas began to watch Beth Marie closely, he soon realized that her hands were swollen, and that she had been trying to hide this from him.

Thomas began to worry about Beth, he felt like she was getting sick, and did not want to tell him. He began to stay home more, he would send Sarah with Thaddeus to Little Valley when she wanted to go the meeting with Roscoe Bennett. Beth begged Thomas to go himself, and that she would be alright, since he enjoyed the singing and preaching of Roscoe Bennett.

The domestic help in Ovington always went to the Gospel meeting, there was a lady that worked for the Harrisons for as long as they had lived in Ovington. They called her Sophie McCall, she was a short, rather stout woman, she always wore something on her head, and stayed to herself most of the time. Sophie was considered a rather strange person, especially when she talked incoherently at times, but she did her work well. Sophie heard about the Gospel meeting in Little Valley, and she asked the other domestic help if she could attend these meeting with them.

The first time she attended, she was humming away as Roscoe preached the Gospel, and she wrung her hands as she continued to praise the Lord. Blue seeing this woman, and believing she was about to get happy, he sort of edged her on, Blue felt like this woman was a shouting person, and he was anxious to see some excitement in this little school house.

Blue was right, Sophie jumped up on the floor, she ran the length of the school house, back and forth, as Blue really stirred her up by clapping his hands, and saying as loud as he could "Praise the Lord". This was surprising to the people, since no one had acted this way at the Gospel meeting before, and they were annoyed at Blue for the way he had stirred up this woman in such a hysteric state. The people at the meeting were trying to calm Sophie down as she shook and talked more incoherently than ever before, and she was finally taken home to the Harrisons.

Carl Benson was still trying to be nice for a change, but he still hated anyone that wasn't White. Carl Benson could hear all the commotion in Little Valley, and wondered what in the hell was going on. He was afraid to bother these people too much, since he knew what these people was capable of doing, seeing how they could slice up a person, and he hardly went to the little creek anymore.

Thomas did attend the meeting when he felt like Beth was well enough to leave, he always went with Thaddeus and Sarah. Richard would not go into the valley without Thomas, since he was still afraid of Blue. Richard knew that Blue watched him, almost daring him to tell about the incident with him and what he had did to Sarah while the

Ovingtons were in Lawsonville. Of course, there was no way that Richard or Geneva was going to tell anything, because they would be in big trouble for not doing their duties as the Ovingtons asked them to do, so Blue need not have worried about them telling anything he had did to Sarah.

Roscoe Bennett and Thaddeus Williams both had a fondness for Sarah, but they were older than she was, but Roscoe seeing Sarah as a beautiful woman, and he knew she had the sweetest voice, and the sweetest smile to go with this beautiful voice, began to look at Sarah in a loving way. Thomas did not want to see anyone falling for Sarah, because he wanted Thaddeus to marry Sarah, and he was disturbed if anyone acted like they were about to get close to her. Thomas could see that Sarah was also fond of Roscoe Bennett, and she never stopped trying to sing with him, and run to him when they would first go into the school house, to see if he would permit her to sing with him.

The meeting got bigger, and the crowd got happier, most of the residents of the valley looked forward to this Gospel time with Roscoe Bennett, he was able to draw crowds that had heard of his preaching, and they were enjoying the excitement, this was keeping their minds off the hard times, and so much worry trying to survive these times.

There was no entertainment on this mountain, except some of the people making their own, and this wasn't all that good, the singing was out of tune, and there wasn't very many string of instruments among the residents, so Thomas always went to any of the gathering in the valley, and at this time, they were into the Gospel meeting and learning to sing like Roscoe Bennett. Thomas always came to the Gospel meeting to be in on the excitement with his friends, and to keep a eye on Sarah, he knew someone was going to take Sarah away from Thaddeus. Thomas wanted Sarah to marry Thaddeus, he believed, if they married, that they would always stay at the Ovington's estate, and this is what Thomas wanted, because he was very fond of both of them.

19

Thomas would travel to Lawsonville about every three months, to check on Fred and Anna, and the businesses in Lawsonville. Fred was always glad to see Thomas, and he would love to hear how Beth was doing. He never ceased to stop talking about Beth, and wanting to know if she was all right. Thomas went to see Anna, who just stared at him and never said a word. Fred was doing his best to take care of Anna, but Thomas could see their time was short. Both of them were getting so old and feeble, and Jeffrey Carter was doing his best to make them both comfortable.

The Bradley brothers were still wealthy, and managed to make money even though the whole state was in a depression. The one of the things that was attractive to Thomas was the new cars he had seen them driving. After seeing the Bradley brothers driving, and Thomas being envious of these brothers, he began to think about owning one of these new cars. Thomas unbeknownst to the residents of Ovington was taking driving lessons. He was learning to operate one of these machines, as Thomas called the car he was learning to drive. This was during the 1930s, and the times were very hard for most of the residents in Lawsonville.

Lawsonville was worse off than Ovington, which was really bad off at this time. Though Thomas was getting scared himself, he decided to take driving lessons anyway, in hopes that someone would be able to afford a new car one day, which was a luxury for only the rich.

Ledia was still in business, and although the times were hard, she had made very good in her business. Thomas had decided when he opened this business for Ledia that he would never see her again. But during these hard times, he was concerned because he had invested a lot of money in this boutique for Ledia, because he had wanted her to do something beside hang around the tavern and live a loose life.

Ledia had taken advantage of this kindness from Thomas. He was surprised to walk in her small shop, and see the way she had managed to run a successful business in these bad times. Though she wasn't a businesswoman when the shop had opened, she had learned the business from the lessons that Thomas had tutored her in operating a small business.

The shop looked good and so did Ledia; Thomas didn't believe that Ledia would ever look so beautiful. During the years of running a stylish dress shop and meeting so many beautiful women, Ledia had managed to wear the right clothes and the make-up, not to mention the beautiful hair style she had learned to do on her own to make her attractive. The older she had gotten, the more beautiful she had become. Thomas was proud of Ledia, and considered her to be the perfect lady that she looked, and he had some of the same feelings for her that he had years ago. But he knew he only loved Beth Marie now, and he wished Ledia well as he hugged and kissed her good-bye.

Thomas would load up food from the farm (there always seemed to be an abundance), so he would take as much as he was able to carry back to Ovington to be distributed among the needy residents. Many of the residents were proud people, but as the times became harder, they had to give in to their pride, and accept some handouts as the people who were not so proud when it came to their families going hungry.

Beth wasn't one to worry about anything, and left the worrying up to Thomas, trusting him to budget the money. There was always plenty of money in her family, and she never worried about any material things in life. Since the Cannons had always had what they needed, or whatever Beth Marie asked for, she would always get it if money would buy the things she wanted.

When Thomas arrived in Ovington, Beth ran to greet him, and as usual she wanted to know the news about Fred and Anna. Beth still was concerned about their welfare, and wanted to know if Jeffrey was seeing after their needs, and if they had sent any message to her. Thomas always assured Beth that there was no cause to worry about Fred and Anna, they were fine, and needed nothing, since the Carters were very kind to them. Jeffrey Carter and his family always sent their love to Beth, and they promised to come to Ovington to see her. Jeffrey wasn't too happy to visit Ovington, since he was living so good in Lawsonville, and he had only bad memories of Ovington when he was living in this little community.

For the past few weeks, Thomas had been after Thaddeus to ask Sarah to marry him, and this was made Thaddeus nervous. He loved Sarah, but he was afraid of marriage. Thaddeus would stutter so bad as Thomas would try to tutor him in proposing marriage to Sarah.

Thomas, Thaddeus and Sarah went to one of the meetings that the dynamic Roscoe Bennett was having. There was a crowd as usual, and Roscoe started his sermon, but he quit preaching and he started to sing as the spirit hit him. Roscoe motioned for Sarah to come up and help him sing. The two sang a duet, and the resident at this meeting really began to get stirred up. Sophie McCall got into her dance step she usually got into whenever Roscoe really stirred up the people, she hollered and wrung her hands, and she jumped up to sing with Roscoe and Sarah. This was one of the times that Sarah really put all she had into this singing with Roscoe Bennett.

Blue sat speechless as he stood staring at Sarah, he could hardly hold his love back for this beautiful young lady. The singing by Roscoe and Sarah touched him so, he felt tears in his eyes, though Blue was only fond of the blues type of music that Sarah sung, he was getting in the same spirit as the rest of the people at the little gospel meeting.

Blue was a happily married man, but he wanted Sarah too. He knew this was an impossible dream: he was older, and he would never mistreat Vera for anyone, but he kept looking at Sarah, and knew there would never be another woman like her.

This was one of the times that everyone was in a good mood at the meeting. The crowd really got into a happy mood as the singing and preaching went on into the night.

Thomas knew this was the right time to really give these people something wonderful to take home with them. He whispered to Thaddeus to ask Sarah to marry him. Although Thaddeus was stuttering so bad, Thomas was coaching Thaddeus to get on with the proposal, though Sarah was a little surprised and seemed uncertain how to answer this sudden proposal from Thaddeus, but she did accept his proposal to marry him.

Thomas waited for the right moment to make the announcement to the people who were gathered at the meeting that night. There was only stillness as Thomas stood up to make the announcement about

Thaddeus and Sarah being engaged to be married.

When Thomas asked Thaddeus and Sarah to come up and stand beside him, there was a shocked reaction throughout the crowd, but there were also tears of joy. Blue felt devastated hearing this bad news when he was feeling so much love for Sarah. Blue left quickly, he couldn't stand the hurt. Even Roscoe Bennett, who was becoming so fond of Sarah, was staring in shocked disbelief.

Blue was getting into his bad moods again, especially since he knew that Sarah was going to belong to Thaddeus. Blue seldom saw Thaddeus, but when he did, his temper almost got out of control. He had stopped picking on Thaddeus, but now he was becoming jealous of Thaddeus because of his love for Sarah. Blue tried to make himself believe that Sarah should be married to someone nice like Thaddeus, but he wasn't one to give up on something he wanted. Even though he knew it wasn't right, and it would not be fair to her to be with someone as old as he was. He was old enough to be Sarah's father, but he still fantasized about Sarah belonging to him. But Sarah should be married, and have a family as most young women always looked forward to.

Blue refused to attend the next gospel meeting that Roscoe Bennett held. The crowd was very big, because everyone was excited about the upcoming marriage between Thaddeus and Sarah, and they wanted to hear any new plans that might be mentioned at this meeting. There was always a celebration when something good was about to happen to these people. They considered this upcoming marriage between Thaddeus and Sarah good news, they loved Sarah and Thaddeus as one of their own.

Thomas was excited when he told Beth about Sarah's engagement to be married to Thaddeus. Beth voiced no opinion, but just looked disappointed. This was devastating news to her because she believed Thaddeus was no more ready for marriage than some child. Because he was as irresponsible as a child, she knew this was one of the worst things to happen to Sarah. Beth knew her husband loved Thaddeus, and he wanted Sarah to marry him because he believed she would help him be more responsible as a man, but Beth considered Thaddeus to be too immature to be the head of a family.

Little Valley was just one big happy place with the meetings going on with Roscoe Bennett. He never let up on his feet-stomping, hand-clapping, and singing his favorite songs to these people. Sophie McCall never missed a meeting. She began to get close to the people in Little Valley, and they seemed to like her more as the meetings went on. Sophie seemed happier within herself, than the way she was when she was withdrawn from the people when she first moved to this community with the Harrisons.

Blue was getting into his mean moods knowing that Sarah was about to be the wife of Thaddeus Williams. Blue seldom saw Thaddeus, but when he did his temper would get out of control, and he wasn't very nice to him. Thaddeus had learned long ago to stay out of Blue's way, and avoided him as much as he could.

Roscoe Bennett would make the meetings a little wild at times, he was so energetic, and he was a dynamic man when it came to leading the people. Everyone in the valley respected Roscoe Bennett, and they were faithful followers of his teachings. Roscoe Bennett enjoyed the way these people treated him, and he never had to worry about a crowd attending his meeting. He always had the school house full of people; almost everyone turned out to hear Roscoe Bennett stir up the people to the point that the crowd could be heard over most of this community. Blue was only hurting himself by refusing to attend the meetings now, but he missed the excitement and seeing everyone together, but he wasn't ready to accept the pending marriage of Thaddeus and Sarah, and it was to hurting seeing them together at the meeting.

The Ovington household was elated about the pending marriage of Thaddeus and Sarah, whom they all loved. That is, everyone was elated except Beth, who wasn't too happy about the marriage at all. But she never let the rest of the household staff know her true feelings.

Beth had asked Geneva to make Sarah a dress for her wedding, she wanted her to have a nice dress to wear on her special day. She allowed Geneva to use the richest material suitable for a beautiful wedding dress. Geneva was excited about sewing this dress for Sarah, she loved to sew, and this dress was to be a special event for her also.

Little Valley, that Thomas loved so much, just wasn't Beth Marie's ideal place to be. She never liked the moonshiners, and she never cared for the people, because she thought that they took advantage of her husband. Every time something bad happened to them, they expected Thomas to solve their problems. Beth had never set her foot on the soil of this isolated place in this mountain, and she wasn't planning to ever go down into the valley, but for Sarah's special day, she began to think about being there beside Thomas to see Thaddeus and Sarah united in marriage.

There was excitement among the residents of the valley as the wedding date neared. Suzette was in charge of the wedding since Sarah had stayed with her more when she was growing up than any of the other residents, and Thaddeus was her nephew.

Roscoe Bennett wasn't used to performing weddings, since he never stayed in one place for long, but he was elated to perform this wedding. He was very fond of Sarah, and if this would make her happy to be married to Thaddeus, he was glad to be the one to marry them.

The servant's quarters were always full with the household help that was hired since Beth always made sure there was plenty of help around the Ovington estate. Beth decided that one of the houses on the estate should belong to Thaddeus and Sarah when they married. Beth was still nervous about Thaddeus working in her house because he always seemed so clumsy and careless with anything he handled inside the house.

Thomas agreed with Beth that one of the servant's quarters should belong to Thaddeus and Sarah, and he went to great expense to see that the small house was comfortable. Thomas was partial to Thaddeus, and he had always loved Sarah. He wanted to give them a good start in their marriage. The measly furniture was upgraded to the finest ever to be put in the servant's quarters because of the Ovington's love for Thaddeus and Sarah.

The Phaeton had never been driven off the mountain down into the valley, the only flat land for miles around this mountain. There was no way that Beth would ever walk the distance into Little Valley, though Thomas and the others in this community always walked when they went down into the valley because of the steep hill they had to go down. Thomas made plans to drive Beth down in the Phaeton, since she always rode in this carriage whenever she went anywhere around the community and she wanted to be at this wedding for Sarah.

The radiant Sarah was beaming with joy as Geneva dressed her for her special day. Geneva was excited as Sarah as she fitted the wedding dress to make sure it was a perfect fit for Sarah. Thaddeus had already been sent to the valley by Thomas. He was so nervous and stuttering ever so much. Thomas tried to calm him as he feared Thaddeus would not go through with the marriage. Thomas was nervous himself and he was so afraid everything would not go as planned. It was taking Beth forever to get ready, and he insisted she hurry.

There were people as far away as Spalding that came to the wedding and to be in on the celebration. Everyone loved Sarah, those that heard her sing since she was a little girl and knew how smart and talented she was wanted to be at her wedding, especially the moonshine crowd that Blue always had hanging around. The people in Spalding had heard the news from Blue about Sarah getting married and they wanted to come to see her. It would give them another chance to see her, the girl they had always admired, saying her wedding vows.

Beth Marie wore her best dress as she planned to attend the wedding with Thomas. The Phaeton was waiting with the finest horses for her comfort, as she visited this small valley for the first time since she had moved to Ovington. Thomas was a little nervous by the steep drive he had to make down the hill to the little school house where the wedding was to take place. Thomas was completely shaken when he reached the crowd of people. All of the people were excited and having the time of their life when the Ovington's arrived.

The wedding was performed by Roscoe Bennett, who was as happy as the rest of the people. Roscoe looked at Sarah, and when he saw the beauty of this young woman, he felt a little sorry that he had missed the chance to marry this beautiful woman. He had always admired and loved to have her with him as he sung his gospel songs. He felt comfortable with her by his side, but now he was performing the ceremony that would make her belong to another man.

Beth Marie never left the Phaeton as the wedding vows were being exchanged between Thaddeus and Sarah. Beth sat looking down at the wedding ceremony and huge crowd of people without any expression of being elated or sad; of course, Thomas was elated as the others. In fact, Thomas was the one to give Sarah away since Sarah had no relatives anyone knew of that would be with her on this special day.

The one sad face in the crowd was Blue. He was beside himself with hurt seeing Sarah, the woman he had loved for so long, being married to Thaddeus. Blue was devastated, though he knew Sarah could never belong to him, and he felt like she deserved a better life than she had. Blue felt sorry for Sarah when she was a child, since she was shifted from one family to another, and then she had to go into domestic work very young to support herself when she was old enough to work.

Richard and Geneva were all smiles as the crowd got wild after the ceremony. They had always loved these people and when they would go into the valley they were always welcomed, because they had no relatives in Ovington. This was like a family affair to them and they were glad to be part of this big crowd and the love they had for each other. Richard went into the valley more than Geneva did, but he never came alone, because he was afraid of Blue. He knew that Blue watched him, and dared him to open his mouth about what he did to Sarah, so Richard was never caught alone in this valley. Geneva felt uneasy in this valley because of the bad memories she had when she had came down to be with Richard and Thomas to bury Grace.

Prohibition was still in effect, but someone had brought some jugs of the liquor that had been made by the moonshiners somewhere on the mountain. There was a still cooking up some mash. The moonshiners were smart because no one knew where they were making bootleg liquor at this time. The moonshiners had moved to the dense woods that were completely hidden from the range of Carl Benson.

The crowd was getting loud, the children were having the time of their life, and all of this commotion had made Beth nervous. She was ready to go home, she had seen what she had come for, and had no further interest in this place. Thomas was having the time of his life, but seeing his wife so uncomfortable he decided to take Beth home. He was having as much fun as the others, but he felt like his wife came first. He could see that Beth was ready to go home. Thomas found Geneva, and had her to prepare to go home with Beth; of course, Richard came along too, having no intention of staying there alone.

Thomas was real nervous going up the steep hill with Beth, Richard, and Geneva as he had been coming down the hill. The Phaeton rocked back and forth as the horses pulled hard to make the drive home, and Thomas was nervous that something would spook the horses and they would have a accident. Tears swelled Beth eyes, and Thomas looked over to see her crying. Beth explained to Thomas that the memories of Grace came back to her as she watched Sarah marrying Thaddeus. This special event had made her sad, and the memories of her own wedding, and her love for him was greater than ever, she begged Thomas to never stop loving her.

Thomas got a little careless as he tried to put his arms around Beth, kissed her, and was in affectionate mood, as the horses were trying to pull the steep hill. This little loving scene was making Richard and Geneva very frightened. They wished that they had walked home. This outburst of affection from Beth had made Thomas feel bad because he knew he had neglected Beth at times, but he assured his loving wife his love would always be with her and to trust him that he would never stop loving her, and would always be with her.

After the wedding and all the celebration that went with it, the Ovington house settled down as Thaddeus and Sarah moved into their own little home to themselves. Thaddeus and Sarah seemed to be happy and seemed to love their little servant's quarters that was fixed up real nice, and they were grateful to the Ovington's for this nice home and the way that they had supplied all the things for their needs for housekeeping and their comfort.

Thaddeus was just as clumsy in his lovemaking as he was in his trying to do house work. Thaddeus was no match for the warm-blooded Sarah. Thaddeus knew nothing about pleasing a woman, he felt embarrassed when he saw his wife without clothes, and he wasn't to sure what he should do, since he wasn't one to jump into bed with a woman to have sex without marriage. Sarah remembered how Blue had caressed her, the way he kissed her huge breasts and the rest of her body until she burned with desire. She still longed for that feeling. Though Blue had hurt her, the memories of that feeling still came back to drive her wild as she thought of that short time in bed with Blue.

Sarah decided to try to teach Thaddeus the things she remembered that Blue had did to her, the way he touched her body. She touched Thaddeus, trying to arouse him to the point that he would want to love her, but Thaddeus seemed embarrassed by his wife's boldness. He would try to embrace Sarah and go along with the way she wanted him to love her, but he seemed to be ashamed to the point he would become impotent at times.

The Williams had trouble with the sexual part of their marriage, but their love for one another seemed to cause no trouble as they were always friendly toward one another. They did their job well at the Ovington's house, and went into the valley to be with Thaddeus' people. Sarah would still sing with Roscoe Bennett, she learned many songs from him, but she made sure she sung the songs that the people liked the best in the valley that would attend the meeting.

Beth never was happy when Thomas put Thaddeus to work in the house to help out. Fearing the women had too much to do, Thomas would put Thaddeus in the house to help them, but Beth would rather Thaddeus work somewhere else around the estate. Sarah tried to do most of the work because she knew that Beth hated for Thaddeus to work inside of her home; although she was still fond of Thaddeus, she could not stand for him to be around her in her home. Richard and Geneva did very little around the house, they stayed in their own servant's quarters as much as possible. Richard loved to work outside, and he wasn't very good working inside of the home, and Geneva never worked all day long, except when she was sewing on something special for Beth or for the house. Sarah was the only one to try to do her job well, and she was very neat, and she loved to do special things for Beth, because she knew that Beth depended on her more than the others employed at the Ovington estate.

Thaddeus always looked forward to traveling with Thomas, since he still took frequent trips to Lawsonville. The times were still getting hard on the resident of this community. Thomas was always concerned about his people in Ovington, and he tried to look out for them. Thomas took Thaddeus to help bring the many items of supplies and the food he always brought home from Lawsonville.

Thomas never had to worry about anything when he went to Lawsonville. Jeffrey Carter and his employee on the farm were always glad to see him. Thomas was highly respected in this community. The people knew him as a favorite person of the late James Cannon, and they knew that he was loved by him and trusted him to take care of his only child, and the only family that he had left. Thomas was surprised to see that Fred and Anna were alive and still a favorite of the Carters, and they seemed to be in good health. The farm had been good for them. Fred was stooped and walking on a cane, but Anna look exceptionally well. She still sat in her rocker and did nothing, and let poor Fred wait on her all day.

Thomas was glad to see the old black couple doing so well. Fred always cried whenever he saw Thomas. The memories of Beth and the Cannon family would come back to him, plus the hurt of losing his loving family brought tears to his eyes. Fred was more of an emotional person than Anna. Now, Anna could be hell whenever she wanted to be; she had gotten involved with Fred and the years that they were so close, and lived as husband and wife, and believed that no one knew what was going on. Anna had Fred eating out of her hand. She gave herself away by her actions around Fred, and of course, Beth Marie was a pretty sharp woman, and she always believed that Fred and Anna were lovers, though her parents never suspected the truth.

The Bradleys still practiced law, though the times were bad for the businesses in this small town. They seemed to be among the few persons or families that weren't hurting too much. The Bradleys still drove the new cars and their home and office were the finest in Lawsonville, except the Cannon estate. Thomas was curious about these brothers, not understanding why they weren't hurting too much, since they weren't practicing that much Law. Thomas seemed to always go around these brothers, though he didn't like them too much.

Thomas would still have the Bradleys represent him as far as business was concerned. Thomas had been upset with them when they refused to help the moonshiners when they were arrested. Thomas always admired the Bradleys, they were well respected, and their reputation was clean. Thomas had never heard anything crooked about them and they also seemed to be good family.

Thomas went to the Bradley's office trying to make amends for the hostile feeling between them. During this meeting, Thomas was advised to purchase more stock in the railroads because the future of the railroads should be profitable. There were many tracks being built throughout the state, and the future of the railroads was going to be big, but Thomas could only see hard times with most of the stock he had purchased. The Bradleys assured Thomas that the main transportation of big businesses in delivery of their products would be by railroad freight and there would be an increase in passengers traveling throughout the state.

The many debts that Thomas had to worry about and the uncertain future of his investment made him a little worried about investing any more of his money. He believed it wasn't wise to invest any more of his wealth at this time, but he assured the Bradleys he would give it some thought.

Thomas still took driving lessons whenever he was in Lawsonville. Thaddeus was scared to death the first time Thomas took him on a little joy ride. Thaddeus was as fascinated as Thomas when he first got into his car, and Thomas showed him how to operate the car. Though he wasn't to good at driving the car himself, he was determined to learn how the car worked so he could purchase one of these vehicles one day. Thaddeus asked Thomas to teach him how to drive, since Thomas was getting better in operating the vehicle. Most of the people weren't able to afford a car, and were afraid to learn how to drive, but Thomas told Thaddeus he would teach him how to drive a car whenever he was able to purchase one of his own.

The absence of Thomas at the Ovington house was always lonely for Beth. She would ask Sarah to stay in the house when Thomas was away, since Thaddeus was always with Thomas, she was really afraid to stay by herself. The Ovington's house was huge, and the nights were long and lonely for Beth. She didn't trust many of the people who wandered up to the estate, and she was afraid of some of them. There were times that Beth wished she could go with Thomas. Trying to keep from getting lonely, was bad for her, she would think about her family and wished that she would get pregnant. She thought it would take some of the loneliness away if she had a child to love and care for. Beth was getting up in age, and the chances for her having a child was getting slim, plus her many health problems would be bad for her to try and have a baby.

Sarah still looked radiant, carrying the blush of a new bride. She and Thaddeus were like two kids together, and though there was no sizzling rumps scenes in the Williams' bedroom, they seem to be very close. Thaddeus was more childlike than ever, he only wanted to stay close to Thomas and do things with him. Sarah was content to stay with Beth and Geneva in the Ovington's house in the daytime, She remained very smart in her duties, and she still played the piano and sung her songs when she had the time to do so, Sometimes she would walk with Beth Marie through her rocked garden to admire the many flowers, or Sarah would love the feeling of just walking around the garden by herself which made her feel better.

Sarah didn't go into the valley as much as she did before she was married. Blue would still try to see Sarah whenever he had the chance. Beth was always willing to let Blue work around the Ovington estate. She really liked Blue, but Thomas wasn't too happy with him being around his house.

Roscoe was still having the meetings with the residents of Little Valley, but he was wanting to move on. He only stayed in one place long enough to help the people know the Lord and all of His goodness. He moved on to another town to do as much good as he could to help the people. Roscoe Bennett tried to pick the right time to tell the people so that he would not hurt them too much. He was sad thinking about leaving the valley. These were his people, and he had earned their respect and love. They seemed like his own family.

On the return trip to Ovington Thomas was tired. He had so many things to attend to, and trying to survive these bad times were taking its toil on his body. Thomas felt exhausted, but he was surprised to see his loving wife's frail body looking weaker and thinner on his return trip home from Lawsonville. Thomas held Beth in his arms as she confessed that she really was ill and feared she was developing the hereditary disease of the Cannon family. Beth was all that Thomas had in this world, he believed that they would grow old together and the threat of death ending their love frightened Thomas.

The Ovington house was immaculate, and all of Thomas' favorite foods had been cooked for him when he returned home. But he wasn't able too feel happy, only scared, he watched the love of his life suffering an illness that had already weakened her body.

Everything was going great for the people in Little Valley, with no great problems at this time. Though Thomas knew there were stills in operation somewhere in the thick and isolated areas, he wasn't ready to deal with that problem. Thomas also heard rumors of Roscoe Bennett wanting to move on from this community. Hearing this news, Thomas was saddened because the meetings were good for the people. It was something for them to look forward to. There wasn't much for these people to do in the valley, they had very little money, and trying to find something to take up their time and entertain them in this isolated valley was hard for them to do. It seemed they weren't too good at finding things to benefit them or make improvements toward their community.

Thaddeus and Sarah were very close, sometimes in the evenings they would go into the valley to see some of their friends and would always go to Suzette Adams' house to see about her. She was always glad to see them and looked forward to their visit. Suzette just wasn't able to travel the valley to deliver babies anymore, she just wasn't strong enough to do this profession now, and she welcomed visitors that came to her house. Even some of the outsiders came to see her and most of these people were babies that she had delivered, now they were grown up to adulthood. Sarah sort of thought of Suzette as a mother, since she had no one else to be a mother to her when she was growing up.

Thomas was always thinking of something to upgrade his community. He was proud of Ovington, and he thought of the town as his own. He was glad that the residents of this community did not change its name, because of his father's disgrace to this small community, and Thomas was wanting to make the name Ovington a name to be proud of. Thomas remembered how his mother talked about his forefathers move to Ovington, and the people wanting the community to be named for the man that founded the town, and Thomas was wanting to carry out the hard job his forefather, Joseph, built. Thomas wanted a community to be for the people and a good place to settle in.

There was no doctor in Ovington and Thomas saw the need for one. He was thinking about his loving wife and the suffering that she was going through. Thomas decided to search for a doctor that would be willing to settle in Ovington and care for the sick in the whole community, but his main purpose was to try to save his loving wife, Beth Marie, who was desperately ill at this time. Thomas knew that he had to get help for her. He knew he could take her off the mountain, but she would have to stay in the town that he would take her to and he knew Beth would not want to stay away from her home and the people she loved around her.

The rumors had reached Sophie McCall about Roscoe Bennett leaving the community. Sophie believed this would stop the little gospel meetings, and she was devastated. This heartbreaking news just about made her sick. She looked forward to going to the meetings, although she didn't communicate too well with the people, she did enjoy the meetings, and the singing really touched her. Sophie was a loner, but she never missed a meeting, and she looked forward to being with the people, and loved to hear Roscoe Bennett preach the gospel. She also had sort of a crush on Roscoe Bennett, and this was her way of seeing him, the only person that she felt close to at this time.

Sophie McCall decided to talk to Roscoe Bennett about the rumor that she had heard. With tears in her eyes, she begged Roscoe to please stay with the people in the valley because they all needed him. Of course, Roscoe Bennett felt sorry for Sophie, knowing that she was a loner and she would miss this time to be with people. He believed that she was able to communicate more with the people since she had been coming to the meetings. Roscoe Bennett assured Sophie McCall that he would stay on a little longer and not to worry about him leaving soon, but one day he would have to move on to other areas to try to reach the people with the word of the Lord, because he felt that this is what he was called to do.

The Cannon wealth was still sizable, and Thomas was careful with the budgeting of Beth Marie's money. James Cannon had trusted him, and Thomas made sure that he took care of Beth; he tried to make sure that there would always be enough money to take care of her. The threat of Beth's illness was causing great danger to her so Thomas decided to use some of Beth's money for her comfort. Beth's pale skin caused by her illness was frightening to Thomas and he believed that she wasn't getting enough sunshine because she stayed inside of the house most of the time. She rarely went very far from the estate. Thomas decided to build an addition onto the Ovington house, which would be for the comfort of his wife. This addition would be built for sunshine to the right side of this estate.

Beth Marie was never one to visit neighbors or walk around the neighborhood as Thomas, but he would make her get out sometimes, and occasionally he would have the Pheaton hooked up to the horses and would drive her around Ovington or take her riding for a short distance to get her out of the house. But this made her tired and she would have to go home and back to bed, making Thomas more frightening than ever.

The shortness of breath that Beth suffered made Thomas decide to purchase a couple of cars to add to the Ovington estate. Of course, this was Thomas' secret because there were no automobiles in the community at this time. Thomas did not want to let anyone know he was going to be the first to purchase a luxury, such as a car during these hard times.

Thomas knew he would have to leave the estate for a few days. He didn't feel comfortable leaving Beth Marie this long when she was in such a frail condition. Thomas felt like Beth's heart was the culprit that was making her so weak. This troublesome condition was the Cannons reason for most of their deaths.

Sarah was asked to stay with Beth all of the time, including the nights, as she was asked every time that Thomas went off the mountain for any reason and took Thaddeus with him. Geneva volunteered to stay with Sarah and Beth Marie also to make sure that she would be available if Beth needed her, especially since Richard was taking the trip with Thomas and Thaddeus.

Thaddeus and Richard took the trip with Thomas to Lawsonville to look for the new cars. Along the way Thomas had advertised for a doctor to settle in Ovington to serve the people of this community. Thaddeus and Richard were excited as Thomas described the advantages of these cars over the horse-drawn carriages.

After many hours of looking and trying out these cars on the joy rides that Thomas took them on, Richard and Thaddeus were elated beyond words, they could not believe the thrill of this ride. Though they were a little nervous by the wild ride that Thomas took them on, Thaddeus was especially thrilled by this fast ride, and he wanted to try and drive also, but Thomas assured Thaddeus and Richard that they would be able to drive as soon as he had the time to teach them about automobiles because they could be very dangerous to drive if you did not know how to operate them. Thomas decided to purchase two Model T Fords; this was the year 1932. Thomas explained to Thaddeus and Richard that these cars would be better than the horse-drawn carriages and they would be faster. Thomas had been thinking about owning a car since the Bradleys purchased a car in Lawsonville, but Thomas knew he should wait until times got better; but he knew after he saw the Bradleys driving around town, he must own one of these luxuries for his estate.

Thomas only made arrangement to drive one of the cars to Ovington since he trusted no one at this time to drive his new cars but himself. The steep mountain to Ovington was dangerous and he was a little nervous himself, but he knew he had to get his automobile home and he would come later to drive the other one home.

The times were difficult for the people, hard times were still upon them, but Thomas would spare no expense to make his wife comfortable and would do anything to make Beth Marie happy. This sudden desire to own these four-wheel vehicles were something that Thomas thought he should do. He was a little jealous of the Bradleys and he purchased these automobiles to show these brothers that they weren't the only ones to own a luxury such as a car.

Everywhere that Thomas went on his trip off the mountain, he placed an advertisement for a doctor for his community. Seeing the need for a reputable doctor, rather than the mountain herbs and home remedies used by these people that were usually useless when the people were truly ill, Thomas' main concern was the illness of his wife, and he knew this community needed a physician to take up residence in Ovington.

Richard and Thaddeus were elated to be riding around in a new automobile that Thomas sported on his way home. The residents of Ovington, seeing Thomas and his two servants drive by in his new car was, mind-boggling to them. This was something rarely seen during these hard times and especially atop this mountain. Of course, Richard and Thaddeus were like two silly children as they grinned and waved at the people that they passed on the way home.

Beth Marie was speechless as she looked at her husband driving the new car and was surprised to know that he could drive a car. Thomas ran, picked up Beth, and carried her to his new car for a little drive around Ovington. Beth was a little afraid to get into the car because she wasn't too sure that Thomas knew how to drive the car, although he had driven home from Lawsonville in one piece. She finally trusted him enough to take a little spin in the car to please him.

After a long and enjoyable time with Thomas, as they rode around Ovington, Beth was elated that he had purchased this automobile. She was even shocked more when he told her he had bought two of these cars, in case she wanted to learn to drive one herself.

The word soon reached the residents of Ovington that there was a new car at the Ovington's estate. The word reached Carl Benson, and the moment he saw Thomas behind the wheels of his new car, a feeling of hatred and resentment made his meanness come out again. Because hard times were still upon him he had to beg the people to buy his dairy products, and money was hard for him to come by.

Thomas decided to switch Richard from outside working to start working some inside of the house. Richard had been keeping the stables clean and caring for the horses on the Ovington estate. Richard always did his job well, but Thomas wanted Thaddeus to work the outside, since he had bought the new cars. He was going to teach Thaddeus how to keep the cars clean and how to operate these vehicles in case he needed help in the transportation around this community. Richard would have done a much better job, but it was the old habit of Thomas trying to save the best for Thaddeus.

Richard was a little hurt and he felt like he was mistreated for Thaddeus to take over his job that he had worked since he had come to Ovington with Thomas and Beth. Richard was very fond of his job and liked to work with the horses, he loved these animals, and they knew him because they were never afraid of Richard. He kept the stables clean and the animals looked good by his careful treatment of them.

These new duties were good for Thaddeus, he wasn't as clumsy as he was inside the house. Thaddeus kept the cars immaculate, and he cleaned the stables as well as Richard. Beth was pleased that Thomas had found a permanent place for Thaddeus to work. Worrying about Thaddeus being in the house working, had made her very nervous when she knew that he was working around her priceless heirlooms.

The word was out in the valley about Thomas and his new transportation, unbelievable to most of the residents that they would ever see anything other than the horse-drawn carriages atop this mountain, but they were elated to see Thomas driving this vehicle. Most people were afraid to ride with him whenever he offered them a ride to try out his new car. Most of them were so use to seeing Thomas walking most of the time, it was hard to believe that he could drive anything, and they certainly weren't sure he knew how to operate this new transportation he seemed to like so well.

Sophie McCall had begged Roscoe Bennett to stay on a little longer in this valley and continue to have his gospel meetings with the people. To everyone's surprise, she began to help Roscoe Bennett with prayer and could sing a song like they had never heard before in this valley. Roscoe was so shaken by this woman's ability to pray such a prayer and sing a song so touching to the people, he began to see this woman differently than the foolish person he believed her to be. Blue was even touched by this woman's knowledge of the word of the Lord.

The gospel meetings went on in Little Valley and the moonshiners were still hiding out in the most dense and dangerous part of this mountain. The two different paths didn't seem to cross much. Roscoe Bennett knew there was bootlegging going on, but he never tried to stop what had been these people's way of survival for many generations. The ones that enjoyed the gospel meetings were faithful in attending and supporting Roscoe Bennett.

Sophie McCall was some years older than Roscoe Bennett, but they became very close. She seemed to support him more than anyone else, and she lived for the time to attend these meetings with the Rev. Bennett. The residents of the valley, though most were still a leery of this woman, were all very nice to her. Roscoe would always get Sophie to help him in prayer and the singing. Sophie even started the shouting among the people attending these meetings, they just seemed to move whenever she moved.

Thaddeus and Sarah would always attend the meetings whenever they weren't needed at the Ovington house. Thomas tried to stay with Beth as much as possible. Seeing her frail body wasted to skin and bones would break his heart, and he knew there was nothing he could do to ease her suffering. She seemed to be in pain most of the time. Beth wasn't one to complain, and she tried to hide her illness from Thomas, since she could see that it disturbed him so. Thomas would take Beth in his arms, and he would assure her he didn't want anything to happen to her. He couldn't see living alone, he was used to having Beth by his side, and she was one to go along with her husband, regardless if she approved of his decisions or not.

Sarah was surprised to see Sophie singing songs only she was used to singing to these people. The change in this woman was surprising to all of the people, but she seemed to be much happier and acted less strange that the people had originally thought. Sophie even started to take pride in her appearance. She really had a crush on the Rev. Bennett, and he seemed to know this, and he handled this in a careful way, and tried to be cautious of her feelings whenever she seemed to get too close to him. Sarah would smile to herself when she would see Sophie trying to get close to Rev. Bennett, and she could see that Roscoe was uncomfortable, and embarrassed during these moments.

Sarah was able to sit and enjoy the gospel meetings since Sophie was taking over the singing with Roscoe Bennett. The people were as happy with Sophie singing as they had been with Sarah. Thaddeus was glad to have his wife by his side for a change, since she was always called to sing and he was left to sit alone; of course, Blue still kept his eyes on Sarah more so than whatever was going on at the meeting.

Blue was faithful going to the gospel meetings, this was Blue's chance to see Sarah, who was more beautiful than ever to him. Geneva always kept Sarah stylish and neat in the dresses she loved to sew for her. Blue would see Thaddeus and Sarah looking so happy together, and his temper would try to rise, though she belonged to someone else, and he had Vera. Blue was a man that never stopped trying to win, whether it was a card game or having a woman he truly wanted for his own. Vera or no one else in the valley knew that Blue had a crush on Sarah, only Richard and Geneva knew that Blue wanted Sarah, and had actually raped this young woman. They were afraid to tell anyone and Sarah was just too young to realize what Blue was up to when he found her alone in the Ovington's house and he took advantage of her. Blue could never forget this moment with Sarah. He wanted her again and sometimes he would get down-right bold with his love for her. No one seemed to pay attention to him, except Thomas, and he would always watch Blue whenever he was around Sarah.

Blue heard that John Smithson had been contracted to build another addition to the Ovington estate. Although, Thomas had made up his mind to never let Blue work at the estate again, John Smithson never did any building where Blue was near that he didn't hire him to work the job. This new job at the Ovington estate would be good for Blue because he was having hard times and needed to work. He was a good provider for his family and he knew that John Smithson would pay him a good salary, plus he would get a chance to be close to Sarah again.

Sarah knew that Blue had a love for her, but she was faithful to her husband. She rarely left the Ovington estate without Thaddeus, or she was with the Ovingtons. Like Geneva she mostly stayed inside of the house most of the day. Beth depended so much on Sarah and Geneva, and they hated to leave her because she stayed home so much herself. They knew that she was lonely sometimes, especially since Thomas stayed away from home so much.

The late 20s and the first part of the 1930s were really hard on most of the residents of Ovington. These mountains could be hard to cope with, the winters were so harsh and work was so hard to find in this tiny town. Thomas was also suffering hardship, but Beth was still well off. She never had any money problems, just her many health problems that kept her from enjoying the things she wanted to do with her wealth. Thomas had made up his mind to build another addition to the Ovington house. He was thinking of Beth's health and hoping he would be able to help her by building a solarium-type of addition for her comfort.

Thomas had wasted no time sending for John Smithson, when he decided to do something, he wanted to start the project right away.

Thomas had decided to build this solarium-type of addition on the right side of the house extending far out enough for a good size room and some extra room for storage, and an extra guest room if needed. The plan was drawn up, and the work was expected to be started as soon as possible.

20

When John Smithson knew he had the job to build this addition to the Ovington estate, he had wasted no time coming back to Ovington for the third time. John knew the money was good and he brought his huge construction company to Ovington ready to do this last phase of this estate. The last few years had been hard on John Smithson. During this time he had suffered and this was his survival to help him over the lean years of the Great Depression. John Smithson had been welcome by Thomas and Beth Ovington He felt close to these people, sort of like family, and it seemed like this house was a part of him, since he had designed the place himself. Thomas always knew that John Smithson would do the best job and he wanted no one else to do the job but him.

The job John Smithson was contracted to do was to build a huge glassed-in porch type room. Since Beth loved to sit in her rocked garden so much, the outdoors would be brought inside as the third and last phase of the Ovington house was finalized by Thomas.

Blue knew he had a job when John Smithson brought his huge construction company to Ovington, regardless of the men he had employed in his company, John always gave Blue a job, if he was close enough for him to get to the job site. Thomas knew that John Smithson would always send for Blue, but he was disappointed to have Blue working on the Ovington estate. He tried not to show his dislike of Blue in front of John Smithson because he knew that he liked him so much.

Just when Thomas was about to panic over his wife's illness, there was a strange couple looking for Thomas. This well-dressed couple rode into Ovington surprising everyone, since most of the people coming to this mountain were looking for handouts or had no plans to stay very long. But this couple came packed and looked like they were coming to stay awhile.

This was a physician coming to Ovington to set up practice. He had heard about the needs for a doctor in this community. The doctor, Edgar Charles Newman, was applying for the position in this community. Doctor Newman, a prominent doctor, had retired from medical practice in the United States Army, and had come through the bloody years of the World War I. He had decided this would be the ideal place to forget the many tormented memories of the human suffering he had seen during his practice of caring for the many soldiers he had tried to save during his long career.

Thomas met the carriage when the Newmans arrived in this town, and welcomed them with open arms, so elated to see that someone had decided to settle in the community to practice medicine. Thomas felt like this was the answer to his wife's serious illness. Lo and behold, beside this physician was a woman that he introduced as his wife, Betty Jean Newman. Thomas was speechless as he stared at this woman stepping off this carriage. She was barely five feet tall, a small woman, but big boned. Her hair was way down her back, but she had pinned it up in a ball high on her head.

Betty Jean was staring at Thomas with her blue eyes and he could see that this woman was unusual. She had a pretty sharp tongue to as she spoke to Thomas, her eyes twinkling away as she gave him the third degree about his town, himself, and his wife. She walked with a steady pace as if she was eager to check this town out. Thomas was amused by this woman, but he was elated to have a doctor added to this community to serve the people.

Doctor Edgar Charles Newman was born in the upper North Carolina mountains, coming from a family of six boys and one girl. He was the only doctor in the family. The family had been shattered by his father's suicide when they were very young. The elder Samuel Newman had shot and killed his oldest child's husband, which was the only girl in the family when the daughter's husband came to his house in a violent state with the intention of harming his daughter. The elder Newman could never forget this devastating tragedy in his life, and after years of guilt and despondency, he ended his life with the same gun that he used to kill his son-in-law.

Samuel Newman had been a big businessman, selling mostly farm products. He also owned a lot of farmland so his children didn't suffer too much financially as they were growing up, but they did miss their father, who was well known, and had been good to them when he wasn't in his guilt moods. Edgar Charles was the only one of the children to go into medicine. When Edgar was growing up in North Carolina, he always had a desire to be a doctor and he made up his mind to study medicine and become a doctor, though his family wasn't able to help him too much since they all married as soon as they were of age to come out of school and find a wife. The daughter of Samuel Newman never married again after the death of her husband, but she was the only one to help Edgar Charles to become a doctor, by supporting him when he was short on money. She worked hard to support her brother until he finished medical school.

Dr. Newman met and married Betty Jean when he was practicing medicine at the County Hospital. Betty Jean was into nursing herself and was very dedicated to her profession as was her husband. Unlike Edgar Charles, she was one of three girls and two of them were into nursing, but she was the only one that wasn't afraid to tackle any illness that came along. Betty Jean would sew up a wound as good as any doctor and she never left her husband's side when he was treating a critical patient, or someone who had serious injuries.

The Ovingtons were elated to have the Newmans as their guests, as well as the new addition to this community. Thomas prepared a place in his home for the Newmans until he was able to find a suitable place for them to live, and set up his practice here in Ovington. Thomas wasted no time having the doctor to see his wife. He wanted Dr. Newman to see Beth as soon as possible because he feared she was truly too ill to live much longer.

Thomas always made someone that was important welcome by giving some type of dinner party, or taking them around this community to meet the residents. Of course, this was a special visit, as he tried to see that all of the residents of Ovington met their new doctor. After Beth was seen by Doctor Newman, he assured Thomas that she should be all right, that her illness was treatable and he should not worry too much about his wife until she had a chance to try his medicine and treatment for her illness.

With John Smithson working at the Ovington house and the new doctor as a guest in the house, the Ovington's estate was one busy place to be. Ovington was active again because whenever John Smithson came to town there was always action going on. He always had a lot of people working, and this was a very active town now. Thomas was excited as he always was when something was going on in town. Anything different happening to him or his community – especially if it was good – just made his day. With Beth feeling better and looking somewhat like her old self, he was feeling like everything was going to be better for him, as well as for all of his friends that needed medical attention, or those that might profit by John Smithson during this new addition to his house.

There were many complaints of sickness in this town. The residents wanted the new doctor to visit and check for any illness they might have. Doctor Newman had no trouble getting started in business because there were some of the residents just wanting to get acquainted with Doctor Newman and his wife Betty Jean. The Newmans wasted no time getting around to the residents. They even went into the valley to visit, and the people in the valley weren't too big with a doctor, but they immediately liked the Newmans, and they welcomed them to their homes.

John Smithson always paid fair wages to the people who worked for him. He employed some of the men that lived in Ovington, which helped this community and, as usual, he employed Blue to work for him. This displeased Thomas, but he tried to hide his true feelings. Beth was happy to see John again. She would sit outdoors and admire the skill of this man who seemed to be able to put a house together so perfectly, and never seemed to be clumsy in doing anything that was to be done to a building when he started his job. He always finished the job according to the plans he drew up.

Doctor Newman proved to be the best around these parts of this mountain. After hearing about Thomas Ovington and his need for a doctor in this community, he immediately decided to apply for this position, especially after all of the things that he had heard about this man that was looking for a doctor for his community. He knew that this man had to be a compassionate person to care for his community enough to seek a doctor that would come to this isolated town, when he would not have a profitable practice, since most of the people would be too poor to pay a lot of money for medical attention. Doctor Newman respected the way Thomas Ovington had built up this community, the way he cared for these people, and he wasted no time to settle and set up his practice in Ovington. He was glad to settle in a quiet town after the many years seeing so much bloodshed during the war.

Betty Jean was always by her husband's side. She loved to sew up a wound, to see the neat stitches she made. She always claimed she was as good as her husband, and wasn't afraid of treating the worst wounds, because she had been by her husband's side during the war. Betty Jean had a bad mouth at times, letting out a string of cuss words you wouldn't believe. She called them, "slip of the tongue words." Betty Jean's husband never tried to stop her bad habit of these cuss words she often used.

John Smithson knew that this was the last phase of the Ovington house. This estate was his pride and joy. No one thought that he would ever be able to build this house on such a treacherous and difficult site when he first came to Ovington to build this house for Thomas, but the money was good, and he wasted no time designing and building this estate when everyone thought it was useless.

This addition was going to be John Smithson's last job. He was getting up in age, and he was hoping this last job in Ovington would give him enough money to retire, and he could turn this business over to his two sons. John Smithson always looked out for Blue, but he warned him this was his last job and he should try to look for someone else to work for, or if he wanted to leave home sometimes, he would be able to help his sons in their own business if they needed him.

Thomas decided to let John Smithson build on his land that was directly across from his estate, and was joining Carl Benson's farm. Thomas' main purpose for building this small house was to let the Newmans move there and have a room for him to have a small office to practice medicine. Walter was always busy with his small business, but he was willing to work along with John Smithson whenever he built anything for the Ovingtons.

William Harrison was surprised to see the way his domestic help, Sophie McCall, had changed the these last few months since she had been attending the gospel meetings. She was more alert, talked more intelligently, and seemed to have a sparkle about her he would have never believed possible. The Harrisons were very fond of Sophie, but they never fussed over her, or made her think she was special. She was somebody that worked for them and there was no communication between them other than the duties that they wanted her to do.

Sophie Mccall was always in a hurry to go into the valley to be there when Roscoe Bennett arrived, so that she would be the first one to greet him and make sure that he knew that she was there. Sophie wanted to be called on to sing or pray to the people. She lived for this time that she would be with Roscoe Bennett. The residents of the valley were becoming very fond of this woman now that she acted less strangely.

She was a warm person to know, especially when you learned her ways. She was a very likeable person to be around.

Thaddeus and Sarah would always brag to Sophie McCall about her singing. This woman could sing a song that would touch you inside and this was special to her to have someone tell her that they enjoyed her singing, and they encouraged her to sing more songs. Blue had ceased to make fun of Sophie, though Blue only wanted Sarah to sing, he felt more close to her and was more used to her singing than anyone else. He sort of resented anyone else singing to these people. Blue felt that Sarah was the only one to entertain these people in the valley, and he wanted her to sing the way that he had taught her when she was very young.

Thaddeus was so proud of his new job, he loved to shine the new automobiles. He loved these cars. He also kept the surrounding grounds neat and up to par. Thaddeus worked very hard, he loved the outdoors and was glad that Thomas gave him this job outside. Thaddeus would always follow in Thomas' foot steps whenever he had the chance. He was very devoted to the Ovingtons, and he rarely did anything or went anywhere before he first checked with Thomas. Since Thomas was getting into middle age, he did allow Thaddeus to do some of his leg work. Thomas was still lean as always, he still did a lot of walking, but he turned a lot of his errands over to Thaddeus. He also let the elated Thaddeus operate the cars at times, and he let him take short drives around the estate.

Doctor Newman was a very good and devoted man to his profession and was always at Beth's bedside. He nursed the frail and weakened woman back to health, at least to the point she was able to enjoy sitting in her rocked garden. Beth was doing very well on the treatment program that Doctor Newman prepared for her condition. Doctor Newman knew that Beth's chronic condition would never be cured, but he was able to treat her with medications that had never been used or heard of on this mountain. The years in the war had enabled him to see and treat many kinds of illnesses and wounds from which he was able to help many people from his experience.

Betty Jean was as smart as her husband when it came to nursing the sick and getting them back on their feet. Betty Jean could deliver a baby and care for the mothers as well as her husband, and she had to deal with the mother's husbands as well, as they always made it seem worse than it was. She made them work if they continued to get in her way and she insisted they comfort their wives to help them through the most difficult times of their birth. Of course, she didn't have too many of these cases, as the husbands weren't strong enough to see the birth through. Betty Jean still had her bad language and she used it when she was excited or angry, but the mothers were very fond of her and trusted her as much as they had Suzette.

The solarium was completed and was the best attraction to the Ovington estate. Thomas had spared no expense with the building and the decoration of this new addition for his loving wife's comfort. Of course, Beth was elated as ever, she was always thrilled that Thomas' thought were of her whenever he built on to his estate. She knew that it was his love for her that he was always doing something to improve conditions for her.

John Smithson also completed the small house he had built across from the Ovington estate that Thomas had built for the new and valuable residents of Ovington. The Newmans had been very busy since moving to this community. Betty Jean had taken over Suzette's job of being the midwife. Suzette's age and her weakened body could no longer do the job; she was always faithful to these mothers, and they had trusted her, and they looked forward to her being with them, but Suzette had to retire from this profession when she became to old to sit the length of the birth with the mothers.

Carl Benson was still trying to see everything he could see over into the valley. He hated these people, and wanted to catch them doing something wrong, so that he could have the law in this town again. There was the threat of trouble with the law if they caught them making the moonshine again, and they indeed were doing just that. The moonshiners were into the bootlegging business with full operation again. The mash was cooking in the valley as always. There were many nights Carl Benson and his bums he kept on his farm would sneak around to see if they could spot any stills in operation, but it seemed that they were well hidden, and most of the residents were to afraid to venture to far into the mountains because of the danger. Even the revenuer were afraid to venture to far into the dense woods because of the many dangerous animals, but these people knew how to look for, and be careful of the danger in this mountain.

The small house that Thomas built for the Newmans was an beautiful addition to this community, but Carl Benson wasn't too happy with it because the house was directly in front of his farm. It cut down some of the view, and he wasn't able to see too much. He wanted a clear view of all he could see at the Ovington estate. Carl Benson wasn't a man to visit doctors and complain about pain, so he wasn't too happy about the Newmans moving close to him and setting up an office in their home near where he lived.

Thomas was well pleased with the completed house that John Smithson had built across from his estate. He would stand in front of his house and look over at the newly built and landscaped home of the Newmans. This was another proud moment in the life of Thomas. The Newmans were elated to be treated so kindly by the residents of Ovington. The house was built for their comfort, as well as an office for treating the residents of this community.

Carl Benson was into his nasty ways again. He never liked Thomas, who loved the people in the valley. Carl, however, wanted to run these people out of this town, but he knew that Thomas would never stand for that. The valley was the most beautiful and the only flat land around this mountain. Carl could see the potential of really doing great things with this land, but these people were known to live a simple life. That is the way they would always be. And since this was the most beautiful land around, he wanted it to belong to him so he could upgrade his farmland.

The dream of getting this land away from the residents of the valley were slim and Carl Benson knew it. So he just ridiculed them whenever he saw one of them out. Thaddeus was the main one he would insult. He would see Thaddeus away from Thomas, and knowing that Thomas was very fond of Thaddeus, he would badmouth him if he were close enough to him by calling him "the Ovington's nigger." Poor Thaddeus would try to defend himself, but he would stutter so badly which would make Carl Benson laugh his head off. Of course, Thaddeus would be so nervous, and would always walk away almost in tears.

Jeffrey Carter sent a message to Ovington about the death of Anna. Thomas was shocked beyond words. He expected Anna to die soon, but he wasn't prepared for this bad news. The main reason he was so disturbed was because of the frail and weak condition of Beth. Thomas hated to tell Beth this sorrowful news, afraid the bad news would only make Beth unhappy and he didn't want his wife to worry about anything now.

Thomas decided to tell Beth about Anna now rather than wait because she would have to be told eventually. This time was as good as ever, knowing it would never be easy to tell Beth about the one person that she loved. Anna was always by her side in most of her trouble before she was married to Thomas.

Beth Marie took the news very well. She only commented that she believed that Fred would soon follow Anna in death. The only details that Thomas knew was that Anna had became very ill and she died shortly after falling out of her chair. Of Course, Fred was devastated. Fred's and Anna's long friendship and love affair they had shared all of these years were ended by death. Jeffrey Carter was having trouble trying to help Fred with his grief over losing Anna. Jeffrey had to bury Anna making all of the arrangements because Fred just wasn't up to par making any intelligent decision about Anna's funeral arrangements.

Richard, Geneva, and Sarah were told about the death of Anna Jackson. This news brought tears to the ladies' eyes. Anna had been a part of this household. Sarah remembered how Anna wanted her to be her child, how she always held her close when she would come up to the Ovington's house to see them and never wanted her to go back to the valley. Sarah had been told how Anna had nursed her to good health after she was born; after she had survived the traumatic birth, and came so close to death when others thought she would die along with her mother. Geneva always felt close to Anna, but liked Fred, and she missed him more because he was more active and seemed to love the people and the men of Ovington's estate more than Anna.

When Richard was told of Anna's death, he held Geneva closely. He was feeling sad as he remembered the tears on Fred's face when he was leaving the Ovington's estate going back to Lawsonville. Fred loved piddling in the beautiful rocked garden that Beth loved so much. Fred made sure the garden was always comfortable for Beth since she loved to sit among her beautiful landscaped grounds.

Thomas had been worried that Beth would not be able to accept Anna's death without a lot of grief to her. He felt more relaxed when he saw that this shocking news had not made Beth more ill than she already was. Thomas asked Beth if she wanted him to bring Fred back to the Ovington's estate. Beth replied that Fred would be better off staying in Lawsonville, and when he passed he could be laid to rest beside Anna.

Sarah was still feeling sorrowful about Anna's death and she decided to attend the gospel meetings held regularly by Roscoe Bennett. This time she went to this meeting. Sarah noticed Sophie McCall sitting close to the sweating Roscoe Bennett as he stomped the floor delivering his message to the people. He was getting happy himself, but Sarah noticed Sophie and she was amused by the weird sounds that Sophie usually made whenever she was getting happy. Sarah looked at this woman and a feeling of love fell upon Sarah for her. She knew that Sophie was alone in the world and she decided to move closer to where Sophie McCall was sitting. All during the meeting Sarah and Sophie were together with their singing and giving the dynamic Roscoe Bennett the support he needed to really get down with the most vigorous meeting since arriving on this mountain.

Everyone, including Blue, was in a state of happiness as they left the little schoolhouse which was the only place for any kind of meeting or gathering of the people in this valley. Roscoe Bennett was pleased with the support of these people. He was wanting to move on, but he sort of felt like family now and decided to stay a little longer in this valley.

21

The times were getting no better, but they and didn't seem to be getting any worse. People were still having hard times, but the residents were surviving the best way that they could. There seemed to be no end to their worry, and Thomas still seemed to worry about the people in the valley more so than anyone else. These people were used to having long periods of surviving on the bare necessities all of their lives.

The end of Prohibition in December, 1933, was of no concern to these people in the valley who had stills in full operation making moonshine in isolated area of this mountain. Thomas had learned long ago that this bootlegging would always be a part of this valley, and he would be the last person to try and stop them from this trade they were used to, and was noted for making clean and the best liquor for miles around.

Kenny Williams was in his late teens and he still was into some sort of mischief all of the time. He would make his father and uncles furious at him for the dumb things he would do sometimes. Kenny always went with the elder men wherever they went; but he always seemed to get into some sort of trouble. His mouth was one of his biggest problem. He would get into trouble with the bums working at Carl Benson's place. He refused to stay away from the little creek where he once got a good whipping when he was younger.

Everyone thought Kenny would grow out of his mischief, but he proved that he was going to be a wild one. He insisted he wasn't afraid of the bums on Carl Benson's farm. This lad was a smart person, but in a more acrimonious way, his temper and manners were getting to be a bit different than his family. Kenny became bold wanting to run some of the moonshine off the mountain, the same thing that got them into trouble in the first place. The worst thing that he did was to start walking the little creek around Carl Benson's farm. Kenny swore he wasn't afraid of Carl Benson, although Carl Benson had threatened bodily harm to anyone who came through his property, who was unwelcome on his land.

Thomas and Beth seemed to be happy with the new addition to their estate. They would sit alone for hours at a time smiling and holding hands with each other. Their lovemaking was at a standstill because Thomas was afraid to love his wife because of her weakness, and fearing her heart just wasn't strong enough.

Sarah continued to see Sophie McCall and be friends with this woman. They went to hear the gospel of Roscoe Bennett together. As for Thaddeus, he was so wrapped up in his new job, and being able to drive the new cars around Ovington, that he hardly paid any attention to his own wife anymore. Blue noticed that Sarah was always alone lately, when she came to the valley, he began to try to get close to Sarah again, always trying to whisper to her and try to get her to be alone with him, never caring if someone was in hearing distance of his proposal.

Sarah was beginning to be lonely. She wanted the love of her husband. Just being in the Ovington's house all day with Geneva and seeing her dodging work by her sitting at the sewing machine most of the day, she was getting restless and wanted some kind of excitement in her life. Sarah would play the piano sometimes like her father, Clayton. She could play a tune just by thinking about a song. She had talent, as well as being a smart woman. She didn't mind doing anything that she was told to do. Sarah was one to ward off loneliness by her ability to play the piano and her singing, but she wanted others to enjoy her talent also, which is why she always wanted Blue to hear her play a tune or sing a song. He let her know how much he enjoyed her talent. Since Sarah grew up with no known relatives, she always enjoyed getting attention from anyone praising her talent.

Beth Marie was feeling better these past few days, and she was able to oversee her house again. She was even able to play her piano, which she had missed so much since she had been ill. Sarah and Geneva were busy with the many chores that Beth Marie assigned to them since she reorganized her house. Beth even had Richard busy with her little rocked garden as he pruned hedges and dug around her flowers until her garden was as immaculate as her house. Thomas was elated to see his wife in such a cheerful mood, and he knew she was stronger when he saw her taking a interest in her home again.

The new strength Beth felt these past few days was exciting to Beth since she was able to love her husband again. Thomas had been patient wanting to make love to his wife, but he had refused to touch her even when she begged him to love her because he knew she was too weak.

The Ovingtons were elated and surprised to see Jeffrey Carter and his family arriving in Ovington. This was truly a rare visit from the Carters because Jeffrey had not been home since he left Ovington with Thomas years ago. The welcome mat was out for the Carters. This was some of the biggest entertaining the Ovingtons had done in a while since Beth had been under the weather, and Thomas made sure the house was quiet because he did not want to disturb Beth.

Beth was the one to beam with happiness. She was so happy to see Jeffrey Carter again she hardly let him out of her sight all through the day. Thomas was glad that Beth had not memtioned Fred or Anna all day. She had forgotten about them since she was so happy to see the Carter family. Thomas had feared that this was not a social call to Ovington, and it proved true when Jeffrey finally called Thomas aside to tell him the sad news about Fred. Jeffrey sat down to tell the Ovingtons about the death of Fred, but he had wanted to warn Thomas first. Beth's joy over seeing the Carters again turned sad as Jeffrey told the two about Fred as gently as he could.

Beth took the news well when Jeffrey explained to Thomas and Beth the circumstances of Fred's death. Lonely and missing Anna so much, Fred just walked around with his head down most of the time. He was not eating very much and ceased to communicate with the other workers on the farm. Fred's death was expected, but everyone was sad when he probably died of a broken heart.

Jeffrey Carter had come to Ovington to tell Thomas and Beth personally about Fred and Anna. He saw that their care was the best, that they did not want for anything because he made sure they were taken care of and did not suffer for medical attention, and he made sure they both were buried properly.

There was no happiness for Fred since he had no one to understand him and his grief over losing Anna. He always seemed to be alone. The Cannons and Anna had been his life, and since he had neither one to be with and love, he ceased to want to live. The Ovingtons knew that Fred would not live long without Anna, they were just too close and they only had each other. Beth wiped her eyes as the tears slowly ran down her cheeks. Thomas held his wife closely to him, as they both thanked Jeffrey for his kindness and the care he had given the Cannons servants. Beth had wanted Fred and Anna to be happy. When she moved them to Ovington, she realized it had been a mistake for her to bring Anna. She had never been happy here, or did any good health wise from the day she brought her away from the farm to the day that she left Ovington.

The community of Ovington had welcomed Jeffrey Carter and his family. Those that had remembered him and his parents and family, he still had a few kin people around, but most of them had left the mountain or died. Of course, the Ovingtons made sure Jeffrey Carter and his family were treated like royalty since they loved Jeffrey so much and appreciated what he had did for Fred and Anna.

Beth had seen her family die out until she was alone now, those that she had loved so much, and the sadness overtook her. She knew she only had Thomas now and a few cousins back East in New York. All through the years Beth had been in Tennessee she had written her cousins to visit her in Tennessee, but there was no response from them, only a promise to visit.

The illness that seemed to keep Beth weak most of the time prompted her to write her favorite cousin, Judith Holman, and beg her to visit her since she felt that the long trip to New York would be too much for her frail body.

Beth was feeling better and able to run her house again. She would see her family heirlooms that had been in the family for generations. She wanted these priceless pieces to stay in the family and she knew that Thomas would care nothing for the Cannon heirlooms. Beth decided to write her cousin, Judith Holman, in New York to visit her here in Tennessee once again. Beth knew that once they started to communicate again Judith or some of her children would visit her, and she would want to see some of her people that she had left before she died.

The Harrisons were getting tired of this mountain. The moonshining was the biggest problem. William knew that there were stills being operated in these woods and he would try to talk to Thomas about these people that made this moon-shine, but Thomas only ignored his warning of the law coming to this mountain again.

Sarah would go to the Harrisons sometimes to see Sophie McCall. She was becoming close to her, she could see that Sophie's life as being a lonely one; she never went anywhere except to the meeting. Sarah would go over to the Harrisons in the evening sometimes just to talk to Sophie. Sarah had found out that Sophie had been through traumatic times in her life. The Harrisons took her in when she had lost her only child, a son of about three years of age, who had died of pneumonia. Sophie was living in a shack, nothing to eat, and barley alive herself.

When Beth Marie heard from her cousin, Judith Holman, she was elated to hear from her again, but Judith had written that her health wasn't too good, either, and that she would not be able to make the trip to Tennessee at this time, but some of the family would try to visit her the first chance that someone would be able to travel the long trip to Tennessee.

All through the years that Beth had lived in Ovington, she had kept in touch with Judith. Beth always wanted to know how her little cousin, Jane Elizabeth, was doing. Beth was partial to this child although she had not seen her since she was three years old, and she was grown now, and with a family of her own. Jane was the one that loved to be on the go all the time. She was asked to visit Beth in Tennessee, since she was her favorite one Beth asked about all of the time throughout the years.

Jane Elizabeth was married to Roderich Bolling, another descendant from the wealthy merchants, in New York. Jane and Roderich were the parents of two boys. Since the Bollings were business people, Roderich had a law degree. Although he didn't practice law in the state of New York, he used his knowledge of the law to help him in his business that he owned with his family.

The Bollings were known to travel to many places in their short marriage, but never to Tennessee, so Jane was elated to be able to visit Tennessee and to see her cousin, Beth Marie. Though Jane didn't remember Beth, she felt like she did because her mother always talked about her and the handsome southern man she was married to. Jane, Roderich, and the boys made the trip from New York to Tennessee via railroad. The trip was a long and tiring one, the railroad depot was about 20 miles down the mountain from Ovington, but Beth made sure that Thomas was at the depot to meet the Bollings when they arrived in town to visit Tennessee for the first time. Although Jane Elizabeth was too young, at age three, to remember Thomas, he had no difficulty recognizing her. The woman talked up a storm for 15 minutes before Thomas had a chance to say hello.

Thomas was amused to see this woman, who he only remembered as a child, a beautiful grown woman now. He never knew anyone that could talk so fast and so long without taking a rest now and then, but he knew that Beth would be elated to see Jane Elizabeth with her family. Thomas was glad that some of Beth's few relatives she had left would love her enough to visit this small town after living in exciting New York. Beth was nervously waiting for Thomas and the Bollings to arrive at the Ovingtons estate. Beth was elated to see her cousin, Jane Elizabeth. Beth was laughing and crying at the same time to see one of her relatives visit her after so many years. She could not control herself as the tears flowed down her cheeks. After many hugs and kisses, the house was in an uproar, as the two Bolling boys checked out the Ovington's house and Sarah and Geneva stared at the elated Ovingtons and the Bollings as they made acquaintance with each other.

Every small town seemed to know everybody's business and the news soon got around that Beth Marie had a cousin visiting from New York. The news was that this woman had shown up in Ovington with all the charm and elegance of the eastern society that she was used to. In fact, she caused more excitement in Ovington than a Mississippi storm about to blow into town.

The tall statuesque, red head strutted around town in the highest shoes you would ever see here in Ovington. She walked the mountain grounds as if she never felt the small rocks scattered around her feet. Roderich Bolling was a rather quiet man, especially for a lawyer. He rarely talked very much, of course, he didn't have a chance around his wife. Jane was thrilled to be in Ovington. She was used to the big city, but this town was different and she loved Beth the minute she saw her. Thomas was everything that her mother had told her about him. He was indeed handsome and she considered him to be quiet intelligent to be able to build up this town, and have the respect and love of the people that lived in this community. The Bollings two boys, Roderich Jr. and James Edward, were very active and the two had the same reddish hair as their mother. Their ages were seven and five years old.

The Bollings were the house guests of the Ovingtons. Beth was beside herself with joy; she loved having children in her home since there had never been any children in her home. Beth and Jane would sit in the little rocked garden for hours at a time, just chatting about events in New York, about relatives and friends, and the things that

Judith, Jane's mother, and Beth had shared together when they were growing up. Beth realized how much she had missed her relatives and friends, but she loved Thomas so much she was willing to give up everything to move to Ovington, to this rural community with her husband, just as she had given up everything to move to Lawsonville. For the same reason, she loved her father and didn't want him to move to Tennessee alone, and she didn't want to live alone in New York.

Beth Marie was wanting the residents of Ovington to meet her cousin and her family so Beth planned on the biggest dinner she had ever given since moving here. Thomas was afraid his wife was getting too excited by all of the planning of a dinner party and trying to keep up with Jane Elizabeth. She was feeling better now, with the good care that Dr. Newman was giving her, and Thomas didn't want his wife to get in the same shape that she was before Dr. Newman came to town.

The once quiet house of the Ovingtons began to have a different routine for the domestic help. Sarah and Geneva were very busy now since there was more cooking and household duties to do. Occasionally Sarah would have Sophie to come over in the afternoon to help with the tremendous loads of laundry they had to do.

Sarah was busy trying to keep up with the two engertic boys of the Bollings. Of course, Geneva found a way to ease the work load because she would get the sewing machine going again as she sewed for the Bolling family, especially for the boys, since they were pretty rough on their clothes.

Thaddeus was still driving the new cars and taking short trips around the community, running small errands for the Ovington household staff whenever they needed something extra for cooking or other things that they needed, and Thomas was too busy to do these errands for them at that time. Richard always felt a little jealous whenever he would see Thaddeus in these cars, since he wasn't allowed to drive or seldom had the chance to ride with Thomas.

After having a crush on Sarah for many years when she was growing up in the valley, now that they were married, Thaddeus was different. They rarely shared the same bedroon together. Thaddeus rarely went to Little Valley anymore with Sarah to see his people or go to the meetings that they always tried to attend together. Thaddeus' love was for Thomas and his duties he did for him. Thaddeus acted like he was the only one to please Thomas, as he continued to run errands for him, and did most of his leg work as far as taking messages to the residents from Thomas. If someone needed help, Thaddeus would try his best to do whatever he could for them, if he thought it would make Thomas happy. Sarah learned to tolerate her husband because she had learned long ago that Thomas Ovington came first with Thaddeus.

Beth had hired two extra ladies to help with the heavy work load in the house, the many chores she had planned for the workers to do was getting to be too much, and too exhausting for Sarah. She would try to keep up the house as she always did in the past, but it was taking its toll on her body as she would fall into bed exhausted.

The residents of Ovington were anxious to meet the new-comers to this community. Those who had seen Jane Elizabeth had spread the word about the beautiful cousin of Beth Ovington. As the dinner was planned and all of the household staff was busy with the many things that Beth had them to do, Jane offered to help with the dinner party. Of course, Beth knew her little cousin was a whiz with planning a party, so she was elated to have someone so talented to help with the many things that she had to do. Beth felt that everything would be perfect if Jane Elizabeth was in charge of this party that she wanted to show off to this community. Jane Elizabeth really liked to cook and fix fancy foods at a party, though she was a little heavy with the seasoning, and talked non-stop as she helped with the pastry, of course, a couple of pans of cookies, and some of the rolls got a little black before they got right, but eventually they were perfect and were a big hit whenever it was time for the dinner to begin.

Everyone invited came dressed in their finest, but they couldn't top Jane Elizabeth in her latest outfit from New York. There were stares and speechless ladies to see such gorgeous clothes on anyone, especially here in Ovington; of course, the eyes of the men nearly bulged out of their heads as they all gathered at the Ovington estate. Roderich Bolling was quiet as usual; he let his wife take over the show, and believe me she did. She continued to entertain the guests as Beth encouraged her to tell the most exciting stories she knew about New York and some of the people she knew there. The Newmans were invited to this dinner party and they loved the excitement of this big night. Dr. Newman was on edge; he hoped his wife Betty Jean wouldn't let herself slip with these little cuss words she was famous for and embarrass him the way she would do from time to time.

The night wore on and the dinner party was a big hit among the residents of Ovington. Thomas felt so proud of his wife. Beth was radiant, thanks to Jane Elizabeth, who had made up her pale face and helped her with her clothes, which didn't fit too well now that she had been so sick in the past. The invited guests were elated to have had this opportunity to be a part of such a lavish affair at the Ovingtons. They would remember this night for a long time in this small town.

Sarah and Geneva had worked hard helping the extra people that Beth had hired for this party. The clean-up was easier because Thomas had Thaddeus and Richard to help the ladies with the enormous loads of dishes and linen that they had used for this occasion. The men weren't too happy, but they knew that Thomas felt sorry for the ladies, seeing how tired they were, and how they had really worked hard helping Beth make this one big affair a success. She really wanted everything to be special and it meant a lot to her to be able to entertain again.

Thomas was as elated by the Bollings being in Ovington as Beth Marie. He took Roderich on a tour of Ovington to see the progress this town had made. Thomas even took Roderich to Little Valley to meet some of these people that were special to him.

Suzette was getting old and feeble now, but she was elated to see Thomas again since he had not been down to her house while his wife was ill. Roderich was getting out of breath trying to keep up with Thomas, but he liked the people he met. Thomas always went to the little school house whenever he was in the valley. He could see the needed repairs to this building. The gospel meetings were taking its toll on this building, especially the floors as the people would sort of get happy and the shouting, it seemed like the jumping around the little tables and chairs were getting a little rough to this little school house.

Thomas could see Blue watching him as he walked these grounds in this valley. Thomas still didn't care for this man, but he knew that he was going to have to ask him to help with the work that was needed on the school house. Thomas tried to be polite to Blue, though Blue had no more love for Thomas than Thomas had for him. He always had animosity toward Blue, but the two were able to talk business as Thomas asked him to work for him repairing the school house.

William Harrison believing the bootlegging was in full operation again and they were hauling out the liquor, he decided to talk to Thomas about these people. William felt like since he was the law, he should do something about these people breaking the law. He was afraid to go into the dense woods where they operated these stills because he wasn't used to these mountain as Thomas and the other residents that had lived here all of their lives. William Harrison was afraid of being injured by the dangerous animals and snakes. When William Harrison tried to talk to Thomas about these people, he was always complaining about the bootleggers, and Thomas would be annoyed at him, and he only got sharp answers from him.

William Harrison was getting tired of this town and all of the trouble that he was having by these people in the valley. The thought of leaving this mountain was strong since he was planning to try to take up residence in another county. William Harrison had not talked to Thomas or any of the other residents, but he was getting tired of fighting a losing battle with Thomas, and was in a hurry to leave Ovington.

Kenny Williams was getting bold, and he seemed to be the worst of these people. He wasn't afraid of Carl Benson and always traveled the little creek when he left this mountain. Even Blue was afraid to mess around Carl Benson's farm, or any inch of anything that belonged to him, but this young man was as bold as any of the people that lived in the valley. William Harrison had seen Kenny William passing through Carl Benson's farm land and he knew this was trouble. Carl Benson still let the bums that worked for him hang out on his place and they would start trouble whenever they could find an easy person to scare and try to get into a fight with them. William Harrison was afraid of big trouble out of Carl Benson and the people in the valley, and he wanted no parts of any more trouble in this community.

The Harrisons had been checking out places to move and decided this was the best time to leave Ovington before they were to old to try to make another life for themselves. The Harrisons had planned to leave Sophie McCall in Ovington, because they had no further use for her work and they believed that she could find suitable work here in Ovington, rather than take her to some place and she would not be able to find another job.

22

The Ovington house began to settle down after the big dinner party was over. Beth Marie was still very frail, but she seemed to enjoy her cousin, Jane Elizabeth. Normally, during the evenings they had long talks in the rocked garden, or as they sat in the solarium. Beth never got tired of hearing the stories that Jane Elizabeth talked about. She told Beth many stories about the people back in New York, and all of the social events that she had attended in the past few years. During this time Beth tried not to show Thomas how much she missed her relatives and the theaters, which she loved so much.

Sarah and Sophie were becoming close friends after visiting, and going to the gospel meetings together. There were times when they comforted each other as friends always do. They tried to cheer up one another after a long and hard days' work.

The Harrison's told Sophie of their decision to leave Ovington. They informed her that they wouldn't be able to take her along with them this time. They told her that she should try to find work with another family since, they would be selling the house. The news devastated Sophie so much that she went running to the Ovington estate to tell Sarah. She became distressed by the news, and afraid that Sophie would have to leave Ovington. She knew Sophie would no longer have a job or, a place to stay, since the Harrison's future was uncertain. They hadn't decided where they would move to. However, they were planning to live in a smaller house so a housekeeper wasn't necessary. They wanted to live a simple lifestyle from now on.

Sophie told Sarah how frightened she was at being left alone on these mountains. The two ladies cried tears together. Sarah didn't have a permanent residence to offer Sophie a home. They both went to Beth in tears. Beth heard their story and assured them she could persuade Thomas to hire Sophie for employment at the Ovington estate. She thought that they could use the extra help, since they were so busy lately. The two felt better, since Beth said she would get Thomas to hire Sophie, and she could live in the servants' quarters. It didn't matter to Beth that the house was getting crowded with the Bolling's living at the estate.

The Harrison's sold their land and prepared to leave the mountain. Thomas was the person who brought their property from them. He was noted for buying property in Ovington, and reselling it to appropriate buyers. He wanted to make sure that no undesirable people move into the area. He was careful about who he sold the property to. Whenever Thomas sold any property, regardless of the person's wealth, he would check out the people before he sold them property. He surely didn't want another Carl Benson moving next door. Carl Benson had been so full of hatred toward him that he was careful not to encourage anyone else like him to move into the community. Carl made Thomas feel cautious of people he knew nothing about.

Carl Benson was getting old and he didn't venture around very much. He had heard about the Bolling's living at the Ovington estate so he decided to nose around and see these eastern folks that everybody was talking about. The wickedness in Carl Benson was taking its toll on his body. He was beginning to walk as though he was stooped down. He seemed to be in pain most of the time. Despite his difficulties he finally was able to meet Roderich Bolling. He seemed to like him, but he told him that he had nothing but animosity toward Thomas Ovington. He told Roderich that Thomas was one person he would like to see ran off this mountain.

Once, Carl was having difficulty getting out of bed. He sent for Doctor Newman to come and examine him. After a few visits, the Doctor had Carl back on his feet. Carl continued to go around the county-seat, and visited the people that came in and out of the building.

Carl seen Thomas and Roderich at the county-seat one day. He mentioned that Kenny Williams had been trespassing on his property. He didn't waste any time telling Thomas that he planned to harm the lad if he continued to encroach on his property. Thomas said nothing but this news distressed him. He thought that Kenny should know better than to mess around at Carl Bensons' place. He felt that he was endangering himself by coming in contact with the bums who hung around at Carls' place.

Sometimes Thomas would ask Jane Elizabeth to drive Beth on little errands. She also drove Beth around the community to help pass time. Jane was a little wild with the car when she put her foot to the gas pedal. She drove the car as she had in New York, since she hated horses. Some of the residents still rode horses around the community. They were less dangerous, since there were so many hills and curves. In these parts cars were very dangerous to drive and one had to be very careful. Thomas never wanted Beth to drive any of the cars so he never taught her to drive. This was okay with Beth, so she never asked.

The Newman's often spent the day at the Ovington estate. They would have their meals there and enjoy the day with Beth and the Bollings, when Roderich wasn't with Thomas. They all just loved to see Jane Elizabeth get stirred up. She would keep them spellbound by her stories of New York. They loved the way she talked, and how she moved around her hands while speaking. Jane always kept one of her fancy fans with her. She probably was a little warm by the way she worked up a sweat by her energetic movement of her body. She was very hyper and she never sat still for very long.

The days were busy for Sarah and by night she was exhausted. Sarah would long for the love of Thaddeus, but he was so wrapped up in his duties and showing off the Ovington's cars. He would forget about his wife and her need to be loved. Sarah became restless due to her loneliness. She had no blood relatives that she knew of and no one was able to tell her much about her family. Grace talked very little about herself or, her background. Clayton had always said that Sarah's mother was his cousin. No one knew for sure that Clayton was the father of Sarah. However, everyone assumed that he was. Tears would swell Sarah eyes sometimes when she thought about having no family to turn to. She felt like there was no person that she could turn to for comfort.

At the next gospel meeting Sarah caught Blue alone to talk with him. Sarah thought that she needed some fatherly advice. She didn't have anyone to tell her troubles to, or ask advice from. Sarah knew Suzette wouldn't understand her feelings since, Thaddeus was her nephew. Blue was happy to know that Sarah thought enough of him to seek his advice. He wanted her to trust him so he could help her with her troubles. He still loved Sarah. He longed to hold her in his arms and comfort her, but the crowd at church was too large for him to disclose his feelings. He could only ask Sarah to meet him in a secret place.

Sophie saw Sarah with Blue. She thought that they were only talking until Sarah told her of their secret meeting for a private conversation. Sarah told Sophie she had to talk to someone about her personal life. She felt close enough to Blue to ask him for fatherly advice. Sophie was so alarmed that she had tears in her eyes. She always assumed Thaddeus and Sarah were happy. She didn't know that they were having trouble with their marriage.

As Sophie and Sarah reached the Ovington estate, they stood talking for a brief period of time. Sophie told Sarah to forget about meeting Blue alone. She said it would only bring her heartaches. She felt that Sarah would be too emotional and Blue would take advantage of this. At this point, Sarah would give into her loneliness. She feared that Sarah wasn't strong enough to say "No" to Blue. She knew that Blue had been a con man in the worse way. Sophie was afraid that soon Sarah would become an adulteress. She knew that Blue was the type of man who figured out a ways to get what he wanted. He was a munipulator, and he would never stop until he got his way with her again.

Sarah swore Sophie to secrecy. At the next gospel meeting Blue asked Sarah if he could walk her home. Normally, Sophie always went with Sarah and they walked home together. Sophie became furious at Blue escorting Sarah home. Blue and Sarah walked behind Sophie as Sarah told Blue of her marital problems. Blue made sure that Sophie walked far ahead of them. Along the path he started to hold Sarahs' hand. He stopped at times to comfort and hold her. There wasn't any advice he could give her about Thaddeus since he hated him. Sophie was very angry at Blue. As they approached the estate she hoped no one had seen him and Sarah together. She thought that these two were heading for trouble. She knew that Sarah was lonely, but she insisted to Sarah that Blue wasn't the answer to her loneliness.

Thomas had allowed Sophie to move into one of the servants' room. She was grateful that Thomas and Beth took her in after the Harrison's had moved out of the Ovington community. Sophie began to help Sarah, which made work it easier on Sarah. She was elated that Sophie was working for the Ovingtons' now. Most of the time Sophie acted as though she was Sarah's sister. She was a big help to Sarah, but she also watched her like a hawk. She was afraid of Sarah doing something foolish with Blue.

He had been trying to persuade Sarah about meeting him in the densest, and dangerous part of the mountains. He didn't care about the danger that he put them in. He never stopped trying to persuade Sarah to meet him every time he seen her in the valley. Blue wanted to convince her to leave Thaddeus. Of course, if she did that, she would have to leave the Ovington estate, and she had no other place to go. Blue told Sarah that Thaddeus would never change. He thought that Thaddeus only loved cars, and things he could do to please the Ovingtons. He explained how Thaddeus would never put aside his duties for the Ovingtons' to be with his wife.

Beth Marie was like a new woman since her cousin, Jane Elizabeth, came to Ovington. There were times that Beth didn't need the service of Doctor Newman. Her health had improved with his medicines. Thomas was happy to see the change in his wife. Lately, he was able to leave for long periods of time as he loved to do.

Thomas loved to travel and make long trips. Sometimes he would ride the trains that came through this mountain. He still rode his horse to the train depot. Sometimes he would travel to North Carolina to see the now retired John Smithson, and spend a day with him. Thomas always stood out among most of the men on this mountain. He was known for his attire, which was always neat, and he rarely wore his coat with his suit, but would often carry it along. Thomas was still a handsome man and he was known to get into some pretty dangerous allegations and arguments, or even a good fist fight now and then, but he always seemed to come through these situations in good shape.

The main reason that Thomas traveled so much was to check on business investments. He always tried to see what he could buy or sell. He would check on prospects for business and financial gains to him, since he always had to borrow from the Cannon estate. Thomas never seemed to get out of his debt to Beth Marie. She never pressured him to repay the money he had borrowed from her father. Thomas always insisted he would repay the loan one day. He never seemed to get enough money ahead to clear the loans he had made from his wife, and her father.

Thomas hadn't been to the farm in Lawsonville lately. He loved to visit Jeffrey Carter and his family. He enjoyed looking over the Cannon farm and thinking about the memories of this beautiful farmland. Most of the people who worked for the James Cannon stayed after Jeffrey took over the farm. Jeffrey was always glad to see Thomas. He asked about Beth and when she would visit Lawsonville again. The workers came to greet Thomas warmly and they appeared happy to see him. He could sense that they were feeling a little leery of him, as most employees are when the big boss comes to town.

Jeffrey Carter and Thomas always discussed the business, and the farm. Beth never mentioned anything about the profits she received from her father's farm, or any profits that came from Jeffrey. Thomas had drawn up an agreement for Jeffrey to pay Beth profits from the farm. Beth wanted Jeffrey to have the farm. She loved him like a son, but Thomas had refused to turn the farm over to him; although he always did a good job keeping the farm up to par. Jeffrey had the utmost respect for Thomas, but he knew that Thomas had become a very clever business man. He wanted to buy the Cannon farm from Beth but, he knew that Thomas would never let the farm go.

Thomas went to visit the Bradley's while he was in Lawsonville. They were still practicing law, and were happy to see him. They didn't see eye to eye on business matters, but their discussions always led to conversations about the railroad stocks. They wanted Thomas to invest heavily in these stocks. They tried to persuade him to sell some of the worthless stock he owned, which was not making him any money. Instead, they suggested that he take their advice and buy the stocks that would make him some money. Thomas had really become interested in the railroad. He loved riding the trains at times, so he decided to get more information on the investment of this transportation that seemed to be getting bigger in Tennessee.

Before Jane Elizabeth took Beth on little errands Thaddeus always had the cars cleaned and serviced for Jane. This little drive with Jane was a treat for Beth. She had always sat at home while Thomas went off on his trips. He wasn't satisfied hanging around Ovington, but he tried to leave someone with Beth. He didn't want to worry when he was away about leaving her alone. There were too many undesirable people that wandered up these mountains. Thomas didn't have the time to drive Beth everywhere she wanted to go. He never took the time to do these things. He felt comfortable knowing that Jane was a safe driver. Jane never seemed to mind taking Beth to the places she had to go.

The Bolling's had not mentioned anything about leaving for New York anytime soon. They seemed to be happy in Ovington, though this town was quite different than the hustle and bustle of New York State. Thomas tried to make them enjoy this town as much as possible. He didn't want them to return to New York.

Thomas asked Roderich Bolling to fill in as Constable until someone was appointed to this position. This pleased Roderich, since it would give him something to do while he was visiting this town. He was beginning to like this tiny community, and the people of Ovington seemed to like the Bolling's too. Thomas felt better since the Bollings were living at the estate, since he never liked to leave the ladies alone. He never trusted Thaddeus or Richard to run things. Most of the time he would take them with him.

Jane had already made friends among the wives of the most prominent residents of this community. The once reticent wives were beginning to speak out for themselves, even having little back yard gossip sessions. Sometimes, Betty Jean was asked to join this group of women. She was favored by most of the women in this community.

Betty Jean had delivered most of the women's babies, or assisted her husband in doing so. She used the same old hard tack technique. She never backed off from her ways of caring for expecting mothers whether they were from prominent homes or, in the valley. She used her mouth to get the work done. Sometimes her language could get pretty dirty. Of course, Doctor Newman was always there to help his wife if needed. Most of the time the mothers only wanted Betty Jean to wait on them.

Roscoe Bennett was asked to stay on in the valley. He managed to beg up enough money to build a small church for the people. Roscoe was well liked by the residents of this valley, and he had become close to most of them attending his church. The meetings in the little school house had taken its toll on the building, and it was time to get out of the school. The money was donated among the residents of this community for another building. The school never was suitable or, convenient for the gospel meetings. It was the best they could offer Roscoe when he came to this valley.

There was no problem getting the men to build the church for they had plenty of time. The men who made illegal moonshine only worked for short periods time. Blue was the most skilled of all of the men who volunteered to do most of the construction on the church. Roscoe was grateful to the residents of this valley. He saw the hard work that was put into the building of his church, and the way the people donated their spare change that they really needed to survive on, but they wanted a church built in the valley, and they went all out to see that they had a decent church for Roscoe Bennett, and hoped this would inspire him to stay in the community.

A few weeks after Thomas came home to Ovington from his little business trip that he took periodically, he was happy to see the church going up in the valley. He hadn't yet given a donation to its building fund. He was delighted to know the people of Ovington were kind-hearted enough to help build their own church. The Bolling's even gave a sizeable donation to Roscoe Bennett.

The Newman's decided to buy the Harrison estate. They were living in the same house that Doctor Newman had his practice in. When they first came to Ovington Thomas allowed them to live in this house to practice medicine in the community. The Newman's wanted to move into a house away from where he practiced and to have a little privacy. Betty Jean had no time to keep house, so she asked Sophie to come back to live on the Harrison estate. She knew Sophie had lived and worked there for several years. Sophie refused to leave the Ovington's house, but she said that she would go over occasionally to help Betty Jean out. Sophie loved the Ovington's house, and she loved Sarah. She wanted to keep an eye on her too, so she wouldn't do anything foolish.

Beth was afraid that the Bollings would be leaving for New York soon and she feared she would never see them again. Jane Elizabeth had become close to Ada Sullivan, Reba Grant, JoyceBoyle, and Jan Nelson. These residents and their husbands were responsible for the few businesses, and helped Thomas with the growth of the community. BeforeJane came to this community, Alfred Nelson's, Fred Sullivan's, Frank Grant's and Albert Boyle's wives were rarely seen outside of their homes. Now that Jane befriended these ladies things were about to change for them. Beth was hoping that the new friendship would keep her cousin interested enough to keep her from getting lonely and wanting to go home.

Jane Elizabeth put her head together with her new found friends. They decided to try to get something going besides the little church picnics the occassionally had. The picnic had become the big event in this little community. Beth's health wasn't the best, but she was thrilled to join in the group sessions the ladies always had where they were always thinking up ways to stir up some kindof excitement among themselves.

The first time they got their heads together was to surprise their husbands. They took driving lessons from Jane so they could buy a car like Thomas Ovington had parked on his estate. Jane Elizabeth was going to be their instructor, including her cousin Beth. They were able to find a big open field to do their driving lessons in, and the lessons were started. There were many scary times with these lessons; trying to learn to shift the gears was quite a chore. Of course, Jane wasn't the best at shifting gears herself, but she kept the hand moving until it got right.

Poor Beth was just too nervous to try and continue with the driving lessons, and she gave it up. The hills were just too tricky to drive, and she feared the danger. She was hurt that she wasn't able to keep up with the rest of the ladies, but they could see that Beth would never make it driving on this steep and dangerous mountain. Of course, Jane would still drive her wherever she wanted to go and assured her that she didn't mind at all.

Thaddeus was having so much fun with the ladies and their driving lessons. He would always have the vehicles ready for them. He lived for the times when they come for driving lessons. He was tickled by how happy they were about doing something adventurous.

Thomas walked around the community and admired the progress that was made since, his childhood. Thomas was able to do what his father wasn'table to do. Willie Monroe Ovington disgraced this town with his behavior, and the sinful way he treated his family. The older people of this community still remembered the man that carried this town's name, but they hated to think about Willie Monroe and his cruelty to his loving wife and son. Thomas had struggled hard to change the bad image the people had of the Ovington name. He was trying to erase the bad memories of his father. He had always tried tobuild up the town his fore father wanted to establish many years ago.

When Thomas financial problems were pressuring him too much, he'd sell off portions of his land to tide him over the bad times. He had sold the Harrison's estate to the Newman's, and he had decided to take this profit to upgrade the little school house in the valley. Thomas was a wise businessman, and he knew how to make money off the property he sold in order to improve the community. Thomas, Roscoe, and the rest of the residents were proud of the new constructed church in the valley which, they help build. The residents of the valley believed the church would improve the bad image of the moon shiners that was beginning to disgust the more respectable residents of this community.

The main supporters of Roscoe Bennett were Sarah, Blue, and Sophie. They rarely ever missed the meetings. Sarah and Sophie were always by Roscoe Bennett's side. The three really stirred the people up when they began to sing. Blue rarely ever missed a meeting. Vera his wife never came to the gospel meetings. Blue had made everything comfortable for Vera at home, and she rarely left her house for anything. Blue was able to provide most of her needs at home, and now that there children were grown, Vera just kept the house for Blue. She seldom visited her friends, or relatives anymore. Blue just came to the meetings to see what was going on. He was no more religious today than he was the first time he attended the church.

The hard times seemed to be with most of the residents of Ovington, but if there was a need, Thomas seemed to find a way to ease the burden of his people. Thomas was considered a temperamental person. He was also a compassionate person to the people he loved, and the community.

After the Bolling's were in Ovington for a while, and had become friends with other young couples in this community, Jane Elizabeth came to Beth all excited and announced the news that she was pregnant. Though Beth was joyful by this good news, she was also sad, because she was afraid the Bollings would be leaving Ovingtonto return to New York. This was also good news for Thomas, he was thinking how nice it would for a baby to be born in the Ovington house. There had never been a baby born, and raised in this house. Sarah was born here and stayed a short while, but the thought was nice to Thomas, if the Bollings stayed in Ovington.

The husbands finally found out about the driving lessons. They were afraid that someone would turn over on these sharp curves, and they were upset. Though they weren't too happy about this little scheme of their wives, they finally calmed down. Thomas told them he didn't see any harm in them learning to drive, since they were having so much fun. He thought the women would be very careful.

Thomas was spending a lot of time in the valley again. He made plans to see that the little school in the valley was enlarged so that the children could go to the school longer than the sixth grade. There wasn't anything for the children to do, once they finished the sixth grade. There were no jobs to do that was worth making a living from, so the children just had a lot of time on their hands that was useless.

Beth was elated when Jane Elizabeth told her that she was planning on having her baby in Ovington, because the trip to New York would be too strenuous on her. Judith Holman, learning the great news about the baby, promised Beth she would make the long trip to Ovington to be with her daughter as her time grew near for the birth of her baby.

With all of the many projects going on, even Roderich was busy with all of the paperwork that had to be done. He always thought that he had an easy job as far as the law was concerned. Most of the residents in Ovington were law abiding citizens. The community even seemed to overlook the few moon shiners as far as the law was concerned, since they rarely caused any trouble.

There wasn't much time for the driving lessons, but the ladies would go out once in awhile to keep in practice, and these little lessons seemed to keep them from getting bored. Beth was really getting annoyed with Thomas. He spent most of his time in the valley, now that he was trying to help the residents with the construction of the new school. Beth knew that she could never keep Thomas from going into the valley, because he loved these people so much. Thomas was apart of these people,he even had their land deeded to them. Although she tried to hide it sometimes Beth resented the time he would spend with the people in the valley.

Suzette was getting a little slow, and the energy she used to have was gone. She had worked so hard in this valley, but now she wasn't able to get around too fast like she used to do. Like her mother, Mattie, she was a rather large woman. Suzette invited Thomas to come to her house and talk with her. She was concerned that Thaddeus rarely came to visit his family anymore. Suzette said that he seemed to be ashamed of his family now that he was driving the fine cars, and living highly. She told Thomas that he had spoiled Thaddeus too much, and he had forsaken his family. Suzette was real angry when she told Thomas that Thaddeus didn't even accompany his wife to the meetings anymore.

Thomas was shocked at Suzette's accusations, since he was partial to Thaddeus. He swore he never wanted him to stay away from his family. He hadn't noticed that Thaddeus wasn't going to the meetings with Sarah anymore. Thomas promised Suzette he would talk to Thaddeus as soon as possible.

The residents of Ovington noticed that Carl Benson hadn't been seen in the stores or, around the county-seat lately. He used to hang around there to see what kind of trouble he could stir up. He never stopped trying to ridicule the people in the valley, so everyone was curious when he disappeared. Dr. Newman continued to go to the Benson farm often, and care for Carl. He would take his dairy products and other food items to sell for him, but he never mentioned anything about Carl Benson. He thought that the people in Ovington disliked him so much that they didn't care to hear about him.

When Thomas noticed that Thaddeus didn't accompany Sarah to the meeting, he questioned him about not going with his wife to the valley. Thaddeus was acerbic when he answered Thomas, saying that he was happy with his life as it was. He didn't enjoy going to the valley to the dull meetings. He always thought that his family mistreated him anyway. Thaddeus remembered his childhood and how his family made fun of him and the way he would stutter. Thaddeus' grandmother Mattie was the only one to take up for him. She treated him nicer than his parents, and the other siblings in his family. Of course, Thomas knew that this was true, he agreed his family didn't treat him too nice when he was growing up. Thomas knew he had taken Thaddeus in because of his family's coldness, and the way he was treated by Blue.

Thomas was hurt that Suzette thought he was influencing Thaddeus to stay away from the valley, and his family. He knew that Thaddeus did have good reason for staying away from them. He knew that they had never made any effort to show him that they truly loved him.

23

Jeffrey Carter made another rare visit to the Ovington estate. This time he was coming to talk business with Beth Marie about the Cannon farm, which he loved so much. Jeffrey had gotten up enough nerve to do what he had planned to do for a long time, but he was nervous about talking to Beth, and was afraid that Thomas would not allow him to talk business alone with her.

Beth was glad to see Jeffrey, although surprised she hugged and kissed him, as a son. When the social visit was over, Jeffrey wanted to talk business with Beth. Thomas, fearing that Jeffrey was here in Ovington on an unpleasant visit, since he only came to this community with bad news, sat quietly in his favorite chair as Jeffrey made his proposal to Beth. Although Jeffrey was very nervous, he asked Beth if she would sell him her father's farm. Beth was a little shocked, but she sat and looked at Thomas for a short period before she spoke.

Jeffrey didn't want to deal with Thomas, since he knew that he was a hard-nosed businessman. The meeting was disastrous to Jeffrey, because Thomas argued that the farm was not for sale. Beth began to cry. She looked at Jeffrey, and believed that he was going to cry, too, as he looked at her. She saw the disappointment on Jeffrey Carter's face. Thomas stood up, and he assured Jeffrey that he could live on the farm as long as he liked, but he couldn't buy the Cannon farm. He thought the farm should remain in the Cannon name as long as Beth Marie was alive. Jeffrey couldn't believe that Thomas would talk to him so abruptly. Beth told Jeffrey to come back later. She would give this serious business deal some thought.

Beth still had tears in her eyes. She thought of Jeffrey as a son, and she loved his family so much. She knew that she didn't need the farm, and would never be able to live in Lawsonville again. She had no love for this land, only her father loved the farm. There was silence between the Ovington's, but when Beth spoke to Thomas harshly, and in the same tone that she had spoken to him when he told her, he had planned to take Fred and Anna back to the farm to live. Beth was just that upset. Beth tried to calm down while she talked to Thomas. She said she had planned to leave the farm to the Carters in her will. She wanted them to have the farm, and for it to remain in their family, since Jeffrey loved this farm as much as her father did. She wanted to be comfortable knowing that this land would always be taken care of, the way James Cannon would have wanted.

Beth cried many tears when she and Thomas discussed this touchy subject. Thomas tried to dismiss this incident as a minor problem, but Beth stood her ground. Beth called Jeffrey Carter back to the Ovington estate to discuss this business deal further. She also called in Roderich Bolling. Thomas, Beth, Jeffrey, and Roderich sat together talking for a long time, discussing the farm thoroughly. Beth decided to make up an agreement concerning the Cannon farm with Jeffrey Carter and his family. Beth had asked Roderich to draw up a contract for Jeffrey and her to become equal partners in the farm while she still lived, and at her death, the estate of the Cannon farm in Lawsonville would be willed to Jeffrey Carter. Thomas sat sternly and he was furious as he witnessed this agreement being made between his wife and Jeffrey. The business deal was finished, and Thomas stormed out of the house as Jeffrey tried to shake his hand. Beth put her arms around Jeffrey, and kissed him the way a mother would her son. She tried to cheer Jeffrey up because he was almost in tears by the way Thomas treated him, and the coldness he felt from him. Roderich Bolling felt uncomfortable by the rudeness of Thomas to Beth and Jeffrey. He wanted to smooth the incident over, but he didn't know what to do, since Jeffrey was a stranger to him.

When Jeffrey was over the shock by the way Thomas was so cold to him, he was elated to know how much Beth loved him and his family. Jeffrey would never get over Thomas' rudeness, he was surprised to see Thomas act this way toward him, since he had never shown anything but love for him and his family. Jeffrey had always looked up to Thomas, and he was grateful to him for taking him from this community when he was so young, and seeing that he was taken care of by the Cannons.

The Cannons were family to Jeffrey, he loved the farm, and he always took care of this land as if it belonged to him. But he always feared that Thomas would sell it, or ask him to leave it if anything happened to Beth. He knew if Thomas lived the longest he would have complete control of the farm. Jeffrey was feeling bad that Thomas was angry with him, but he decided to forget the hard feelings between them and hoped that they could remain friends because Beth loved them both. He knew she wanted them to remain friends.

Jane Elizabeth was still tutoring the driving lessons, though her time was limited because of her pregnancy. They still had fun as Thaddeus always made sure the ladies had everything they needed, and the cars were ready to go. Doctor Newman was busy running to Carl Benson's farm and keeping an eye on Jane, he was always trying to make her slow down. He always kidded her by saying that her baby was going to come into this world running, since she was running around most of the time trying to do more than she had the time to do it in. There was still some concern about Carl Benson, but Doctor Newman never mentioned his name, or his condition.

Sarah and Sophie were like sisters, they worked good together, and went places together. Sometimes they would learn new songs to sing at the meetings. The greatest delight Sarah and Sophie had was helping Betty Jean. Sometimes they would go with her to deliver a babies, and they loved the way she would try to calm the fathers. Betty Jean acted more like they were little boys than grown men, but she never left a home until she was sure everything was right.

The Ovington's house was busy as the Bollings and the Newman's were at the house most of the time. Of course, the Bollings still lived at the estate, Beth fussed over them as if they were little children. She was so elated to have someone close in her family with her, she had suffered so much loneliness since she had moved to Tennessee. Occasionally, Beth would sit at the piano and play some of her favorite classical arrangements for her guests. Sometimes Jane would try to take over some of the entertainment, but playing the piano just didn't seem to be one of her best things to do, and she even tried to sing. Sarah would usually come to the rescue, and sing some of Beth's favorite songs she would always ask Sarah to sing.

Thomas was still walking around a little hurt by his wife's decision to make Jeffrey an equal partner to the Cannon's farm. He was hurt that she didn't trust him to carry out her wishes at her death. He knew that

Beth didn't trust him to keep the Cannon's farm as it was before she changed it. He knew she feared that he would make the Carters move from the farm if she were to pass before he did, or he would sell the farm out from under the Carters. The tension was a little strained between them.

The house stayed full of music as Beth played the piano, and Sarah sanged. They were trying to ease the tension between Thomas and Beth. All of Jane and Roderich friends were anxiously waiting the birth of the new baby. Beth was able to keep busy, and didn't seem to pay any attention to Thomas as he pouted around her. She remained busy shopping for the new baby. She would get Jane or Roderich to take her off the mountain to some of the bigger stores to buy fancy clothes and the things that was needed for a new baby. Geneva was even sewing little baby clothes herself, and excited that she could be at her sewing machine instead of doing the heavy housework.

Judith Holman had made Beth Marie a promise that she would visit Tennessee near the birth of the baby. She wanted to be with her daughter, since she had decided to stay in Tennessee to have this baby. Beth was looking forward to having her cousin at the Ovington house when this happened. This time would be different compared to the time when Sarah was born.

Thomas had been feeling sad since Jeffrey Carter had come to the mountain, and he felt left out in the cold. This was the first time that Beth had made a decision on her own, and he felt like this was serious. He didn't think Beth should have given the farm to the Carters. He would have made them pay something for the valuable land, and the equipment that was left on the farm. Thomas tried to ease his hurt by hanging out in the valley again. He would always go to the people he felt the closest when he was feeling down in the dumps. He began hanging around the new school house, and made sure everything was up to par. He would stop by to see Suzette who scolded him for things she thought that he should do, or hadn't done.

Thomas paid the money for the needed repairs in the school. He had the building enlarged by adding on more classrooms for the children. He sent for Walter who could build some bigger tables and chairs so that the children could go to school longer than the sixth grade. Blue even came to help with the school after he had finish working on the new church. This little valley was beginning to look beautiful with the cooperation of the residents trying to improve their community.

The Newman's were in and out of the Ovington house trying to keep a eye on Jane Elizabeth. Doctor Newman made sure that Jane remained in good health. She was excited about the new baby, and the doctor didn't want her to overdo anything and make herself sick.

Beth was really concerned by Thomas' quietness and the way he pouted around her. She loved Thomas too much to see him so hurt. She even noticed the coldness he had began to show toward her. Beth knew that she had done the right thing signing over the farm to the Carters, and she didn't regret it, but she felt like Thomas was being childish acting the way he had been these past few months.

Beth had made up her mind to makeup with her husband. She could not stand the tension between them. She loved Thomas and wanted things to be the same as before between them. When Beth approached Thomas, he was as anxious to make up with her. Thomas soon cooled his head, and he made up with Beth, he assured her that he was glad that Jeffrey and his family would always be on the Cannon farm. Thomas always loved to visit the farm himself, but now he wouldn't be able to rule the operation of this farm anymore.

Thomas and Beth missed each other, since they were apart, both sleeping separate in beds. They started sharing the same bed again, and they could not wait to renew their love. Beth missed the warmth of her husband, and the passionate way he would love her, though she was still frail. She assured Thomas she wanted his complete love, and to spare nothing to make her feel his love again.

As the time got close for the baby's birth, Jane had to quit teaching driving lessons. Sometimes the ladies would get Thaddeus to take the cars out for them to drive. This was the most fun they had. Thaddeus was having a great time too with the ladies. They continued to depend on him for their lessons, whenever they were brave enough to go out on their own.

Roderich Bolling was a good man for the Constable job. However, he still refused to take the job permanently. He had hopes of returning to New York just as his wife desired, once the baby was born. They both wanted to revisit New York when the baby was old enough to travel. There was a lot of respect for this man among the residents. He was a smart man, and he really knew the law. He took care of the bad business deals for the people. Thomas tried to persuade Roderich into staying in

Ovington. He wanted him to take the job of Constable permanently, or set up his own law practice.

The community was quiet, it was one of those days when everything seemed perfect. No one seemed unhappy or worried by these bad times that was crushing everyone. Beth and Jane Elizabeth were sitting in the solarium. Jane was talking a mile a minute as Beth listened. Sarah and Sophie were doing household chores, and Geneva was hitting the sewing machine pedal at a rapid pace. Thomas was down in Little Valley, walking and admiring the remodeling of the school, and seeing the beautiful church, when all hell broke loose on this mountain.

There was a crash that would split your ears open. When all of the residents heard it, they froze in fright, believing it was a tragedy of some sort as the explosion rocked the mountain. The husbands of the wives taking the driving lessons was fearful at the explosion. Some believed that Thomas was the one who crashed in his car. Beth was pale because she knew her husband was gone forever. Jane Elizabeth almost lost her baby over the excitement, and over trying to calm Beth. She was trying to get a hold of her nerves because she believed that it was Thomas, or some of her friends in that awful crash.

Sarah along with all of the others ran to the crash site, but no one was prepared for the shock. They learned that it was Thaddeus Williams that had run off the mountain in Thomas Ovington's car. Thomas ran up the hill from Little Valley, his heart was beating so fast, as if it was coming out of his chest. He never stopped running until he reached the crash site. Thomas pushed through the crowd of people to see who had crashed. Seeing Thaddeus, he reeled in shock, and broke down crying so hard. Thaddeus was dead, having been thrown free of the car, which was burning in flames. Thaddeus was dead from a broken neck, and internal injuries, which were so bad he was unable to survive.

Sarah had ran to the crash site as the others did, and she never would have believed it was her husband. She was shocked to see Thaddeus Williams so still, and she knew that he was dead. Most of the residents were sad when they learned it was Thaddeus who was in the car crash. Everyone felt sorry for Sarah who was left alone once again.

The Williams and the rest of the residents in the valley were in a state of shock. They were used to having traumatic times but, they were devastated by the terrible shock to this community. All who knew

Thaddeus would be hurt by this tragedy. They knew Sarah would grieve for Thaddeus.

Thomas Ovington's car was upside down and burning away, but at least Thaddeus was not burned in the wreck. He had been thrown clear out of the car and no burns covered his body. The residents had to carry Sarah, and Thaddeus's body back to the Ovington's house. Doctor Newman examined Thaddeus, and he assured the Ovingtons' that Thaddeus didn't suffer, he died almost instantly. Sarah was put to bed, she was in a state of shock. Sophie tried to comfort her as best as she could. The Ovington's and the Bolling's were in and out of Sarah's room most of the time, they did their best to comfort Sarah.

Thomas was in shock himself, but he tried to hold up for the sake of Thaddeus relatives. They were grieving beyond words for him. They had heard the crash, but they never dreamed it was Thaddeus. They knew that he could drive, and they never expected he would have a fatal accident. When they heard the crash, and saw Thomas running up the hill, a few of the residents followed. They were unsure of what was going on and was not prepared for the shock.

The men all got together to discuss the tragedy, and what to do about getting Thaddeus down into Little Valley for his burial. No one wanted the hard job of carrying his body down the steep hill. The relatives and friends of Thaddeus all huddled together weeping.

Thomas was trying to do what he could to help the family, but he was weeping as much as Thaddeus' family. He cared for Thaddeus and had looked after him since he was fourteen. Thomas remembered Mattie and her love for her grandson. Thaddeus had been the one person that had tried to look after her when she was sick. Thaddeus had always tried to make Thomas proud of him. He even married Sarah to please him.

Walter was asked to build a casket for Thaddeus, as he did for many people. He built him one of the best boxes that he knew how to build for Thaddeus to rest in. There wasn't much of a funeral as Thaddeus was put to rest. Sophie was in shock herself, but she sung and prayed along with Roscoe Bennett. Everyone was in grief and shock, but the ceremony was soon over. The Rev. Roscoe Bennett tried to console the family and do what he could to ease the grief. The Bolling's stayed with Beth, and Thomas went to the funeral with Sarah. He was trying to do all he could to lessen her grief. Thomas was still in shock himself. This was just another blow to his long and troublesome life. He seemed to have suffered many bad times in his life, but he always seemed to find a way to survive these devastating times.

Sarah wasn't able to get over the shock of Thaddeus's death too soon, and she had many problems. Sophie was trying to help Sarah, but she wasn't able to do much to get Sarah over her depression. Blue and Vera would come up to the Ovington house to see Sarah during these bad times. It surprised to everyone to see Vera get out of her house, since she rarely left home for anything.

The whole community was saddened in Little Valley. Everyone realized it could have been any one of the ladies, or even Thomas himself could have been involved in this terrible accident. Everyone wondered how Thaddeus had such a bad accident, because he knew how to drive, and he certainly knew the mountain. Thomas trusted him to take care of the vehicles, and he would drive the cars to do small errands for the Ovingtons and other residents of this community.

Roderich Bolling tried to talk to Thomas, who just walked around in a daze most of the time. He missed Thaddeus, the one person who admired him. Thaddeus had loved Thomas much more than anyone else, because Thomas was the one to see that he was taken care of after the death of his grandparents.

Richard and Geneva were hurt as everyone else. Although Richard had been so hurt when Thomas had given his job to Thaddeus, he believed that Thomas would let him go back to his old job now that Thaddeus was dead. Geneva was trying to do what she could to help Sarah; she had known Sarah since she was born. Seeing Sarah so unhappy made her grieve as much as Sarah.

After the shock of Thaddeus' death wore off a little, Thomas allowed Richard to go back to his old job. This made Richard ecstatic to be able do chores outside of the house again. Richard certainly didn't like being inside of the Ovington house with all of the chattering ladies.

Since Kenny Williams was into everything he could do to get himself into trouble. Thomas asked him to come to the Ovington's estate. He offered him a job, even though it wasn't a very attractive job to Kenny. But, his family made him take the job. They feared he was headed for trouble if he didn't take it. Kenny was still hanging around Carl Benson's place. He loved to walk through his land, as he would travel around the little creek down the mountain to Spalding.

Most of the residents of Spalding were fond of Little Kenny Williams, but he could be a wild one whenever he wanted to. The young man would drink moonshine, and he would get into one of the worst moods. There were times that he would have to be put to bed. He would stay in this little town until he straightened himself out enough to travel back home to his family.

Spalding was Kenny Williams' second home now that he had made friends there. He was seeing a mulatto woman in Spalding named Cassandra that he really liked. She was highly intelligent, and had taken some college courses which was rare among the Colored people. Cassandra Brooks came from a well established family, and was very popular among the residents of Spalding. Why she fell for the hell-raising Kenny Williams was mind-boggling to these people.

Thomas put up with Kenny, giving him a job to keep him out of trouble. He only did this because his family was so worried about him. At the Ovington estate, Kenny tried to comfort Sarah, and he helped her whenever he could. He would tell her jokes, whenever she seemed lonely, and unhappy with her life.

The more Sarah tried to forget Thaddeus, the more she seemed to feel sorry for herself. Sarah had never left this mountain, and the worry of never having any family began to haunt her. The love she had for the Ovington's and the other household servants wasn't enough to make her satisfied as far as family was concerned. Sarah began to think of her father and wondered if he was alive, or just who was her father. The love Sarah had for Blue was more of a fatherly love than an intimate love, but her body cried out for fulfillment. Though she knew it was wrong, she just wanted to make love with Blue to satisfy herself.

The deadly car that took Thaddeus' life was hauled off the mountain. Thomas didn't want to be reminded of the tragedy that had caused so much hurt to so many people. He knew he would never get over the death of Thaddeus Williams. He thought that removing the car so that he wouldn't see it could start the healing process for him, and the rest of the community.

Roderick and Jane Elizabeth were anxiously awaiting the birth of their baby, their third child. Of course, Beth was all radiant herself as she shopped, and helped prepare the nursery and acted more like the grandmother than the cousin. Cousin Judith Holman promised that she would be in Ovington for the birth of her grandchild. Beth believed she would never make the trip to Tennessee, but she prepared for her visit anyway, just in case Judith did indeed come to Ovington.

Doctor Newman was pleased by Jane's condition. She seemed healthy and full of energy. The Bolling boy's were full of energy, and they kept the household staff and Beth on their toes as they tried to keep up with them.

Roderick Bolling was real popular among the residents of Ovington. He was a real smart man, and he helped the people in solving problems that were frightening to these people that had invested their money. It seemed the times were getting no better, and they were very frightened that they would lose everything they had during this period of depression. There was very little money circulating through this little town, and this was beginning to make times hard for everyone who lived there.

Sarah would go into the valley every chance she would get, and of course, she had Sophie right behind her. She was afraid that Sarah was up to something that would cause her trouble or heartbreak in the end. Sarah would visit the residents' homes in Little Valley, something she rarely did since she had moved to the Ovington's estate when she was still a child.

There was no relief in the depression that had affected most of the families. Walter had little work to do, and though he was semi-retired, he still tried to do jobs to make extra money and to ward off boredom. Beth asked Walter to build a cradle for the expected baby. Of course, he was elated to build anything for the Ovington's and this was special. He hadn't built anything for an infant, since his own children were in their younger years.

Since Kenny Williams couldn't stay away from Spalding and Cassandra Brooks. He was finally able to talk her into marrying him and moving to his home down in Little Valley. Everyone in Spalding knew she must have loved him very much to leave home and move to such an isolated place. Her new home wasn't as comfortable as the one she lived in while in Spalding with her parents. Kenny's family welcomed Cassandra, and hoped that the responsibility of a wife would cure some of his wild ways. They expected him to stay home more. However, knowing Kenny, Cassandra would have to be a patient woman to stay married with him. When Thomas learned that Cassandra had been a college student, and had mastered some courses in teaching he asked her to take the teaching job for the newly constructed school. Ester Kennedy just wasn't up to par teaching these children anymore, especially since she wasn't able to stay awake through the whole day.

Doctor Newman made his daily trips to the Benson farm. Everyone knew something was going on there, because no one had seen Carl Benson for awhile. Betty Jean never went with her husband to the Benson's farm, but she spent her time at the Ovington's house, her favorite place to hang out, since she didn't have to cook. She always took Doctor Newman a plate of whatever was cooked at the Ovingtons. Betty Jean always fussed over Jane, trying to make sure she didn't overeat, and to get plenty of rest, but this was hard for Jane to do. She loved to move around, and she had the two boys to keep up with. Therefore, she never was one to stay in one place for too long.

The letter Beth wished for finally came. It was from Judith Holman, writing that she was coming to Tennessee in a week or two, to be with her daughter when she was ready to deliver the baby. She wanted to keep her promise to Beth and visit her. This was good news to Beth, and she was elated. She wore out everyone as she planned for Judith Holman's arrival.

With all due respect to Carl Benson, as with all of his patients, Doctor Newman kept Carl's medical problems confidential. He didn't even discuss his private marital troubles with others. No one in this community knew that Mable, Carl Benson's wife, had left his home with the help of one of his bums that he kept hanging around his place. When Carl Benson became so feeble, he called upon the good doctor to come to his home for medical treatment. Of course, Doctor Newman wasted no time seeing to his medical needs. He treated Carl as best as he could, but the pain he was suffered now was more emotional than anything else. In his disabled condition, the bums ran his place. Mable didn't trust many of the men, and was afraid of most of them. She confided in one of the few men that she did trust, and he helped her leave the farm she hated, leaving in the black of the night. When Carl found out one of his men was also one of his enemies, as far as his wife was concerned, he was devastated. Mable had slipped out in the middle of the night, and had gone home to her family. She had always been afraid to leave Carl, because she feared her husband would find, and harm her if she left him. But in his feeble condition, she took the chance and left him and the farm, which she hated so much.

Doctor Newman's dedication to his profession kept him visiting the Benson's farm. He believed Carl Benson would never be able to care for himself as he should. He also knew the riffraff working for him would eventually steal everything he owned, so he just came daily to care for Carl and to try to keep a eye on his property.

The Ovington house was all up in an uproar, everyone seemed happy with company coming, and the arrival of a new baby, plus Beth was in full control of her house again. Sarah was not in a humorous mood as the other household members. She missed Thaddeus, although they hadn't been very close the last few months of their marriage together, but he was her husband, and he was someone to call her own. The need to be comfort was stronger for Sarah each day as her nerves were on edge. She felt like she wasn't going to make it much longer, so Sarah decided to go into the valley by herself. Sarah had to slip off from Sophie, because she never let her out of her sight. The only person Sarah felt comfortable with and felt like she could talk to was the Rev. Roscoe Bennett. Blue was married to Vera, and Sarah didn't want gossip about her and Blue to start. She would never do anything to hurt Vera who was devoted to Blue. Sarah realized that she trusted him to do no wrong to her and the children.

Sarah found Rev. Bennett in the little church hall, he was in the long room behind the church building. There was a long hall and a room big enough for Roscoe to sleep in and have a small table and a chair in, which he used to counsel the members in. Roscoe knew that Sarah was having a difficult times at this point of her life. He asked Sarah to sit down and talk to him about herself, the way she was feeling, and to pray with him. The emotional Sarah could only cry, the tears were so heavy on her face. Roscoe came around the table to her side. He held her and tried to comfort her as Sarah held on to him so tight. He wasn't able to pull away or, rather he didn't want to.

The tears on Sarah face were kissed away by the Rev. Roscoe Bennett as he lost all control of himself. When he held her in his arms, Sarah lost control herself, and let him undress her as he hurriedly dropped his trousers. He was as starved for the love of a woman, as Sarah was for a man. Sarah kissed the muscular body of Roscoe as he fondled her body. He lost all control of himself, and wasn't able to think about the shame he would suffer later, since he was a minister for the people, and was to lead them in the right direction. When Roscoe and Sarah were able to gain control of themselves, after the long and fulfilling copulation between them, their shame for what they had done frightened them. He was a minister and was expected to set an example for the people. They each blamed themselves for being too weak to stop this shameful thing they had done.

Sarah slowly dressed and walked home, taking small steps as she walked up the steep hill to the Ovington house. Sophie had been looking for Sarah. When she saw her coming up the hill from the valley, she ran to meet her. She looked at Sarah with disgust, Sophie believed she had been with Blue. Sophie lashed out at Sarah, because she knew she had bedded down with a man, and Sophie assumed it was Blue. Sarah swore to Sophie that she didn't see Blue, and he had not touched her in any way, and that was the truth. Of course, Sophie was certain Sarah was telling the truth, but felt like Sarah had done something shameful.

24

Beth had been busy with all of the preparation for the coming baby, and Beth's cousin Judith Holman was on her way to Ovington. It was a joyous day for Beth when Thomas went to meet the train that was bringing Judith to Tennessee. Roderich went with Thomas to see that Judith made it to the Ovington's estate safely, and Thomas persuaded the ladies to stay at home, which was hard for them to do. Beth Marie could hardly wait to see her cousin again. The times were wild and busy at the Ovingtons.

The train pulled into the station about 20 miles from the mountain. The sight of the Tennessee hills excited Judith as she looked out into the beautiful mountain. This was a thrill to Judith to be in Ovington, and to be able to see her cousin Beth and her husband after so many years. Best of all, she would see her daughter and her family again.

Judith had always been fascinated by Thomas' good looks, almost to the point of being spellbound. Seeing Roderich and Thomas at the station, she ran to hug and kiss both of them. Of course, Judith was holding on to Thomas a little longer than her son-in-law, and this made Thomas a little nervous, but he was elated to see Judith Holman, and to have her visit them in Tennessee after so many years.

Sitting between Roderich and Thomas, she was as bad as her daughter, chattering all the way up the mountain. Judith was excited, she knew that she would soon see her daughter and grandsons. She asked Thomas many questions about Beth: whether she had changed, whether she had gained weight, and so on. This was making a nervous wreck out of Thomas, but he was glad to see Judith, even though he knew she was a nuisance at times.

Sarah was walked around in a daze, feeling depressed and guilty, believing that she had led the Rev. Roscoe Bennett on, knowing that he was a minister for the Lord, and she had made him commit one of the sins that he preached about to his people. The Rev. Bennett, knowing that he was a minister of the Lord, felt like he had taken advantage of her loneliness and he felt ashamed of himself. The next meeting he had, he did not see Sarah, and he could not do a good job when he stood up to preach. Rev. Bennett knew he must try to talk to Sarah, and try to amend for what he had done to her.

At the Ovington's house, the hugs, the kisses, and laughter filled the house when Judith arrived. Jane Elizabeth was elated to see her mother again, and was thrilled that she would be with her on the pending birth of her baby. Beth was speechless as the tears were heavy on her cheeks. To see her cousin again was the biggest thrill since she had married Thomas. Beth was excited beyond words as the two ladies talked non-stop for hours. This was one time that Jane was quiet as she listened to the chatter of these two people who she loved so much, who had not seen each other for many so years.

Sophie tried to get Sarah to confide in her about what was troubling her. Now, Sophie was sharp when it came to people. Sophie was always withdrawn because of the many times she was mistreated by the people she had loved. Sophie believed Sarah was suffering some sort of trouble or guilt, but Sarah never let her in on her secret. She was never going to tell anyone about her relationship with Roscoe Bennett.

Betty Jean had almost moved into the Ovington's house, she was at the estate from sun up to sun down, and she told the Ovingtons she was ready to help her husband deliver the Bolling's baby. She was keeping a eye on Jane Elizabeth to see that she was alright, and did as the doctor ordered her to do. Of course, this kept Betty Jean from going home to do duties in her own house, since she was waited on in the Ovington's house, and had no duties to do, but to enjoy the luxury of the estate.

There were days when Thomas walked this community just to ease his troubled mind. Since Thaddeus was killed, he had been suffering within, he missed him so much. Thaddeus was always running behind Thomas and stuttering so much as he tried to talk. Thomas wondered how Thaddeus could have been so careless. He knew how steep these hills were. Sarah was no better off as she worried about the way that Thaddeus had been killed. Sarah was suffering guilt also and it had taken its toll on her body. Thomas and Sarah were both restless; they missed Thaddeus more than anyone else in this community.

There was no quietness in the Ovington household. The two cousins were so excited seeing each other after so many years. Jane Elizabeth was on the quiet side, she felt awful as her swelled body kept her from moving too fast, and her feet felt so heavy as they swelled also.

Judith finally settled down to try to comfort her daughter, since she could see the discomfort she was having as the days were getting close for the coming baby. Judith was getting a little nervous. She was hating to see the labor she knew her daughter would have to go through to bring this baby into the world.

Roderich was walking around a little nervous, although this was the Bolling's third baby. He was still nervous about the labor, and to have to see Jane suffer so much as he had seen with his sons. Roderich was hoping they had made the right decision to stay in Ovington for the birth of his baby because he was a little leery of small town doctor, but Jane was willing to stay in this small town, and felt comfortable having Doctor Newman take care of her.

Jane's friends came to see her often, but they never mentioned the driving lessons since the accident that claimed Thaddeus' life. They were a little scared by this terrible tragedy and were thankful they never had an accident in the car. The ladies were afraid to drive through these mountains again, so they were very quiet on the subject of driving. Ada Sullivan was pregnant also, so these days the talk was mostly about babies.

Sophie and Sarah were as busy as ever. Geneva still did as little as possible, she had just about run out of anything to sew. Geneva had the biggest pile of baby clothes she had sewn. Beth always kept Geneva supplied with the finest cloth, and she was a perfectionist when it came to sewing, the stitches were always straight. She loved to pedal the machine and admired her work that she completed. Beth was always pleased by her work. She realized Geneva wasn't too fond of other duties of this enormous house, but Geneva helped her by her ability to be able to make anything out of a piece of cloth.

Richard and Geneva were devoted to the Ovingtons. They rarely caused any trouble and whenever they finished their days' work, they would go to their little quarters, and you never saw them until the next morning. They were always at work and on time the next working day. Richard was elated to be outside again. There was only one car now, but the Ovingtons still kept the Phaetons and horses parked that was used to travel this mountain sometimes, so, Richard still had plenty to do out-side.

Richard's hurt feelings were on the mend now that he was outside. He missed Thaddeus and was as hurt as the rest of the people who had loved him, but he was always a little jealous of the love Thomas had for Thaddeus. Thomas gave Richard a little raise in pay when he went back to his old job. He always felt a little sad when he saw how much he had hurt Richard when he sent him back inside of the house to work, know-ing he loved the outside, but Beth hated for Thaddeus to be inside of her house working. She just never could feel comfortable when Thaddeus was around her priceless heirlooms. Thomas was always fond of Richard, but he loved Thaddeus more. When Beth kept begged him to get Thaddeus out of her house, he knew he had to find him a place to work outside and he felt like the stable and the animals would be the best place to put him.

Thomas wondered why babies had to start coming into this world at night. Roderich woke Thomas up to go to the Newman's house and ask them to hurry to the estate, his wife was beginning to experience labor pains. They were getting to be close. Thomas hurried to the Newman's house in the black of the night, as he had hurried out in the night to get Suzette when Sarah was born. Thomas was a little fright-ened remembering the tragedy of that night. His heart raced as he walked, rather than drove, to the Newman's house. Of course, Doctor Newman was a little nervous himself as Betty Jean let out a string of cuss words. She aimed her cussing at Thomas for not driving the car to pick them up, but she wasted no time walking back to the Ovington's estate with Thomas. By this time, he was turning a little pale and he was scared that something would go wrong with this labor and delivery of the Bolling's baby.

Beth had worked hard preparing the place for the pending birth to take place. Since it was Spring and still a little cool in these mountain, Beth had the solarium made into a labor and delivery room. Everything was in place, plenty of clothes and sheets. The bed was prepared, including pillows for Jane's comfort.

Doctor Newman, Betty Jean and Roderich were in the room with Jane, and the long wait was on as Roderich tried to comfort his wife, but it was the other way around. He was in a state of nervousness himself and had to be comforted by his mother-in-law, Judith Holman.

The long wait was on as Jane's travailed labor went on into the night. She was still in better shape than the Ovingtons and the rest of the others that were anxiously awaiting the birth of the new baby.

Sophie and Sarah waited up through the night as Beth had them brewing tea and getting other treats to set on the table as the crowd got bigger. Richard and Geneva even stayed at the Ovington's house during the night, which was rare for them to do. Betty Jean would come out for a breath of air as she let Sophie and Sarah in on Jane's condition and how close the baby was before it would make its entrance into this world.

Judith was nervous, but she was in better shape than the others. Beth would look in the room from time to time, but was too excited to try and sit with the others through the whole labor. Thomas wasn't brave enough to stay with Roderich. He walked around the house and outside a couple of times when he knew the time was near. Doctor Newman assured the anxious relatives everything was going fine with the mother and baby.

Doctor Newman wanted the little one to come on. Between the father and the other people in and out of this house, he was getting a little worn out himself, and having to listen to Betty Jean was hard on his nerves, too. Betty Jean hadn't let out any of her famous cuss words yet, but she knew that she had better hold her tongue and not use any of her words she used at the birth of the babies she usually delivered. Dr. Newman wasn't taking any chances of making her mad, and she put on one of her little shows she usually put on.

Early in the morning there was a cry, a joyful cry as the Bolling's baby came into this world. The baby was a girl, and a beautiful one. There were cries of joy and Beth acted like the grandmother more so than the cousin, She shooed everyone out so that she could bathe the baby and fuss over Jane. Of course, Judith was all smiles and wanted to hold her granddaughter as soon as Beth finished bathing her. Roderich had his chest stuck out a mile, elated to have a daughter after two sons. Thomas just stood motionless as he watched the others make over the new baby. He made no effort to hold the wailing baby since she was actually as mad as she could be by all of the things being done to her. She was being passed from one person to the next since all wanted to see her and hold the new addition to the Ovington household. Dr. Newman was worn out himself; he often let Betty Jean do most of the work whenever he delivered a baby, but he knew this was one case he would have to carry the job through himself. Of course, Betty Jean was too busy with the ladies awaiting the birth, trying to keep them up on what was happening in the delivery room. Betty Jean didn't let out any of her cuss words, she was so excited herself, and this was a blessing that she kept her mouth shut for once. Betty Jean kept Sarah and Sophie informed on the condition of the mother and how soon they could see the new baby; otherwise, Betty Jean did little of anything else on this case.

The next couple of weeks Dr. Newman was busy trying to see that the mother and daughter were on the mend and trying to assure Beth that Jane and the baby would be fine, since Beth was worrying him so much about the condition of the two. Dr. Newman was also trying to make his daily trips to the Benson's farm to see about Carl.

Carl Benson was Mr. Nasty before he became ill, but now that Mable had left him, he was even worse. There was little he could do since he really had no true friends he could depend on except Dr. Newman to help him in his disabled condition. The bums still hung around his place, and they did as they pleased. Carl Benson did search for his wife, but no one told him where she was. Mable was happy now, and wanted no part of her ex-husband and his cruelty to her in the past. Although Dr. Newman worried about Carl Benson, he did not try to stop him in his continuing hatred of the Ovingtons and the people of this community that he hated, especially the people in the valley, or anyone that was Black, or looked Black.

Beth Marie kept the household staff and even Thomas in a nervous state as she tried to keep everything up to par, but it was disaster at time with two energetic boys and the extra guest in the house. But everyone tried to please her since she was so happy at this point to have her relatives with her.

Sophie and Sarah were like two peas in a pod as Sophie was trying to keep up with Sarah, and she tried to see what Sarah was doing all of the time. Though Sophie was curious about Sarah's reluctance to attend the meetings anymore, she wasn't smart enough to guess the real reason why.

When Rev. Bennett missed Sarah a couple of times, he knew he must do something about Sarah avoiding him. Roscoe Bennett spoke to Sophie about Sarah, and asked Sophie to see if Sarah would have a meeting with him, though he was feeling bad about their last meeting together, he knew he must do something to ease the shame between them. Roscoe knew their secret was safe as far as people were concerned, but Rev. Bennett felt like he had taken advantage of Sarah in her depressed and lonely frame of mind.

Traffic was heavy at the Ovington's estate as the friends and the people that knew the Ovingtons and the Bollings wanted to see the baby and to congratulate the Bollings, since Roderich and Jane Elizabeth was well liked in the community.

Thomas was getting restless, he missed the farm, he had not made a trip to the farm in Lawsonville in a long time. Thomas had gotten over his quarrel with Jeffrey, and he wanted to see the Carter family again, and to make amends with Jeffrey, who was like a son to him.

The newly constructed school in the valley was also Thomas' pride and joy. He was proud of Cassandra for her ability to control and teach these children; although some were a little old for grade school, they were eager to learn. Cassandra had very little trouble out of the older children. Thomas would sometimes help Cassandra with projects she would have the children to do to keep them interested in the classes. Cassandra was strict with the three R's, but she made the classes seem like fun at times.

Kenny Williams and Cassandra were very close, wild as Kenny was always known to be, he seemed to take marriage seriously. He still worked the Ovington's estate, but the job wasn't his greatest love. Kenny managed to get along with everyone, he tried to cheer Sarah up, he knew her grief, but he managed to make her smile sometimes with his jokes.

After Roscoe Bennett failed to see Sarah at the meetings anymore, he became very concerned about her. He decided to walk the steep hill to the Ovington's estate. He was able to see Sarah at her worst. She looked awful, the work, the guilt, and the shame within herself made her look older than her years, as she had no meaningful goal in her life now. The first thing Roscoe wanted to know was why she did not attend the meetings anymore. Refusing to answer, he asked her to please talk to him. He also apologized for some of her suffering. No one could refuse to talk to Roscoe for long, his rich mellow voice, and his years of being a minister, and the patience of dealing with people, enabled him to draw Sarah out of her little shell.

Sarah looked at the concerned Roscoe Bennett, the person she had given her body to. She could see the suffering within himself because of the guilt he felt like he had caused her to be hurt. Sarah put her arms around his body and assured him she felt no shame anymore, that they should forget the incident that was causing them both shame and suffering, and to go on with their lives. The Rev. Bennett knew that everything would be normal between them now if Sarah could talk about the problem and assure him she was alright. He would accept the fact that the problem was solved.

The little school was growing with children as more parents were sending their children to the school. The parents were more comfortable since Cassandra was in charge of teaching the children. Ester Kennedy had not been responsible running the school, and the children had done as they pleased while she took her daily nap, and their parents weren't too happy with her being over their children.

Thomas always made sure he checked everything to see that the school was in good shape as far as repairs and supplies because he was pleased by the way Cassandra had taken charge. Thomas loved the way that she could control these children. Thomas would look at the beautiful woman, seeing the dimples in her round face. Sometimes this would make him think of Rose Ann, the one person he didn't like to think about, but he loved Cassandra, and loved to see her smile. He would go to the school to talk to her often. Thomas loved to hear Cassandra's soft voice and the intelligent way she was able to express herself.

Thomas felt like Kenny Williams would never be worth a damn, but he was beginning to have second thoughts about him amounting to something with Cassandra by his side, and with a little help and encouragement from him, he was sure Kenny would amount to something and be as smart as some of his family.

Thomas told Beth he was going to make some changes around the estate, which made Beth nervous, as she never knew what Thomas had on his mind. Thomas had decided he would bring Sarah back inside the house, and she would no longer live in the little servant quarters that Thomas had built and furnished with the best of furniture of any of the housing he had for the domestic workers on his estate. He had built this housing for Thaddeus and Sarah, but now that Thaddeus was dead, he wanted Sarah to move back inside of his house to one of the rooms he had for the servants. When he told Sarah to pack all of her personal things so that Kenny could move them into one of the servant rooms, she was speechless. She never dreamed that she would be asked to move out of her little house. Sarah was devastated, and looked at Thomas with tears in her eyes, but she assured him she would pack as soon as possible.

Beth wasn't too pleased with Thomas' decision to move Sarah out of her little home, but she learned long ago when she tried talking with Thomas about Fred and Anna, when he told her he was taking them back to the farm in Lawsonville, how she had begged him to let them stay in Ovington. Thomas was a head-strong person, and once he decided to do something, you could not change his mind.

Sophie went with Sarah to help her pack her belongings. The tears fell on Sarah's cheeks as she tried to separate Thaddeus' things to be discarded from her things. Sarah remembered how, as a child, she was shifted from family to family, and now as a woman, she was still shifted around from the home she loved to a room in the Ovington's house. Sarah fell on the bed crying uncontrollable tears. As Sophie tried to comfort her, she wiped tears from her own eyes.

Kenny moved Sarah to the Ovington's house, and he was as sad as Sarah when he saw her tears. Kenny tried to cheer her up, but she never said a word, or tried to smile as she usually did. She was too crushed at this time to even act like she even heard him.

Beth went to Sarah's room and put her arms around her; she tried to cheer her up by promising her anything new that she wanted to fix up her room. Beth told Sarah she would have Geneva to sew whatever she wanted. Beth wanted Sarah to be happy, she felt real bad for Sarah. This arrangement was bad for Sarah after she had gotten used to a bigger place, but she had no other place to go, so she had to stay at the Ovington estate because she had no other means to support herself.

The baby with her wailing kept the once bored household moving. Jane Elizabeth carried little Judith on her hips as she tried to pacify her and Judith Holman was walking behind them trying to calm them down. Of course, poor Beth, frail and nervous, wanted to hold little Judith to try to calm the latest addition to the Ovington's household. Geneva was the only one that seemed to be able to pacify the baby, she was good at working sitting down, and Geneva would rock the baby until she seemed happy again.

The handsome Thomas Ovington was still admired and loved by

most of the women he met. His dark hair, now mixed with grey, made him more distinguished among most of the men his age. His body was still slim, and his ability to walk many miles at a time kept him in good physical condition. Thomas still wore his traditional vest without his coat, his style that he was noted for most of his life. He gained the highest respect among the residents of this community.

Now, Betty Jean was too fond of Sarah not to be hurt when she saw the tears on her face. When Betty Jean found out that Thomas had moved Sarah out of her little house into the one room that was offered her in the Ovington's house, she went into one of the worst cussing fits you would ever want to hear. Betty Jean tried to comfort Sarah in her little room, calling Thomas every kind of a son-of-bitches, but a white one, and she wasn't too quiet saying it either. You would have to have two tongues to beat Betty Jean cussing. She could say some pretty nasty words. Sarah was glad Thomas wasn't around to hear Betty Jean talk about him in this degrading way. Sarah tried to make Betty Jean be quiet, afraid the Ovingtons would hear her talking ugly, but she didn't seem to mind them hearing her say these terrible words, and calling Thomas such bad names as she did. Betty Jean finally went to Beth and told her that they were wrong to make Sarah move out of her quarters, since she still worked for them. Beth had tears in her eyes as she listen to Betty Jean, believing she was telling the truth about hurting Sarah, and she should be allowed to stay in her home. But Thomas was the head of this estate and she always obeyed him, and respected his wishes concerning his home.

Jane Elizabeth was feeling better and was wanting to get out of the house; she was bored with Judith Holman and Beth chattering all of the time, and both of these ladies wanting to spoil little Judith. Jane could see that her mother was getting bored by the way she would prance around and wring her hands. Judith tried to make Beth happy as long as she was here in her home, she knew Beth missed her relatives in New York, the few that she had left, but Judith Holman was not happy here in these back woods, and the people were not of her social level.

Judith didn't want to leave Jane Elizabeth and the children here in Ovington when she left for New York, she knew that Roderich would follow his family wherever Jane went, but she worried that her daughter would not want to go back to New York with her, since she was so fond of her cousin Beth.

When Thomas saw Sarah with the swollen eyes and the sad expression on her face, he felt a little hurt by his decision to move Sarah back inside of the house, but he had plans for the servant quarters that she lived in, and he quickly blocked it from his mind. Thomas could not understand some of the things he did himself, but once he made up his mind, he usually carried the plans through whatever it was that he wanted to do.

Judith Holman would try to touch Thomas whenever she could get close enough to him, but he had learned to stay out of her way, Judith had to do something to ward off boredom on this lonely mountain. Beth knew her cousin had a crush on her husband, but she felt like she was no threat to her marriage.

Kenny was shocked at Thomas' suggestion that he move his wife into Thaddeus' and Sarah's little servant quarters, the one that he had made Sarah move out of. Kenny told him he would have to talk to Cassandra, but un-be-knownst to Kenny, Thomas had already spoken to Cassandra. Thomas had asked her to move with Kenny to Sarah's old quarters, so that Kenny would be close to the estate, in case Beth needed him for something, and would not have to wait until he came up from the valley. Of course, everything Thomas said to Cassandra was fine with her, she would be glad to move out of the shack that Kenny provided for her, into some decent housing.

Sophie and Sarah started going to the meetings together again, even though poor Sophie never knew what was going on. She had been shocked when Sarah refused to go with her before, but since Roscoe and Sarah had their little talk, everything was back to normal.

Sarah told Blue that she had moved back into the Ovington's house. Of course, Blue was smart enough to figure this one out without Sarah telling him why. Blue knew that once Thaddeus was dead, Sarah was just another servant to Thomas, he didn't have the love for Sarah that he had for Thaddeus. Blue was as bad as Betty Jean since he raved over the way Sarah was treated by the Ovingtons just as much as Betty Jean did.

Beth tried to find a way to keep everyone happy with all of the tension in the house, she wanted peace. Beth started to play her piano again, and she encouraged Sarah to do the same. She was trying to help her get over her sadness and grief from losing Thaddeus. The days were long for Sarah, she tried to keep up everything, Sophie tried to sing and keep Sarah in a good mood, and she encouraged Sarah to play some of her beautiful songs, and they would sing together to keep from being so bored now that she had to stay in one room.

Geneva had found a way to sit most of the day, since she had sewed most of the cloth that Beth had around the house. Geneva always liked to sit and do her job, she didn't like to move around. Geneva took over the job of tending to little Judith, Geneva would sit and rock the baby, a wailing baby who demanded lots of attention. Geneva had never liked to do straight housework, loving instead to do something that you could sit and get the job done.

Jane Elizabeth was on the mend, and that meant she was raring to get with her friends and stir up something to ward off boredom. Judith was still begging her daughter to pack and go home with her. Judith Holman had taken about all she could of this rural community, this was the dullest place she had visited, and she had traveled a lot these past few years. Every day Judith begged Jane to reconsider going home, hoping she would win in the end. Judith could not understand Jane wanting to stay in Ovington for this long.

Roderich hated to see his mother-in-law leave for New York, he liked Judith, she never gave him any trouble, and she was always there when they needed her; although she tried to get him to pack up their belongings and take his family back to New York with her, he wanted to wait until his wife was ready to leave Beth, since she was so fond of her cousin. The Bolling boys adored their grandmother too. She had kept the boys back East, and they were her favorite grandsons, she had spoiled them, and was always buying them things that they didn't need, just to do something for them.

A day didn't pass that Beth didn't beg Judith to stay in Ovington. Beth was so happy now that she had some of her relatives with her, she had been really lonely in Ovington, but she would never leave, because she loved Thomas so much. Judith Holman tried not to hurt Beth's feeling, but she wasn't the type that could live in a small town. Judith dreaded the day she would leave because Beth was so tense these past few days, she knew the good-byes were going to be hard on Beth and she would be feeling bad too.

Dr. Newman was staying at the Benson's farm a lot these days, but Betty Jean never went with her husband to the Bensons. She loved hanging out at the Ovington's house. Dr. Newman felt sorry for Carl

Benson, his wife never came back to live with him, and he was alone most of the time. Carl had sent word to his wife to come home, and told her how ill he really was, but there was no response from her. There wasn't a lot of the bums hanging around now that Dr. Newman had gotten rid of the troublesome ones, and he kept the ones capable of running this farm, since Carl was unable to run things himself.

Sarah travailed from sun up to sun down, she arose before daylight in order to do the work for the many people that were always in this house during the day. Sophie tried to help out, but she was no match compared to Sarah when it came to work.

Thomas had left most of Thaddeus' and Sarah's furniture in the home they shared. Sarah had left the place spotless, even though she was unhappy moving, she still took the same time to make sure the house was in the best of shape. The day that Kenny and Cassandra moved into the little servant quarters was rather painful for Sarah. Sarah felt like the world was on her shoulders, but she didn't cry anymore, just looked sad most of the time.

Beth looked on with remorse as she saw Kenny with his wife moving their small possessions into their new home that Thomas only let his favorite help occupy. Beth could not understand why Thomas was so fond of Cassandra. She was a little educated, but she wasn't a part of the people that lived in Little Valley, those people that Thomas was so partial to. Thomas didn't seem to care that much for Kenny, since he considered him to be irresponsible, but with Cassandra, it was different, she seemed to have made an impression on Thomas that Beth had not seen in a long time in her husband.

The time was coming to an end for Judith Holman's visit to Ovington. Judith was packed and ready to go back to New York, and to some decent living. This little town was just too boring to her. Jane Elizabeth showed little concern that her mother was going home to New York, but Judith was very sad knowing that she was leaving her daughter and her family here in this small town without a home, and all of the things she was used to in New York. Judith knew the Ovington's estate was comfortable, but she also felt like Jane and her family had lived much better in New York, and she never stopped trying to persuade her daughter to come home with her. Beth Marie had sweet-talked Jane into staying longer with her, and Judith feared that Jane would not return to New York as long as Beth was able to talk her into staying in this small town. Judith knew that she had enough of this small community, and she was ready to return home.

Judith assured the Ovingtons that this had been a wonderful trip, that she had enjoyed this visit, that she loved the people she had met in Ovington, and that she would always remember this visit to Tennessee. Judith told the Ovingtons she would never forget the people in this community, and the way everyone tried to make her trip a pleasure.

Jane Elizabeth insisted she and the boys accompany her mother to the depot to see her off to New York. Thomas and Roderich Bolling loaded Judith's many packages into the car. The tearful goodbyes between Beth and Judith were long and Thomas insisted they had to hurry. Beth watched from the front porch until they were out of sight. The tears were falling down her cheeks, and she had a sinking feeling this would be the last time she would ever see her cousin.

25

The land surrounding the Ovington estate was all cleared and landscaped, but Thomas was concerned about the crash in the car that took Thaddeus' life, so he decided to clear the land that he had purchased years ago, which was nothing but rock, woods, and thick bushes surrounding small shacks further on down the mountain. These shacks that the poorer people lived in were an eyesore to Thomas, and he decided to try to buy most of these people out that he knew would never do any better as far as improving themselves, or trying to fix up these shacks they lived in for so many years.

There were still some of the hill people scattered around this mountain, but Thomas went to them, the ones that were the closest to his land, and made them an offer. He bought up the land, and wasted no time tearing the shacks down that they had lived in. Some of them were so bad that it took very little work to tear them down. Some of these hill people weren't too happy selling their land, but Thomas would go back to their home time and time again, until they would finally gave in and sell their land to him. As some of them moved, the others would soon give in to sell, since they knew that Thomas would pester them until they did give up their land.

When Thomas told Beth of his plans to clear the land further down the mountain, Beth knew that Thomas was still thinking of Thaddeus. Thomas told Beth that he would have a better road built, because the curves were too dangerous to travel, and the people of this community would be afraid to drive down the steep mountain after the terrible accident that had claimed Thaddeus' life.

Thomas made arrangements to clear his land that he felt would benefit Ovington. This town was growing with people and better businesses would follow. Thomas went through the same procedure he did when he cleared his land for his home site. He employed the best men from the valley to do the job, since it was still dangerous. Thomas brought boots and thick gloves for them to wear to make sure they had some protection from injuries, because this would be a dangerous job, and he wanted no more tragedy in Ovington if it could be avoided.

Sarah improved with time; she wasn't as depressed as when she first lost Thaddeus, and the unhappiness she suffered when she had to move out of her little home. She was attending all of the meetings of Roscoe Bennett. There were times that she wanted to stay home, but she wanted to be close to Roscoe, and he would always look for Sarah first in the crowd, and his heart would race faster when he would see her walk in the door. Roscoe knew that he was falling in love with Sarah. Poor Sophie never caught on that there was an intimate closeness between Roscoe and Sarah, only they knew about, but Roscoe could hardly preach sometimes, his feelings were so strong for Sarah. Roscoe also felt sorry for Sarah, he could see how unhappy she was most of the time, and he wanted to help her, but he also was afraid to approach her, since he knew what happened the last time he tried to help Sarah.

Beth was finally calming down since her cousin Judith had left Ovington. She missed her cousin so much, but she still had Jane and her family, so she tried to be happy. But she thought often of the good times that she and Judith had in New York, and the many times they had concerts together when they were young, and the theater had been her greatest love. Thomas was Beth's life now, but she wished he would take her to New York one more time, but Thomas had no love for New York, he had never mentioned taking another trip to New York once he returned to Lawsonville after their marriage.

Betty Jean never missed a day coming to the Ovington's house. She felt at home, and like she was one of the family. Beth knew it was use-less to try to calm her down whenever she was upset about something, which was often. Betty Jean loved Sarah and Sophie, they loved to spoil Betty Jean, and loved to hear her talk up a blue streak about some of any and everything she could think of to talk about, and they would pamper her so, until she wasn't about to miss this treat from the Ovington's household.

Dr. Newman was still making his trips to the Benson farm. He knew that Carl was an evil man, but he learned to like the man, and he felt sorry for him now that his wife had left him. Carl was a broken, pitiful man, and a very sick man also. He never showed regret or sorrow for all of his past meanness, but he was helpless now, and he needed someone to help him, and Dr. Newman didn't feel like he should judge the man, he was dedicated to his profession to treat people who were sick, and Carl Benson was truly a sick man.

Jane Elizabeth was still busy with the two energetic boys and a new baby. Jane always tried to help with the many things to do in this house since there were so many people living at the Ovingtons, but the more she tried to help, the more attention her children demanded of her. Beth wanted to take some of the burden off Jane, but she was no match for these boys, and their never ending energy, and little Judith had the best lungs, you had no trouble hearing her. Geneva seemed to be the only one to calm the wailing baby down.

Beth would send for Blue to do work around the estate, she knew how smart Blue was, and she was always pleased with his work, although Thomas still wasn't to happy to see him on his land, but Thomas knew there wasn't a better man when it came to doing anything to a house. The residents of Ovington had a lot of respect for Blue, even though they knew what a bad reputation Blue had in the past, they would send for Blue if they needed something done to their house.

Blue was older, up in his 50s, and of course he was still black as ever, but he looked better in his middle age than when he was in his younger years. Blue was still rather thin, very tall, his black hair was mixed with grey, this older look on Blue made him look like the perfect gentleman. It was hard to believe the terrible things that he had done in the past.

John Smithson always wanted to hire Blue when he could, and he paid him good money. Blue had made a lot of money working for John Smithson, also he had made a lot of money gambling, this was big money for someone to be poor, but he had not wasted his money as everyone believed, or rather Vera had not let him waste the money.

Blue and his family always lived better than anyone else in the valley, and he was in a better position to do for his family since he had a trade. This trade paid better than the men that were trappers, or the money the men made bootlegging moonshine. Vera knew that she was Blue's life, by his kindness to her, although he was guilty of adultery, he never mistreated Vera or his children, and Vera knew a man that never let her want for anything, he always treated her nice when he was unpleasant to others.

The building was over for John Smithson, he would not be back to build anything for the Ovingtons or any businesses, since he had retired. Blue would not be making big money like he was used to making in the past, but he had a big sum of money he had saved. Blue was thinking of building a real nice home in the valley for his wife, he knew that he may die and leave his wife, and he wanted her to be comfortable, and have a better house to live in.

Thomas was busy with the men in the valley that he had hired to clear the land, and tear down the shacks scattered around the mountain. Thomas was able to buy the land when others lost out, of course, he was still in control of the Cannon's money, and he could always use some of the money if he needed it, so he never missed a opportunity to buy land if he thought he could make money on his purchase, because he usually sold the land for a big profit.

Sarah was quiet most of the time, but she never missed a meeting these days, her thoughts were of Roscoe Bennett, and the warm feeling she had for him. The Rev. Roscoe Bennett had planned to remain celibate since he had devoted his life to the Lord, and only wanted to serve the people preaching God's word, that is until he had held Sarah, and knew the closeness of her body. Roscoe wasn't able to keep his mind off Sarah, and he actually lusted for her, and he knew how wrong this was, and he had began to have second thoughts about remaining celibate, since he knew that taking the love of a woman sexually without marriage was a great sin.

The beautiful, newly-built church was Roscoe's pride and joy, and was his whole life. There was quite a crowd these days, but even the support of the people just wasn't enough to keep him from thinking of Sarah. He knew that if he touched Sarah again, he would never be able to preach to these people again. Roscoe knew that he had nothing to offer Sarah if he asked her to marry him, but he knew that he could not go on any longer in this frame of mind.

Thomas had been working very hard, but his mind would wander to the Cannon farm. Thomas missed going to the farm, and he knew he had treated Jeffrey very badly, but he wanted to make up to him, the Carters were like family, and he missed them so much. Beth never mentioned the farm, she was satisfied with Jeffrey running the place, but the Cannon farm was still one of Thomas' loves, since knowing the Cannons, this was the turning point in his life, and he would never forget James Cannon, and Beth Marie was his whole life now. Thomas made up his mind, he would return to Lawsonville to try to make amends with Jeffrey Carter.

There were plenty of rocks scattered around the mountain. Blue worked very hard as he gathered the best of the rocks to use for building the new home he planned to build for Vera. Blue told Sarah of his plans to build Vera a home. Sarah was elated, knowing Blue was such a smart man, and to think he loved Vera so much he wanted to build her a better and more comfortable home to live in.

The most vigorous and rewarding service in Roscoe's ministry was after he approached Sarah and Sophie as they came into his church and he asked to speak with Sarah alone. Roscoe asked to hold Sarah's hands. He was trembling as he spoke, asking her if she would marry him. Sarah was shocked and unable to answer Roscoe immediately, but when she recovered from the shock, Sarah hugged Roscoe, answering that she would love to be his wife. No one at the meeting knew why Roscoe was so happy as he preached and sung so long to the people. He wore the people out, even poor Sophie didn't understand why the service was so long.

After Roscoe was worn out himself, he asked Sarah to come forward to stand beside him. He told the hushed crowd he wanted to make announcement to them. Sophie sitting quietly, was on edge, she wondered just what was going on. After stumbling on his words a few times, Roscoe told the crowd that he and Sarah were planning to marry. The people were shocked speechless, and Blue was shocked out of his seat, this was the second time he had to listened to this announcement of Sarah marrying someone. The people soon recovered from their shock, and they rushed to kiss and hug the couple and congratulate them. Sophie sat alone as the people went up to Roscoe and Sarah. She was unable to move for a while. The hurt and disappointment of Roscoe and Sarah marrying stunned Sophie, and it seemed like it was forever before she could move to congratulate the couple.

Sophie was lost for words. She never dreamed that Sarah would ever marry Roscoe Bennett. When Sarah and Sophie were ready to go home, Roscoe walked the steep hill to the Ovington's estate with the two women. Sophie wasn't able to question Sarah about her relationship with Roscoe. Sophie suspected that Roscoe must be the one that

Sarah was meeting in secret, but she was glad that the two were marrying.

Sarah refused to discuss her relationship with Roscoe with Sophie, although Sophie tried to press Sarah to tell her the full details of her decision to marry Roscoe. Sophie was a little jealous of the pending marriage between Roscoe and Sarah, she even had a few tears in her eyes, but she shed them in private.

The Ovingtons always arose early, this was a busy house now, and Beth wanted everyone to eat breakfast together, and Thomas was a person that wanted to start the day before daybreak, and the Bolling boys had to go to school, and of course, little Judith was always wanting attention.

Sophie wasted no time telling Beth about the announcement of Roscoe and Sarah planning to marry. She told Beth that Roscoe had Sarah to stand beside him as he told them last night at the meeting. Sophie shocked Beth as much as all of the people at the meeting were shocked, and they were planning to marry so soon. Beth was speechless, but she wasted no time running to Thomas to tell him what Sophie had told her. There had been many devastating times in Thomas Ovington's life, but this one was bad for him. He believed that Sarah would be with him and Beth in the Ovington house for the rest of their lives, or as long as she lived, and they depended on her so much, and with Beth so weak most of the time, Thomas wanted Sarah to stay with them.

Thomas called Sarah into his office, he put his arms around her, and he told her he wished she would not marry Roscoe Bennett. Thomas thought Sarah should respect her memories of Thaddeus, and not rush into a marriage so soon. Thomas knew Roscoe had nothing to offer Sarah, and he didn't even have a place for her to stay, or any money to offer her a decent life. Thomas pointed out all these things out to Sarah, hoping that she would change her mind.

Beth was beside herself with worry at the thought of Sarah marrying and leaving her just about put her to bed. Beth remembered Clayton, and the love she had for him. Beth loved Grace also, but in a different way, because Grace was a person you could not get close to, and Beth had lost both of Sarah parents, and now she feared she would lose Sarah. Beth tried to act happy for Sarah, but she wasn't too good at it. Sarah assured Beth she wanted to be happy, and felt like Roscoe

Bennett would fill the lonely void in her life, and she believed he would always love her and be good to her.

Jane Elizabeth was happy for Sarah, knowing that Sarah had been through a lot of traumatic experiences in her life, and she hoped this pending marriage would be a rewarding one for her. Of course, the biggest shock was to Betty Jean, she knew her being waited on so much by Sarah in the Ovington house just might come to an end. Betty Jean wished Sarah happiness, but she pulled Sophie off to one side, and said, "Sarah should not marry Roscoe, since he had nothing to offer her."

The trip Thomas usually made to Lawsonville were long overdue. Thomas knew he must go to the Cannon farm to make up with Jeffrey Carter. Thomas wanted to get away from Ovington for awhile. Beth Marie was in good hands, and Thomas had no worry about leaving her since, the Bollings were there and all of the domestic help that was at the estate. Thomas was getting bored, and he had to find something to do to ward off boredom.

Thomas asked Kenny Williams to see that the ladies had whatever they needed for the operation of this house while he was gone to Lawsonville. Thomas also asked Cassandra to do a good job with the children, who were still his pride and joy. Cassandra was still running the school, and she continued to make a good impression with the parents. The children were progressing with her strict methods she used to teach them, and even had a few students smart enough to help her with the many projects she had for them to do. Kenny wasn't a very smart person when it came to books, but he would go to the school with his wife sometimes to help her.

Beth usually felt sad when Thomas left Ovington, but she never asked to accompany him on these trips, and of course, Thomas never asked her to go with him. This time was bad for Beth, she was worn out from worrying about Sarah marrying, and the workload of her house was taken its toll on her frail body. Beth asked Thomas to refrain from doing anything foolish when he visited the Carters. Thomas assured Beth that he was going to Lawsonville on a friendly visit, and to stop worrying so much about him.

Beth wrung her hands as Thomas drove down the driveway away from the house, because this time he took no one with him as he usually did when he took the trips to Lawsonville. Beth had a scared feeling for the first time. She had seen Thomas leave this mountain many times, and never had this feeling before, and she wondered if she should have gone with him.

Jane could see how worried Beth was, and she tried to do something to cheer her up. Thomas took the one car now, so they were unable to leave on a trip. Jane tried to encourage Beth to play her piano, but it was a bad time for Beth to want to play the piano.

Sarah tried to cheer Beth up when she saw how unhappy she looked. She asked Beth to be happy for her, because she believed her upcoming marriage would be good for her. Sarah had been so lonely, and she needed to have someone to love her; and she hoped that Roscoe would fill that need in her life. Beth knew what it was to be lonely, and she had been so happy with Thomas, although she let him have his way most of the time. But she loved her husband with a passion, and never wanted to be without the love of Thomas, and she hoped to pass first, and not to be left alone without him. She had suffered so much these past few years health-wise, but she hung on to life to be with Thomas as long as she could, just to be with him.

Sophie had been quiet since she had heard about the pending marriage of Roscoe and Sarah. Sophie was older than Roscoe, but she did have a crush on him. She never expected to marry Roscoe herself, but to know he was marrying Sarah sort of devastated her, and she found herself crying at times. Although she wanted Sarah to be happy, she never wanted to see Sarah marrying anyone, because that would mean that Sophie would be left alone at the Ovingtons. Sophie had been happy at the Ovingtons, she would never forget how they took her in when the Harrisons left Ovington, and she had no place to stay or a job, and Sarah always seemed to cheer her up, and they would work so good together, and always found something interesting to talk about.

Dr. Newman tried to get Betty Jean to help him at Carl Benson's place. Betty was a trained nurse, and he wanted her to help him with the care of Carl, as well as taking care of the house. Carl was in no position to be mean now, since pain was a constant thing with him. Betty Jean wasn't willing to give up the comfort of the Ovington's house everyday to accompany her husband to attend to Carl Benson, but Dr. Newman put his foot down, because he knew she was needed at the Benson's farm.

After Betty Jean knew that her husband was serious about her helping him, and she was going to have to stay at the Benson's farm with him, she let out a string of cuss words that would have made your ears burn, which she did when she was displeased about something, and this request from her husband sure did displease her. Betty Jean did go along with Dr. Newman to help him with Carl Benson, and she did do a little housework, but she sure did miss going to the Ovington's everyday, and the good treatment she received there.

The workers, or bums as Doctor Newman thought of most of them, meant Carl Benson no good, and he trusted none of them, but they were surprised to see Dr. Newman bring his wife. The workers were used to seeing him around, but they were annoyed by a woman being around this farm, especially one as outspoken as Betty Jean, and they were almost scared of this little cussin' woman, since she gave them a daily dose of degrading words she would call them.

It was hard for Sophie to take, but she knew that Roscoe and Sarah would marry, and she felt like it would be soon. Sophie felt like the Ovingtons would let her stay at the estate as long as she wanted to, but it would not be the same without Sarah. Sophie was used to talking to Sarah when they had moments together, and Sophie loved to tell Sarah about some of the things that happened to her in the many places that she had stayed, and most of all Sarah loved to hear about the people that lived off this mountain. Sophie liked Richard and Geneva, and all of the others who worked this estate, but it was easiest to talk to Sarah.

Beth did everything she could to run her house efficiently, and to keep everyone happy. Everyone seem to miss Betty Jean, since she was always running her mouth about something, and would say some of the worst and funniest things to keep them laughing.

The nights were the worst since Thomas was gone to Lawsonville, Beth missed her husband lying next to her, she felt like Thomas was her strength. In the day, there was so much going on that Beth didn't have time to think about being lonely, but the nights were so bad. She would lie awake, the house seemed so quiet, and she would start thinking about Thomas, and her life with him, and her love that she shared with him, although there was always a house full of people around her, she felt so lonely when Thomas was away from her.

Thomas could stay away for days at a time, but he could always find things to amuse or entertain him, there was something interesting going on around him wherever he went. Thomas had promise himself he would never be intimate with another woman as long as he was married to Beth, but there were always women trying to get his attention.

The Carters knew Thomas was coming to Lawsonville, and they were a little nervous, since they knew their relationship was a little strained now since, Beth had changed the contract of the Cannon farm, and Jeffrey and his family were to inherit the farm at her death.

Thomas walked around Lawsonville shooting the bull with some of the old timers he was acquainted with before he went to the farm to see the Carters. Jeffrey was a little nervous when he saw Thomas walking toward the house. As soon as Thomas saw the Carters, he was elated as ever to see this family he loved so much. The Carters and Thomas were as close as ever, all of the bad feelings were forgotten as the Carter family and Thomas had the best visit since he left Jeffrey in charge of the farm years ago. When the Ovingtons married and went to New York for the first year of their marriage, Jeffrey and the others on the farm were the ones they thought of all the time.

The Bradley brothers were semi-retired now, they were well off, and didn't need to work as hard. Thomas always went to see these brothers whenever he was in Lawsonville, although they just pissed Thomas off sometimes by the dominant way they would behave toward him, and other businessmen they had dealings with.

The Bradleys acted elated to see Thomas, and they even encouraged him to stay for dinner. The dinner went along fine, and Thomas enjoyed this time with the brothers more than any other time he could think of. The brothers discussed some business advantages to him, and investments to benefit him and make him a big profit in the future. If someone mentioned profit to Thomas, he was always eager to know what the business deal was.

The Bradley brothers were fond of Thomas, but they didn't consider him to be their best friend. The Bradleys admired Thomas, they knew he only had money because of the Cannons, they felt like Beth should have allowed someone else to manage her money, and they were thinking of themselves.

Thomas stayed for a long time talking to the Bradley brothers, he knew how smart they were, and he was wanting to get all of the information he could from them, believing they were smart enough to advise him in a profitable and financial advancement in the future from the many investments that were available in the latter years of the depression.

The Bradleys loved the railroads, they were fascinated by this transportation in Tennessee, and believed that the passenger and freight, and not to mention the mail transit would grow tremendously very soon, and the future of the railroad stock would flourish to persons holding investments in the this transportation.

Thomas listen to the Bradleys attentively, and he decided to take the advice of these brothers, and he left their house with a good feeling, unlike the usually despicable feeling he had for these brothers when he had visited them in the past.

Ledia Summer's Boutique was Thomas' last place to visit. He always looked forward to seeing Ledia, she was one of his favorite persons to see in Lawsonville, and he was a little nervous going to see her again. Thomas always wanted to hold this woman and hug her in a friendly way. After all, she was the one who taught him not to be afraid of women, and what a beautiful thing love was. After Thomas saw the way his parents lived, and the lonely marriage they had together, he had been confused about love. As Thomas approached the Boutique, which looked more fashionable than ever, he saw the most beautiful and stylish woman he had ever seen in Lawsonville.

The long beautiful blond hair was to her waist, and her voluptuous body sent shock through Thomas as he stared at this lady. Thomas stumble on his words as he asked to see Ledia Summer. The surprised look on the woman's face frightened him, because he feared something had happened to Ledia.

The smiling lady told Thomas her name was Vickie Lynn Richman, and she was the new owner of the Boutique. Ledia Summer had married and retired from business, and she no longer lived in Lawsonville. Thomas was shocked and disappointed that he would not see Ledia. Vickie could see the disappointed look on Thomas' face, and she preceded to show him her well stocked business. By the time Vickie Lynn was through with Thomas, he had bought a bulk of clothes for Beth, he was feeling good about purchasing these latest styles from Vickie. Thomas knew Beth was still wearing her clothes she had for years, of course, she never went anywhere and never wore her clothes out.

With all of his business taken care of in Lawsonville, and friends and acquaintances he wanted to see behind him, Thomas was ready to go home. Thomas went to the Carters to say his goodbyes, and they had a letter ready for him to take to Beth. They all hugged Thomas when he said his goodbyes, Jeffrey was glad that he had made up with Thomas, because he had been miserable since he had last seen Thomas. The jubilant Carters all waved to Thomas until he was out of sight.

The Ovington's house was as wild as ever, but Beth Marie was rather calm as she anxiously awaited the return of her husband. Beth would walk to the front porch periodically as she looked for a sign of Thomas down the mountain. The way Beth worried about Thomas was ridiculous, Jane shouted, she said that Thomas could very well take care of himself. Beth had worked herself into a nervous state, and she had made Jane and the others in the house nervous to by the way she walked to and from the front porch.

Sarah tried to persuade Beth to relax and find something to do to ease her fear of thinking that something would happen to Thomas as he made his trip home. Of course, this was a useless suggestion, since Beth would only relax when Thomas returned home. Beth knew that she was going to have to sleep at night, the circle around her eyes were making her unattractive, and she didn't want Thomas to see her this way.

Dr. Newman was worn out. He was trying to take care of Carl Benson, although Betty Jean was still helping him, her complaining, and the workers were complaining telling Dr. Newman to control his wife's mouth, all of these things were taking their toil on him mentally. When Dr. Newman tried to talk to his wife, she only replied she didn't like the riffraff hanging around this farm, and she would continued to speak her mind.

Rev. Bennett was getting impatient to marry. Every time he saw Sarah he knew he wanted her to be his wife, and soon. When Roscoe pressured Sarah to marry him, Sarah went to Beth, and she told her she was going to marry Roscoe as soon as possible. Of course, Beth always got upset when someone mentioned that Sarah was marrying Roscoe, and she asked her to wait until Thomas returned.

Blue had completed his foundation on his house, and Vera was excited, she knew Blue loved her, and to know she was getting a new home made her feel most important. Blue had some of the men in the valley to help him with his foundation, but he was going to build this house himself, and the way he wanted the house to look, he knew this was his way of showing Vera that he truly did love her, and he wanted her to be comfortable in case something happen to him.

Jane Elizabeth was trying to think of something for Beth to do that would keep her from worrying about Thomas all the time. Jane knew Beth loved the theater, and she knew this was her favorite entertainment. Jane offered to take some of the workload off Beth by helping with the planning of the meals for this enormous household. Jane would shop for the house, there were two big ice boxes in the Ovington's house, but Jane would cram so much into them, it was hard to put the ice in the boxes.

Thomas arrived in Ovington, and the jubilant Beth was relieved that he was home safe. Thomas gave Beth the letter from the Carters, and Beth was so pleased that they wrote to her, she felt so close to the Carter family, and she wasted no time reading the letter. The Carters expressed their love for her, and thanked her for the kind and loving way she had made sure that they would always enjoy the farm that she had wanted them to have.

The Carters invited Beth to come home to Lawsonville and stay for a few days with them, and to be their guest, and they could enjoy each other's company. They also asked Beth to bring Thomas if he wanted to come. This pleased Beth to know that the Carter family thought of her as family. Beth put the letter in her little jewel box, this was truly one of her treasures.

Beth wasted no time telling Thomas they had been invited to visit the Carters for a few days. Beth did want to take another trip with Thomas, she would not worry about the estate, because the Bollings were here, and she knew they would take care of things that needed to be done. Beth loved going places with Thomas, but he rarely took Beth away from the mountain, although he did take her riding around the community at times. Thomas gave Beth no answer about the visit to the Carters, he was elated to make up with Jeffrey, and he did enjoy the visit, but he wasn't ready to make any commitment to stay a few days at the Carters. Of course, Beth knew she would never fulfill the invitation after seeing the look on Thomas' face, and he spoke very sharply when he said he would give this kind suggestion from the Carters some serious thought.

Beth asked Sarah to continued to come to the estate each day to work, and she would be paid a higher salary. Sarah assured Beth she would try to come to the estate each day, although she would have to walk the steep hill from the valley. Thomas finally told Sarah he was happy for her, and wished her happiness. Beth was feeling sad, Sarah was the only one she could count on to run the house the way she liked things done whenever she wasn't able to do the job herself.

Roscoe and Sarah made plans to marry in a few days. They wanted to belong to each other. Roscoe promised himself he would not touch Sarah again in an intimate way until she was his wife, but this was hard on him when he would see the voluptuous body and remembered the way he had loved Sarah; he wanted the marriage to be very soon.

When Jane heard that Sarah was marrying in a few days, she was elated for her. Jane asked Roderich to marry Roscoe and Sarah, since Roscoe was the only minister in the valley, and could not marry himself. Sarah was jubilant knowing she was about to become Roscoe Bennett's wife.

The Ovington's didn't offer Sarah the wedding and all the fine dress and fine furnished living quarters that they did when she married Thaddeus. The Ovingtons hardly congratulated the Bennetts after the marriage. Geneva was the only one to cry over Sarah marrying, Sophie was more hurt than happy for Sarah, she felt like they wouldn't be close like they were before she married, because Sarah would be with her husband more than at the Ovington's estate.

Roscoe or Sarah had nothing to start housekeeping, there was only the one room Roscoe lived in, and it was the church property, but they wanted to be together, and they hoped they could work out a living arrangements after they married.

Blue wanted Sarah to come back to the valley to live so bad, he made room in his house for the couple until they could find them a place to live. Roscoe was pleased that Blue let them move into one of the boy's rooms; since they were grown, only he and Vera lived in the house now. Roscoe would be at the church all day, and Sarah would be at the Ovingtons during the day, and they would rarely be at home, only to sleep at night.

This arrangement worked fine for the Bennetts, although it was hard on Blue knowing Sarah was in the next room, and in the arms of another man. Blue still cared for Sarah, but he knew he must get rid of all of his lustful thoughts of Sarah. Blue knew that Sarah was another man's wife, but he would think of her at times, he would lie awake at night, thinking of his love for Sarah over the years, but he knew his real love was Vera, and the way she had stood by him when others talked raucous of him, Vera always defended her husband.

Betty Jean sure did miss the Ovington's house, she loved having Sophie and Sarah wait on her. The Benson's house was nothing like the Ovingtons. There were men that cooked and took care of the house inside. Carl Benson had no other women on the farm other than his wife, and she refused to come home, even when Carl Benson had became so ill and flat on his back.

Betty Jean helped Dr. Newman as much as he needed her, she always had been by her husband's side through the years, but she had gotten spoiled when she moved to the Ovington estate, and she was waited on by all of the domestic help they had working in their house.

Sophie missed Sarah so much, and she didn't think to much of Sarah and her new husband moving into Blue's house. Sophie knew Blue liked Sarah, and she was afraid Blue would try to persuade Sarah into doing something shameful, since she was living in his house. Of course, Richard and Geneva had never trusted Blue since Sarah was no more than a child, and Blue had raped her, she was innocent at the time, and didn't realize what Blue doing to her.

Roderich Bolling had never accepted the constable job on a full time basis. He only took the position to help this community when the Harrisons left this town. Roderich told Thomas he wished he would get someone else to be the constable of this town. Roderich was thinking of opening his own law office, or go into some other business, if times got better. Thomas wasn't too happy with Roderich's leaving this position, but he assured him he try to find someone to take the job.

None of the residents in Ovington ever visited the Benson's farm, since Carl had been such a hard man to get along with, but some of them went to his residence when they heard how ill this man was, and they knew how tired Dr. Newman and his wife were trying to take care of him. There wasn't much they could do, but the Newmans thanked them for offering to help out, and they were so worn out, but Dr. Newman felt so sorry for the man, he was willing to sacrifice his time to care for him, plus all of the other patients he had to care for in this community.

Sarah would faithfully walked the steep hill from the valley to the Ovington's estate each day. Sarah was strong, and she never seemed to mind this strenuous walk before she started her work day. Sometimes Roscoe would walk with her, but he would soon give out of breath, and had to abandon this time he wanted to spend with his wife.

Beth was always glad to see Sarah, she missed her living in the house. Sophie and Geneva worried Sarah when she first married Roscoe, they even had the nerve to ask Sarah personal questions about the details of their intimate relationship, if the Rev. could do it good, etc. This questioning from her friends embarrassed Sarah, but she only smiled, and changed the subject to other things.

Thomas tried to find someone to take the job of constable of Ovington. There weren't a lot of jobs available, but no one was eager to be responsible for law and order in this town. Most of the residents knew of the moonshining in the valley and they didn't want to deal with the bootleggers, especially when they knew Thomas would never cooperate with the law, when it came to trying to stop this operation by his friends in the valley.

Thomas was happy to be home, to be with his wife and to greet all of the household staff. Thomas wanted to trust Kenny Williams as he had Thaddeus to do his leg work, and all the errands he had to depend on others to do for him sometimes, but Kenny wasn't as crazy about Thomas as Thaddeus had been, and he let him know he wasn't too fond of all of the running around he had him to do, plus having to do so much work for the ladies in the Ovington's house. The residents of Ovington would send word to the Ovington house for Kenny to do errands for them, as Thaddeus used to do, Kenny also told Thomas he was tired of doing so much for everyone in this community, and he wasn't too happy living in the nicely furnished servant quarters that he made Sarah move out of, Kenny said he felt uncomfortable in this house. Cassandra loved living in the small house, since she was used to living in a decent house in Spalding, and the house that Kenny provided for her wasn't substantial for comfortable living. Cassandra didn't know Sarah before moving to this community, and she had no guilt feeling about moving into this house. Cassandra told Kenny that she refused to move back to the valley, and the home he had provided for her there.

Dr. Newman notified the constable of Ovington that, he had found Carl Benson dead in his bed early in the morning when he came to check on him. Carl was a vile man, and lived an ignoble life, but the man died peacefully in his sleep. This should not have surprised the Newmans finding him dead, since he had been so sick, but it was still a shock to them, and Dr. Newman had trouble getting used to the idea that Carl Benson was finally dead.

Many of the community residents came to the Benson's farm to help the Newmans with the many things they had to do trying to prepare Carl Benson for burial, and to make arrangements for someone to be here at all times. The workers on this farm were devastated, although they were considered no more than riffraff, this was the only home they had, and they seemed to be in shock, they were wondering what would happen to them next.

There was trouble finding Carl Benson's wife, Mable, she was the only relative close to him, and they thought that she should be the one to see that he was given a proper funeral, but she refused to come to Ovington, or anywhere near this mountain. The decision was left up to Dr. Newman as to where Carl would be buried, and to take care of all of his affairs, since he was the only one to stick by Carl Benson these past few months while he had been disabled.

Betty Jean let her husband know right away, she wanted nothing to do with the Benson's farm, and sure didn't want to clear out any of his damned junk. There was a lot of furniture and clothes in this house, and dust to go with it. Dr. Newman asked some of the men to clear out some of the things that were of no value to anyone, and to take them away from this house. The workers were willing to do anything for Dr. Newman, because they were afraid he would make them leave this farm, and they had no other place to go at this time.

Thomas Ovington felt badly as everyone else about Carl Benson's dying, although they never did get along. Carl Benson had been dead for hours when his body was found. Thomas felt pity for Carl who lived such a ignoble life and he treated Mable, his wife, the same; and because she was not by his side when Carl died, she will never know whether he would ask her for forgiveness. Thomas never went to the Benson's farm during Carl's funeral and burial. Thomas would gaze from his estate over to the Benson's farm, he noticed all of the people over there, but when Carl was living the only people welcomed on the land was his kind of people, and they weren't very good people.

Dr. Newman did his best at the Benson's farm. He knew it was left up to Mable Benson to make a final decision so that his estate could be settled, but Dr. Newman was going to let someone else take on that headache.

When Dr. Newman talked to Roderich Bolling about the Carl Benson's estate, he said he would try to talk to Mable and work out a solution with her to dispose of the farm, if she did not have plans of living in Ovington again. Of course, the farm was worth a lot of money if anyone was able to afford the price, or talk Mable into selling the farm cheap.

Thomas had been thinking of purchasing Benson's farm, but he was totally broke at this time and he was up to his neck in debt with all of the land he had purchased lately. When it came to land, Thomas went into debt to buy as much as he could possibly buy, but he would always try to sell the land at a big profit. The Benson farm would be one of the best pieces of land to buy on this mountain, but it was completely out of the reach of Thomas so he quickly forgot the thought.

Sarah was happy even though she had no home or anything of value, but she had the love of Roscoe Bennett. Roscoe worried all of the time because he wasn't able to give Sarah a decent place to live, and she was the one with the money to spend. All the money Roscoe could earn or collect in the church was used to maintain the church. Roscoe felt badly seeing his wife work and support him and having to live with Blue and Vera wasn't a good way to start off a marriage, but he wanted Sarah to be his wife. Roscoe never thought of having to fear Blue around his wife, and Blue never tried to touch Sarah or say anything out of the way to her. Blue had lusted for Sarah for years, but he gave her the highest respect now that she was living in his house.

As soon as Betty Jean got over her stay at the Benson's farm and rested a little she began experiencing physical exhaustion, because her husband had started working her hard at the Benson's farm. This was the hardest she had worked since moving to Ovington. Betty Jean was too tired to go to the Ovingtons the way she once loved to do, she wanted to get back into her old habit of sitting out her days with the household staff waiting on her all day and Beth trying to please her.

Blue was working hard on his house, everyone that passed him and saw the way he sweated on his job would stop to talk to him and offer to help. Blue thanked them for the offers, but he was determined to build this house alone the way he wanted it to be built. Vera would follow her husband to their new home sometimes would sit and watch him as he would travail the day through as he toiled the hardest job of making sure everything was right before he would hammer the nail. Vera's love for Blue was one of the best, she always took up for Blue when others knew he had a mean streak in him, but to Vera and the children he was a great man.

Roscoe did his best for the church, he wanted to have a decent place for Sarah but work was scarce around Ovington and he knew the only money-making jobs in the valley was the trapper business and the operation of the moonshine, but this was totally out of his line so he just kept preaching as Sarah went to the Ovington's house each day to work to support them both. Sarah never seemed to mind the work because she was happy with Roscoe staying at the church each day.

The Newmans were not wealthy, but they weren't too poor either. Betty Jean was so worn out helping her husband at Carl Bensons, she knew that nursing was getting to be too much for her to handle. Dr. Newman was also fatigued and Betty Jean feared he would get sick and be unable to care for himself and the burden would be on her to take care of him, coupled with the expectation of supplying the community with professional medical care.

Betty Jean started to think of Sarah and her life. It seemed that she had gotten herself in a worse predicament since she married Roscoe. Sarah was having to live with Blue, of all people, and she was tired by the time she walked the steep hill each morning to the Ovington's estate. Having to support her husband, Roscoe, seemed pretty damn hard to Betty Jean.

Beth let out a sigh as Sarah walked in the house. She felt sorry for Sarah and wished that she still lived at the estate with them. Sarah was smiling at Beth because she knew that Beth had something on her mind and it wasn't easy for her to say it, but Sarah tried to act cheerful so that Beth would say what it was that she was so hesitant to say to her. Beth wanted Sarah to move back to the estate until she was able to afford a home of her own. Beth felt like the living arrangement that Sarah and Roscoe had wasn't too good, in fact, they had no privacy of their own.

Sarah always assured all of the concerned people that she was happy, and things would get better for her. Roscoe was doing his best for her; he was trying to support his church, and he had very little money

Sophie was quiet these days. She never went anywhere, except to attend Roscoe's meetings and back home. Geneva tried talking to Sophie, but she wasn't as easy to talk to as Sarah. Sophie was always elated when Sarah would take a few minutes to chat with her. Sarah knew that Sophie missed her and she still wanted to be friends with her, but Sarah was always in a hurry to be with Roscoe and she would run home when her duties were completed at the Ovingtons.

Betty Jean made a special trip to the Ovingtons to talk to Sarah in private. When she was able to get Sarah alone, Betty Jean asked her if she would consider a new and rewarding job. Sarah looked at Betty Jean dumbfounded as she talked excitedly about her going into nursing. Sarah didn't take Betty Jean seriously, but she remembered how Suzette always took her along when she had to deliver babies in the valley and she always wanted her to take over the midwife business when she became too old to sit and care for the mothers during the long labor and delivery of their babies.

Sarah was reluctant to answer Betty Jean, but she told her she would talk to her husband before making a decision. Betty Jean told Sarah that she and Dr. Newman needed someone to help them, since they weren't able to handle the workload of the community, and she would teach her everything she needed to know about home nursing.

Sarah was excited as she thought about Betty Jean's proposal to teach her home nursing. She knew that Betty Jean would be a tough teacher, but she would love to learn the proper nursing procedures since she loved taking care of people. Sarah loved the Ovingtons, and this estate and all of the household staff and she loved Geneva and thought of her as a mother, but she loved the ideal of becoming a nurse.

When Betty Jean told Dr. Newman about training Sarah to help with the workload that she wasn't able to keep up with anymore, Dr. Newman looked at his wife and wondered how she could think up so many unpredictable things to do. Of course, Dr. Newman was thinking this wild thought that Betty Jean wasn't a good one. To get her off his back, he said he would have to think about it some more.

Geneva was the only one that Sarah trusted to ask her advise about taking the home nursing training from Betty Jean. Geneva put her arms around Sarah and hugged her tightly, and with tears in her eyes she told Sarah to accept Betty Jean's offer, though it would be quite a challenge to undertake this training from Betty Jean. Sarah believed this was the right decision after talking to Geneva, especially after she assured Sarah that she was a smart person and would be able to learn all she needed to know from Betty Jean.

Sarah was feeling better after talking to Geneva, but this was a good time for Geneva to tell Sarah some sad news that she had been dreading to tell her and the others that she had been around for so long, including the Ovingtons. Geneva told Sarah that she and Richard were thinking about moving home to Lawsonville. The shocked Sarah was speechless for a minute, Sarah always assumed that Richard and Geneva would always be around–they were a part of her life–and to lose them was like losing family.

Geneva explained to Sarah that Richard wasn't able to stay out in the bitter cold as he cleaned the barn and other surrounding buildings, plus take care of all of the animals on this estate. Richard would cry out at night from pain as he tried to rub the pain away in his joints. Geneva said that they wanted to go home to their people because they had lived on the mountain for many years and they had a little money saved since the Ovingtons supported their needs as far as housing and food were concerned. She stated they could live out their lives on the money they had saved over the years. Sarah was distraught as she listened to Geneva, but she wished them happiness in Lawsonville and stated she would miss them but would always love and think about them.

When Beth was told of Sarah's leaving to work with Betty Jean and that Richard and Geneva were planning to move home to Lawsonville, she had to be put to bed. When there was something unpleasant happening to Beth, she would get in such a state of shock they would have to put her to bed because this bad news was very unpleasant to Beth.

The Ovingtons didn't try to stop either Sarah, Richard or Geneva from doing something they thought would make them happy, although this would be a very big loss to them and they would be missed very much. There were many people who worked for the Ovingtons, but none was as close as Sarah, Richard, and Geneva because they had been in this house since it was first occupied by the Ovingtons. Thomas was really disturbed, but he knew that Richard and Geneva were getting older and would want to go home to their relatives.

Thomas decided to walk to the valley; he was in a state of despair. He went to the school to see Cassandra because he knew she would cheer him up with her smile. Cassandra never seemed upset, though she had more students to teach, the children always loved to see Thomas. He still helped out at the school; he enjoyed the company of these children and the way they thrived with the strict teaching methods of Cassandra. Thomas was real proud of Cassandra and always thanked her for the hard work she did advancing the children's education.

26

The people in the valley were jubilant since they could walk the path along the little creek through Carl Benson farm again, as this had been their shortcut for many years to the outside of their valley on down the mountain before Carl Benson had stopped them. The men dared not walk through the Bensons' farm while he was living. The grown up creek bank was cleared by the men in the valley, they took this job upon themselves to clear this path even though no one asked them to do the job.

The few workers left on Carl Benson farm were still living there, but they had a different personality than when he was living, unlike the vile way they would treat people in the valley, they were always pleasant now and ignored the people when they came through Carl Benson's farm.

Roderich and Thomas went to see Mable Benson a couple of times to ask her to do something about the farm since she was the next of kin to Carl Benson. Mable refused to make the trip to Ovington to clear out the house or do anything about the farm. Roderich asked Mable if she would be interested in renting this farm. She replied that she would sell the land and all of the surrounding buildings for whatever price they would give her.

Roderich decided that he would talk over the sale of the Benson farm with Jane to see if she would consider his buying it. If she approved, he said that he would like to buy the farm. Thomas had no desire to buy the Benson farm, because he could not afford any more debt, and he would not be satisfied with anything that belonged to Carl Benson, he wasn't too fond of the man and wanted nothing that he had owned.

Thomas told the Davises he would take them back to Lawsonville when they decided to make the trip home. Geneva had written to her people, and told them they were coming home, and they were elated to have them home again after so many years. Richard would think about the years he had lived in Ovington and thought of this little town as his own, but he had few relatives left in Lawsonville, and he wanted to go home to be with them.

Sophie wasn't that close to the Davises, but when she heard they were leaving to go home to Lawsonville, she was devastated. This was another disappointment to her. Sophie had no close relative that she could go home to if she decided to leave Ovington, and often wondered what would happen to her when she was unable to work.

Betty Jean was pressuring Sarah to resign her job from the Ovingtons so she could start her training. Roscoe had agreed for Sarah to take the training he believed would be a better chance for her to make more money and a better pay for all the hard work she was used to doing, and Sarah would be able to take care of some of the people in the valley without the people having to put up with Betty Jean all of the time.

Blue was jubilant to hear that Sarah was leaving the Ovington's estate. Blue was so devastated the day he saw Thomas taking Sarah to his house to work when she was still just a child. Blue was as anxious as Betty Jean for Sarah to leave the Ovington's estate to take on her new job with the Newmans.

Beth Marie was unable to believe so much was happening to her all at once. The Davises were still planning on leaving Ovington soon, Sarah was leaving, and Roderich Bolling was planning on renting or buying the Benson farm. This would almost clean out the Ovington house.

Beth wanted Thomas to talk to Roderich Bolling about taking over the Benson farm, she didn't want the family to leave the estate. "This is a selfish thing you want me to do," shouted Thomas. He didn't want the Bollings nor any other household members to leave, but he didn't want to persuade them to stay if they decided to leave. Beth was thinking how lonely it would be, but there were already too many people living on the estate. There was never any quietness in this house.

Beth thought about the letter she received from the Carters. This was a chance for her to visit the family if the Davises moved home to Lawsonville. Beth asked Thomas if he would let her ride with him and the Davises to Lawsonville to visit the Carters and stay for a few days.

Thomas knew it would be selfish for him to say no, Beth did want to accept the invitation from the Carter family. This would be a chance for her to stay on the Cannon home place and the farm that her father had loved so much.

When Sarah first started working with Betty Jean, she believed that Betty Jean was impossible to learn anything from. She drove Sarah hard and the hours were unbearable. Sarah and Betty Jean started early in the morning and sometimes worked late into the night, according to how sick the patients were and if they could handle the case without Dr. Newman.

Betty Jean was trying to prove to Dr. Newman that Sarah would turn out to be a good nurse. Dr. Newman protested so strongly against her training Sarah, so Betty was trying to prove to her husband that she wasn't wasting her time training Sarah in this profession. Betty Jean taught Sarah how to treat a wound as best as she could and she taught her to bandage a bruise or help bandage a sprain. The work was hard and the hours kept Sarah exhausted, but Sarah was enjoying her new job because she had a chance to meet some of the people in Ovington she never knew. She was more popular than ever in the valley since she was at one of their houses each day. She even talked some of them into attending the meetings with her and to meet her husband.

Blue was pleased that Sarah was doing so well; he never complained to anyone because he never received a dime from Roscoe Bennett for them living under his roof. He took care of them as if they were his children. This was rare for Blue to do, since he always was trying to con someone out of their money. But he was sitting on a lot of money that he had made throughout the years and he wasn't as greedy after money as he once was.

Roderich finally told Jane Elizabeth he would like to rent or buy the Benson's farm. Of course, Jane looked at Roderich as if he had said something dreadful to her. Jane had no idea what she would do on a farm. Roderich explained the boys would be happy and this would give them a chance to have plenty of room for pets of their own, and he would enjoy his luck growing a little garden. He was planning on having a big fruit orchard.

Jane wasted no time running to tell Beth, but she didn't realize that she already knew this was Roderich's plan. Jane loved the Ovington's house, and didn't like the idea of leaving to move to the Benson's farm, although the farm was a big place and had a rather big house. Beth wasn't surprised by Roderich's decision to move, but she wanted the Bollings to stay with her. She would miss the children so much. The Bollings had never mentioned moving back to New York; although Judith wrote often asking them to come home.

Dr. Newman had to admit to Betty Jean that Sarah was a good little nurse. She was a compassionate person and always did her best with her patients. Sarah was more of a friend to them and they trusted her more than Betty Jean because Sarah had a nicer personality. She never talked ugly to the patients.

Sarah did take a lot of the workload off Betty Jean, once Betty trusted her to be on her own. There were times that Sarah had to rely on the Newmans to care for the critically ill and there wasn't much hope for them, but to see that they were comfortable.

Blue would diligently keep the hammer nailing as he rushed to finish his house. Vera stayed with Blue most of the day and sometimes she would get in the building spirit and hammer a few nails, but Blue never asked her to do anything to the house. He seemed to enjoy her presence as he worked on their home.

Sarah was always tired at the end of the day, but she never refused to love her husband, she was happy with Roscoe and rushed home to be with him. For the first time in her life Sarah felt loved and needed. Roscoe was tender toward Sarah; he never spoke harshly to her, and he never let her forget she was special to him.

Thomas and Richard took a trip to Lawsonville to find housing for Richard and Geneva's move back home. Thomas was feeling a little sad and would rather they stay in Ovington, but he knew they were getting up in age and wanted to be with their people.

Richard was excited as they drove through the community to visit old friends, relatives, and old acquaintances, as well as looking for a suitable house to live in. Richard had been gone so long there were many people that were strangers to him, most of the younger people were strangers, but they were friendly to him, and insisted he and his wife came back home soon.

Thomas knew he would have to visit the Carters and tell them about Beth wanting to visit with them for a few days. The Carters were surprised that Beth was accepting their invitation to spend a few days with them, but they were all jubilant that Beth Marie would be coming home to the farm once again.

Thomas always loved to visit the Boutique when he came to Lawsonville, but since he knew that Ledia wasn't there anymore, he decided not to go near the Boutique. Vickie Lynn was a beautiful woman, and certainty was a smart business woman, since she was smart enough to sell Thomas a nice wardrobe for Beth. He was shocked when he realized how much money he had spent in Vickie Lynn's Boutique.

This was one time that Thomas didn't hang around Lawsonville too long. As soon as Richard was finished with his business, he was ready to drive home. Although Richard wasn't satisfied with his housing that he had found, it was the best that he was able to do at this time and he was hoping Geneva would be pleased with his choice of the little house he had rented. At least the house was near his closest relatives.

Roderich Bolling had finally talked Jane into buying the Benson's farm. As soon as Thomas came home to Ovington, he had to make another trip with Roderich to see Mable Benson. Of course, Roderich had all of the necessary papers ready, this was the advantage Roderich had being a lawyer. He had prepared all of the necessary papers before Thomas came home. Roderich was ready to make the trip to see Mable and he was hoping to close the sale of the Benson's farm as soon as possible.

Geneva was all smiles as Richard told her of his renting a small house for them and their old friends and relatives were waiting for them to move home. The Davises didn't want to leave Ovington, but they knew it was time to go home. They had stayed in Ovington nearing 30 years and there was talk of war coming, and they had very few relatives left so they wanted to spend their remaining years with them and their home town they had grown up in.

The ignoble workers that were still on the Benson's farm were keeping the place up to par. The house had been cleaned out and was in a immaculate condition. The small buildings on the farm that some of the workers stayed in were cleaned and the men even took it upon themselves to paint some of them. No one had asked any of the workers to leave and they received no pay from anyone, but they continued to stay on the land, and worked harder now than when Carl Benson was living.

Sophie was always glad to see Sarah when she had the time to visit the Ovington's house; although she was busy, but she came when she found the time. Betty Jean was a slave driver, but Sarah was enjoying her new job, it was a chance for her to go out into the community instead of being in one place all of the time.

When Roscoe would see his wife come home so tired he would feel badly, but he was assured by Sarah he had a much bigger job trying to help the people by his kindness to them in troublesome time, and to comfort them with their problems, and his ministries to them was a comfort. Most of the residents were still living from hand to mouth and Roscoe did try to give them hope that things would get better. He tried to do things to interest the younger people to keep them in the community, since they were beginning to leave the mountain when they became of age to leave home.

Every time Thomas came to the valley he would see Blue working on his house, but he never attempted to go near him. If Vera saw Thomas, she would wave to him or call and invite him over, but Thomas only waved back to Vera and avoided going near them.

Cassandra was really trying to improve conditions at the school; although she had little money for supplies, but whatever Cassandra wanted for the school Thomas was with her all of the way. He even dug into his own pocket to help her with finances when it was some special project Cassandra wanted to do for the children. Cassandra was never afraid to ask Thomas for anything for the school because she knew that Thomas would see that she was able to get the things she needed, and was behind her with any new project she wanted to try for the children.

When Cassandra mentioned letting the children do small plays at the school, Thomas was surprised, but he agreed this was something different for the children. Thomas remembered the theater in New York and how he hated these plays Beth wanted him to attend, but a little school play would be different, and he knew that the children would be jubilant to do something different. Thomas agreed that this was a great way for the children to express themselves and he had the aging Walter to build a flexible stage for the school plays. Cassandra along with her husband spent long hours every afternoon after school practicing with these children as they spent time on their lines they were to do for the little plays for their families.

The show was on for the valley to see their children do their parts in the plays, and Thomas never missed the plays. He tried to get Beth Marie to attend these little plays since she loved the theater so much, but she insisted the steep hill to the valley was to dangerous to travel and she would not enjoy the plays when she was so nervous trying to get to the school.

The little house was always crowded when the children put on a skit for their parents. Roscoe and Sarah loved to go along with Blue and his family to enjoy the children doing their play acting. They tried to get Sophie to come along to see the children, but she was getting into her old habit of wanting to be alone again.

Beth was looking forward to seeing the Carters again and staying a few days with them. This was the first time Beth was homesick for Lawsonville. She missed James Cannon more so than she missed her mother and her only brother. Beth was so close to James Cannon, she was able to rule him, being so spoiled, and she always had her way when he was around. He saw to that. Of course, when Beth was growing up she never wanted for anything that money could buy, but in later years, she didn't have any desire to want for anything as long as she had Thomas. Beth did want to go to Lawsonville one more time to walk the land that her father loved so much and was happy on this land in his last days.

Roderich was thinking of Carl Benson farm. He loved the Ovington estate, but he wanted a place of his own since Jane refused to go home to New York. Roderich had decided to stay in Ovington and try to establish a suitable business in this small town that would make a decent living.

Jane Elizabeth loved to be with Beth and she loved this estate, it certainly was comfortable, and she loved all of the household help, and was forever trying to do something to help out. The household staff loved Jane, but they hated the days that she wanted to help them out. Jane could do a lot of messing in the kitchen before she got the dish right and she always had Beth to come and sample her favorite dish before she put the finishing touch to her work. Beth was always proud of Jane when she took on this little task to help out the ones that was doing the cooking.

No one was able to make Sophie happy these days. She stayed in her room more than she used to when Sarah was living at the Ovington's. Sophie was in her old habit of being alone. She still did her work, but Beth was getting worried about her because she wanted to be alone too much. Beth remembered how the people of this community avoided her because of her strange behavior when she first moved to Ovington with the Harrisons.

Geneva still spoiled and pampered little Judith. Beth wondered what they would do when Geneva moved back to Lawsonville, and they had to try and keep the baby happy. Geneva was a patient person and she seemed to be able to get along with most of the people around her, including the babies.

Roderich didn't let Thomas rest until he had the deed to the Benson's farm in his hand. Thomas and Roderich would make the trips to see Mable Benson and they talked of nothing but the negotiating of the farm that Roderich wanted so bad, but they didn't try to cheat her. Roderich was willing to pay top dollar for the farm. Roderich felt sorry for this woman, you could see she was very unhappy.

At the last and final signing of the farm over to Roderich Bolling, Mable cried. She hated the farm and all of the unhappiness she had suffered there and she thanked Thomas and Roderich for their kindness. It was a relief to Mable to get rid of the place she hated so much. She never had any friends in Ovington because of her husband's meanness and never intended to live there since her husband's death.

Most of the Benson farm was cleared and leveled off, but a portion of the land was nothing but hills and rocks. The house and surrounding grounds were beautiful and Roderich had many plans for this land he hoped to make into one of the best investments he had ever made in his career of doing business.

In the valley, everyone that came to visit Blue to see his work and admire him as he sweated and put all he had into building his new house. Some were even a little jealous of him. Blue still welcomed Sarah and Roscoe in his home, and he treated them with such kindness. It was unbelievable to most of the residents that knew him for a long time that this act of kindness was coming from Blue. They were seeing a changed man.

Roscoe would offer to help Blue, he would feel guilty sometimes, he had nothing to give Blue and he felt ashamed to be living off another man. Blue always refused any money from him and he certainly wouldn't take any money from Sarah. Vera would ask Blue to charge them a little something to make them feel better staying with them, but Blue refused to ask or take any money as long as they lived in his house.

Sarah was almost on her own, Betty Jean rarely went with Sarah on her jobs she was doing in Ovington and she was beginning to make a little money. Sarah thanked Betty Jean for training her and helping her by the jobs she would send her on, and Betty Jean would assure the people that Sarah was as reliable to do the job as she was, and to trust Sarah to do the right thing, and if they were in doubt, she would call on Dr. Newman.

Thomas would go to the school house to help Cassandra since she was having the children doing these plays, and he would do little jobs around the school. Kenny wasn't another Thaddeus, he didn't run behind Thomas as Thaddeus used to do, but his wife was just like Thaddeus. She was all smiles when she saw Thomas and tried everything to please him. Cassandra wanted Kenny to be more appreciative of Thomas, but he had a lot of hell in him and never acted like he cared for anything or appreciated some of the nice things Thomas did do for them. Cassandra looked up to Thomas and admired this man that tried to do everything he could to make them comfortable and sometimes Kenny did get a little jealous of the way his wife acted around Thomas.

When Thomas was in the valley for any reason, he never failed to admire the wonderful work he could see Blue doing on his house when he was finished. This would be one of the finest home in this valley, unlike the many poorly constructed homes scattered throughout this valley. Thomas knew this man did have some good in him; although he never cared for him, Blue was the only one to offer Roscoe and Sarah a home when he knew they had no other place to stay when they married. Thomas wondered why the two married without a home or suitable things to start housekeeping.

Beth reminded Thomas the Davises were ready to move back home to Lawsonville and she had already written the Carters a letter that she was coming to visit them very soon for a few days. Thomas was hoping that he would get out of this staying at the Carters for a little visit, but Thomas knew he owed this favor to his wife. She asked very little of him and rarely went anywhere. She always stayed at the estate while he did all of the traveling since he had moved her to this little community and many times he had left her alone with just the domestic help to keep her company.

When Thomas saw how excited his wife was about making the trip to Lawsonville and to visit the Carters, he put his arms around her small waist and tried to act elated as she was because he knew he owed his wife this joy that she was feeling to her. Thomas assured Beth they would visit and shop and do all of the things she wanted to do on this trip. Beth went to Geneva to assured her that she and Richard would have her as company when they travel to Lawsonville.

27

The day it was announced the Davises were moving home to Lawsonville was shocking, but not as traumatic as the time that Fred and Anna left Ovington. The Ovingtons wanted the Davises to stay in Ovington, but they didn't try to persuade them to stay when they wanted to go home to their people. The couple had given the Ovingtons many good years of service, they were devoted to them and always did whatever the Ovingtons ask them do.

Geneva sent for Sarah. She hated to leave Sarah and wished she could take Sarah with her, but she was married and Geneva knew they would never take Roscoe away from the valley since the people depended on him so much.

When Sarah heard the news that the Davises were leaving Ovington soon, she ran into the arms of her husband and cried tears of despair. Geneva was the mother that Sarah never knew. Anna was the one that wanted so badly for Sarah to be her child, but Geneva was the one that was there when Sarah needed a mother when she was growing into her early teens. So many of the things she didn't understand about her body as she grew into womanhood was the time she really needed a mother. Sarah remembered all of the cute dresses that Geneva made for her out of the few scraps of material that she sewed for Beth. All of these things were the love of a real mother.

Roscoe went with Sarah to see Geneva; Richard came in later, but Sarah wanted to be with Geneva alone for awhile. They had a chance to talk over old times and shed a few tears together and between talks and even hugged and kissed as Roscoe looked on uncomfortably. Richard came in and Sarah ran to hug and kiss him. She told Richard she would miss them so much and wished they would stay in Ovington.

The Bennetts and the Davises were having their last visit they would ever have in Ovington, but the Davises invited them to visit them in Lawsonville whenever they wanted to, and if they would like to come to live there, they would help them find a suitable home to live in.

Roderich was itching to move to his farm, but Thomas asked the Bolling to stay at the estate while they were visiting the Carters, and he would help them move to the farm when they returned. Roderich had hired people to paint and to do the necessary repairs to the house and Jane was already in a decorating mood; although she loved the Ovington's estate, this would be a chance for her to have her own home once she got used to the idea on living on a farm.

Beth Marie was so excited as she packed her bags to make this trip she wanted to be special to her. The Davises had been packed for weeks, they only had the small chest and the sewing machine that they moved to Ovington with so many years ago, which had been used so much doing work for Beth, and the small dresses and other children clothes that Geneva loved to make. Beth had given Geneva a few things to start housekeeping in their own home which included some of the finest linens that Beth pulled out of her chests that were only used for special occasion.

Geneva tried to talk to Sophie, to tell her she was leaving Ovington and to come visit her sometimes, but Sophie was so unhappy and cried so much Geneva had to leave her alone. Geneva could see that Sophie was having trouble coping with her loneliness, and she did miss Sarah so much. Sophie wasn't used to making friends, she didn't trust people, she was always afraid she would be hurt by people without knowing them first or getting out meeting new friends.

Thomas made arrangements with a friend to help the Davises with their belongings since the car would not hold all of the things that they had to move to Lawsonville. Beth Marie was packed and ready to travel with the Davises. This was truly a happy day for her, and she tried to greet the many people that came to the estate to bid the Davises good-bye.

The Davises had plenty of company the few days before they left as old friends and acquaintances that knew them for so long came to say good-bye. Richard looked sort of sad, but Geneva was all smiles.

This time it was Beth Marie who told Thomas to hurry as she rushed to the car, since he was making no effort to get started as he usually did. The Davises kissed the Bollings, and Geneva held little Judith tightly to her as she knew this was the last time she would be in Ovington.

As the two couples made the trip down the mountain, it was sort of sad for awhile as Richard looked over the land he had worked for so long and loved. This beautiful mountain was Richard's heart and he would never forget this part of his life, but he didn't want to die here and be buried in this mountain. He wanted to go home to live out his last days. Geneva held Richard's hand; she could see the disappointment on his face. He was leaving behind his home for so many years.

The trip was pleasant enough and Beth was chattering away as Thomas was on the quiet side, but he would look at his wife and smile. He wanted Beth to be happy, and whatever it cost, he would see that she was indeed happy. Thomas asked Beth if she wanted to go to see the Carters first and drop off her suitcases. Beth wanted to spend as much time with the Davises as she could, and she told Thomas, she would wait until they let the Davises out and they would go the Carters together.

Richard had rented a house and all they had to do was to move into their new home, but they would have to buy some things to start housekeeping. The Ovington's took the Davises to their new home and helped them with their small possessions. They also bought them a bed and stove to give them a new start. It had been a long time since the Davises had been out on their own. The good-byes between the Davises and the Ovingtons were sad, but they promised each other they would keep in touch. The Ovingtons told the Davises to never want for anything they needed, just to let them know and they would be more than willing to help them.

The Carters had been looking for the Ovington's car. They were all jubilant when they saw them drive up to the farm. Jeffrey ran to the Ovington's car, and he helped Beth out and took the small woman up in his arms and he was all hugs and kisses as the rest of his family joined him. They tried not to forget Thomas as they shook his hands, but Thomas looked uncomfortable seeing this affection between his wife and the Carter family. They all went into the house as they all tried to talk at once. Of course, the Carters had prepared for this special day with the Ovingtons, and it was a big day as they all gathered around the spacious dining room for the best time they would ever have, and even Thomas had to admit this was a joyful day at the Carters.

Beth took short walks around the old home place with Jeffrey. She enjoyed these walks with just the two of them. Jeffrey would stop to put his arms around Beth and thanked her for the good life he was enjoying on this farm and the great start in life she had given him when she had educated him when he first moved to Lawsonville.

Beth looked with pride at the good condition of this land her father loved so much. Beth was never very happy here, but James Cannon was at peace here on this farm, and he lived out his last days here after having so much stress in New York trying to keep up with his many businesses. The worry of coping with the people he disliked that was running some of these businesses.

This was one time that Beth was happy on this farm, with Jeffrey Carter following her around. Beth loved every minute, as he showed her the changes he had made to upgrade and expand the operation of the now Carter's farm. The people still called it the "Cannon's farm," but Beth wanted Jeffrey to think of this land as his own now.

Thomas had plenty to do in Lawsonville as he usually did. He never failed to visit old friends, but some of the people were leery of Thomas, knowing he had a quick temper, and he was hard to deal with at times. Jeffrey tried to include Thomas in his time he spent with Beth, but Beth seemed to only want to be with Jeffrey. In the evening the Carters and the Ovingtons would be together and have a nice time, but Beth looked forward to being with Jeffrey as they took short walks around this enormous farmland.

Thomas asked Beth if she would like to visit the Boutique where he brought her last clothes. Beth thought it would be nice for her to try on some of the latest styles. Beth was elated with all of the attention she was receiving from her husband and Jeffrey Carter. Beth agreed immediately to visit the Boutique with Thomas.

Thomas asked the Carters if they would like to come along on this shopping trip. Since Thomas had promised Beth to take her shopping, he wanted to include the Carters, but the Carters declined the invitation. Although Ledia was no longer the proprietor of this Boutique, Thomas still loved to visit her shop. Vickie Lynn was thrilled to see Thomas again and for him to bring his wife to shop herself. Beth was thrilled at the well stocked shop and she enjoyed this time she could browse through the shop. Beth tried on a few pieces, and Thomas paid for the few dresses and suits she selected. Beth adored Vickie Lynn, and promised her she would visit her establishment again.

After about ten days, Thomas was ready to make the trip home. Beth was having such a great time. It didn't seem like she had been in Lawsonville that long. Jeffrey wanted Beth to stay longer and he would take her home later, but Thomas wouldn't hear of this suggestion, and Beth did want to go home with her husband.

Jeffrey Carter loaded the car with so many treats for the Ovingtons from the farm. Beth was so proud of the way Jeffrey had run this farm and she was so glad that she had spent this time with the Carters. Beth didn't go to her father grave or mention Fred and Anna in any way. She wanted this trip to be one to remember for a long time, and she did not want any sad memories to cloud this visit.

The Ovingtons did not go back to see the Davises before they left Lawsonville, because it was painful enough when they left them to go visit the Carters. The trip home was thrilling for the Ovingtons. They remembered years ago when they moved to Ovington. The trip to the mountain was much rougher with the horses than with the car today, and the beautiful scenes up the mountain was breathtaking. Beth was so happy that she had made this trip, the Ovingtons would always remember this time they had together.

Roderich was glad to see the Ovingtons when they arrived at the estate. The Bolling boys were packed and ready to move to their new home, especially after their father told them of the many things they could do living at their new home.

The house was immaculate, Roderich had seen to that. Most of the furniture had been moved out of the house, but there was a couple of pieces that were too nice to throw out because they were heirloom pieces in the Benson's family for many years, so Roderich kept them in his home. There was a lot of furniture in the Ovington's house so Beth asked Thomas if she could share with the Bollings. Beth knew that they didn't need all of the many pieces of furniture in each room, and she cleared out some of the furniture she would never use.

The Newmans came to see the Ovingtons. Dr. Newman was worried about Beth Marie while she was visiting the Carters in Lawsonville. He still treated Beth, but he was proud that she was doing so well lately. Betty Jean was going to miss Geneva. She was always a part of this household, and she missed her the moment she walked in the house. With Sarah and Geneva away from the estate, it wasn't the same as when she would spend her days at the Ovingtons. Betty Jean saw Sophie and she felt sort of bad when she saw her looking so lonely and sort of depressed.

Dr. Newman watched Sophie as she went about her duties, he could tell she wasn't her old usual self, and he was concerned about her. Betty Jean tried to talk to Sophie, but she had little to say. Sophie was always glad to see Betty Jean in the past, and couldn't wait to hear about her nursing cases that she had been on.

With the Bollings and the Davises move home to Lawsonville, Sarah living at Blue house was rather lonely. The Ovington's house was different. The absence of the children on this estate was so lonely for Beth. She missed Jane and the children the most because they were always underfoot, and kept everyone busy.

Beth was looking for more help since Sarah and Geneva weren't a part of this estate anymore. Beth asked Thomas to see if anyone from the valley would stay with them. Thomas knew that there were few people from the valley that would come to work for him, since they didn't like to leave their home.

Thomas went to see Cassandra. He wanted to ask her if she knew someone who would take Richard and Geneva's places. The Davis's house that they occupied always looked so lonely when Thomas passed it, and he missed them more than he realized he would.

Cassandra did have a couple in mind that she thought would be suitable for this job, but she would have to go home to Spalding to have a talk with the couple to see if they wanted to leave Spalding to take a job away from home.

Cassandra assured Thomas she would try to fine him a reliable couple to come to this estate to live.

Beth would have Thomas to drive her to the Bollings just about every day to see the family. She missed them so much. Beth was so lonely now that so many of the people she loved so much had moved away from the estate.

The Bolling's house was one wild house as all of the family were trying to do their own perspective thing to adjust to their own home after living with the Ovingtons so long. Jane was in a frenzy since, she was trying to get everything in order and to keep up with her little family.

Beth Marie tried to do her best to help out at the Bollings, but she only got in the way, and made things worse. She was in no shape to keep up with the Bollings. Thomas knew Beth was wearing herself out and he worried about her, but he knew that she enjoyed being with the family. He didn't want to hurt her feeling by insisting she stay home more.

The Ovington's house suffered with no help and Beth spending most of her time at the Bolling. Sophie did very little because she was caught up in self-pity and would stay in her room most of the time, but she would still attend the meetings of Roscoe Bennett. She always seemed to live for the time she would be with the people that attended these meetings.

Blue finished his house after working long hours, and many bruised fingers and sore hands as he never let up until he had the house just as he wanted it to look, and he made sure he had each room as he and Vera planned them. Everyone was shocked and amazed to see a house of this standard in this valley, and from a man like Blue. The residents were forgetting where Blue got his training because John Smithson was one of the best builders this side of the mountain, and although he knew that Blue was a ignoble man at times, John Smithson liked him. There was nothing that he would not do for Blue.

Beth Marie's trip to Lawsonville was one of the most rewarding ones in her life. It was nice to have someone like Jeffrey Carter make over her and spent so much time showing her the most admiration and respect any man could show a woman. In fact, Beth was becoming quiet feisty, wanting to be on the go more, and wanting to follow Thomas, something she had never did before. Beth made him take her to the Bollings and sometimes she visited some of the other residents.

When Cassandra told Thomas about a couple that would love to come to Ovington to work, they were willing to leave Spalding and move to Ovington to take this job because they were both in need of employment. Thomas thanked Cassandra, and agreed to go with her to Spalding to meet this couple.

Sophie was becoming more withdrawn than ever. Thomas decided to try to find the Harrisons to see if Sophie had any people to contact about her condition. Thomas hated for anyone else to leave this estate, but he was very concern about Sophie's condition and he didn't know how to help her.

There was so much talk of war that Thomas was getting very nervous, because he didn't know how a war would affect Ovington since things were already bad as far as the economy was concerned. There had been many a bad day for this community, but they all stuck together and tried to make the best of hard times. There had been many newcomers to this little town and some of the older residents had died or left the community, but Thomas was proud of his town and wanted only prosperity for its remaining residents.

Sarah always found the time to visit the Ovington estate to see the Ovington's and tried to visit with Sophie and cheer her up. Betty Jean kept Sarah busy, but Sarah did miss the estate more than ever since Geneva wasn't there anymore. She thought of all of the good times they had together, and poor Richard was scared of his shadow, but he acted like he would tackle a bear until the time come for him to show his masculine strength, and he would turn the other way. Richard was always afraid of Blue, but behind his back, he would act brave about defending himself against Blue.

There was excitement in the valley when Blue and Vera moved into their new home. One could not believe the way Blue and Vera would be living now that they had a more modern home to occupy. Blue allowed Roscoe and Sarah to remain living in their old home and he still never mentioned them paying him any rent.

The Bollings had just about adjusted to their new home. The workers left over from Carl Benson were grateful to Roderich for letting them stay on at the farm since they had no place to go, and it worked out for both Roderich and the workers, because Roderich knew nothing about running a farm. Roderich always loved the Benson's farm since he first came to Ovington. He had hoped running this farm would be a success and he was willing to give the workers a chance, at least they acted more civilized now since they didn't have Carl Benson around to encourage them into meanness.

Thomas and Cassandra went to Spalding to talk with Steven and Estella Douglas, the couple that Cassandra had told Thomas about. They were anxious for Thomas to hire them since they were in dire need of a job and this sounded like a good opportunity for them since they would be given housing with the job.

The Douglases were so anxious for Thomas to hire them, they never asked about the pay or working conditions, but Cassandra's word was good enough for Thomas that they were reliable and if she thought they were good enough for the job. Thomas believed they were and hired them on the spot. Steven and Estella needed a few days to get their belongings together, but Thomas promised them he would return for them and move whatever they needed to move to Ovington.

When Beth heard from Thomas that he had hired this couple from Spalding to take Richard and Geneva place on the estate, Beth was elated, but she rather Cassandra wasn't the one that found the couple for them.

Thomas wasn't able to tell Beth very much about the couple, but he did mention that Estella was a robust woman compared to her small husband, Steven, looked like he only weighed a mere 125 pounds compared to his wife's 200 or more pounds. Thomas assured Beth that he felt like the couple would be good help and seem friendly enough and he believed they would be as faithful about being on the job as Richard and Geneva.

Although Sarah was working hard and Betty Jean was doing less as she trusted Sarah to be on her own more, the Bennetts never got out on their own. Roscoe was comfortable living in Blue's house on the money Sarah made. She gave most of it to her husband for the support of the church. Vera questioned Blue about getting some money from the Bennetts, but Blue only told Vera he was trying to help them and give them a chance to get on their feet. Vera wasn't one to question what Blue did and she was satisfied enough that she never mentioned the Bennetts paying for their housing again.

Cassandra was pleased that the Douglases were moving to Ovington. She missed her hometown and her people. Kenny was her only reason for leaving her family in Spalding, but she loved Kenny enough to move to Ovington with him and she adore Thomas, but kept her distance from Beth.

Roderich wasted no time getting the farm in shape and he and the workers were getting to know each other better each day. They knew that Roderich was a different type of man to work for than Carl Benson. Roderich gave the men respect and treated them fair as far as paying them fair wages and expected no more out of them than the days work agreed upon.

Roderich was very elated that he had been able to do so well on the farm in such a short time, but he gave the workers the credit for helping him because he knew nothing about running a farm. He was a businessman and he had planned to open up some type of business in

Ovington, but he wasn't sure what the best business to start at this time.

Roscoe was preaching harder than ever and seemed to put all he had into his work. He truly performed his duty to his people. When Sarah wasn't too tired she was at her husband's side, the sweat would cover his body, Roscoe would get so emotional. Sarah would worry about Roscoe, but the people would get so excited even Blue would get emotional and seem to be in the same mood as the people, but he never let Roscoe know how he felt. When Roscoe wanted to baptize Blue, he only laughed at him. Sophie, one of the most faithful members in the church, mentioned to Sarah how hard her husband worked to please the people. Even Sophie worried that Roscoe preached too long and too hard.

The Douglases let the Ovingtons know that they were ready to move to Ovington and Thomas was in a hurry to move them, since he couldn't keep Beth Marie home anymore. Thomas knew if Beth had new people to train in her home she would be there to see that they did things as she liked for them to be done, and was very strict about doing the house duties as she liked for them to be done, and she took great patience to train them well.

Beth was pleased with Steven and Estella Douglas. She loved the jolly and energetic Estella and her size didn't keep her from doing what needed to be done. There were days that didn't go too well, but Beth liked to see Estella always in a good mood. She would sort of smile to herself when she saw the way Steven tried to hang around his wife, as if he was going to lose her.

Estella had to be someone special to get Sophie out of her moody spells, but Sophie seemed to like Estella from the first day she moved to Ovington. Sophie seemed to like Estella just as much as she liked Sarah and she would hang around her and talk to her. She even seemed to like Steven and would talk to him almost as much as she did to Estella. Beth was pleased that Sophie liked the couple. She had been worrying about Sophie, fearing she was getting in a depressed state, and they would not be able to keep her living at the estate.

Steven wasn't as good outside as Richard, but he was trying to do a good job, and Thomas let him do as much as he was able, since Beth liked Estella so much.

28

The first years of World War II were as full of turmoil to Ovington as the rest of the world. All of the confusion, young men going off to War leaving the women to do what only men had did before. Thomas was too old to serve in the war, but he promised the husbands that did have to leave for the service that their families would be cared for by the remaining residents.

Kenny Williams was one of the first young men to be called to the service from the valley. He wasn't too happy leaving his wife, but Cassandra assured him she would wait for him to come home in Ovington, rather than go home to Spalding, especially since the Douglas' moved to the Ovington's house. Cassandra knew she would be lonely without Kenny, but she did have a big job trying to teach and control all of the children that were coming to school in the valley.

Beth was quite busy these days. She never stopped trying to pamper Thomas, and she did things she thought would make him happy. After the Ovington's trip to Lawsonville, and the thrill Beth got from walking with Jeffrey around the old home place, Beth had begun to follow Thomas around for short walks, something she had never enjoyed before, but she would walk with Thomas to the surprise of the neighbors, and when the Newmans saw Beth getting out more, Betty Jean asked her husband what kind of pills he was giving Beth.

There were still people that came up the mountain to Ovington, either they heard of this town, or just curious and came to check out the town. There were few people that hadn't heard of Thomas Theodore Ovington. He was a person you could never forget, he seemed to stand out among other people. Many people were fond of Thomas and he had the highest respect; even people who weren't too fond of him, respected him.

During the war years, Thomas many investments he had made for himself began to pay off. In addition, the Cannon money he had invested scored beyond belief, and for the first time in his life, Thomas began to make money on his own. These were good times for Thomas, and he was elated to be able to have his own money, and not have to borrow from his wife's money that had originally come from her father. This made the short-tempered Thomas a little more cheerful and he didn't have to feel guilty spending the Cannon's money since he had a lot of money on his own.

There were so many new faces in Ovington these days. Although there weren't business places to work, this seemed like a nice little to be. Many of the people from the valley invited people to visit since many of the men left Ovington to work in other towns where work was good and they made more money than anywhere near Ovington.

Beth was getting more energetic each day, she was excited since she had Estella in the house, she was one woman that could do just about everything, and she was always smiling as she worked, and she joked to the others working with her. Sophie loved this woman, and seemed like a new person these days. Beth felt comfortable leaving Estella to run the house while she would go to visit the Bollings. She just could not stay away from the family, and made it her daily thing to do to the surprise of her husband.

Thomas tried to show Steven the things he needed to do outside, but he was having a hard time trying to do all that Richard had done. Steven knew his wife was well liked, and she had no trouble with her job.

There were times when Steven was so frustrated, he would take his frustration out on his wife. Although he knew he was no match for Estella, he would get up enough nerve to try and slap his wife around a little, and would pay dearly for his mistake. Estella would grasp Steven with both hands, and she would just about whip the poor man to death until she felt sorry for him. It was funny, because Steven knew he was no match for his wife, as far as strength was concerned.

Cassandra was so fond of the Douglases, but she knew when Steven was bashed around by Estella, and she smiled to herself, and wondered when Steven would ever learn his lesson.

Thomas would go to the valley and walk around to see some of the old-timers. There were a few families that were deceased and their homes were mere shacks that stood isolated and unusable. They were just standing and looking like the wind would blow them away. Thomas would ask their relatives or some of the men to tear the houses down. After seeing the beautiful home that Blue built in the valley, Thomas wanted to change the image of this valley with all of the shacks that needed repairing. This was still Thomas' favorite place to be in Ovington.

The smartest thing that Roderich had done in Ovington was to take a chance and hire the workers left over from Carl Benson. The Bolling farm became one of the most beautiful and rewarding places for miles around. The work was hard and the hours long for the Bollings, but Roderich had seen the potential for a great farm with a little hard work before he bought this place for his family. The Bolling family were enjoying the farm, especially since they were showing a profit from all of their hard work.

Jane Elizabeth was into selling everything she could, and she was a pretty good salesperson. The Bollings had more than they could use, and the money was needed. In fact, there was another baby on the way, and Jane was thinking ahead and planning the time when she would have to take it easy. When Jane told Beth of the new addition coming, she was elated, and wanted Jane to start taking it a little more easy now.

When Sarah saw a little change in Sophie, she was happy that she and Estella was becoming friends, because Sarah was so worried about Sophie, the way she was letting herself become a loner again. Sophie persuaded the Douglases to attend the meetings with her, and they loved to hear Roscoe preach the gospel, and Estella wasn't able to keep still in her seat when Sarah got up to sing with her husband.

Occasionally, Thomas would attend some of the meetings. He was making money now, and he was doing a lot of traveling, was working hard trying to keep up with his new wealth. Most of the time Thomas took Roderich with him to make sure he was doing business in a legal manner.

Blue was rather quiet these days, the way he worked on his house in all kinds of weather, seemed to have taken a lot out of him. Vera acted like a different person, she seemed like she was a little above everyone else in this valley, since Blue had built her this nice and beautiful home, and Blue treated her like she was truly very special to him.

Roscoe and Sarah were still welcome to stay in the Johnson's other house, and Blue treated them like they were his children, he didn't treat his own children any better, and Vera was a little concerned with the way he took the Bennetts under his wings. This didn't seem like Blue to do so much for anyone.

Vera never knew that Blue wanted Sarah, but she could not understand the way that Blue let the Bennetts stay in their old home rent free; however, she was one to never question the things that Blue did, most of the time she accepted them. Deep down in his heart, Blue still wanted Sarah, but he felt guilty about the way he had treated Sarah when she was so young, plus, he still felt sorry for her, she seemed to have had a very hard life from the time she was born when her mother died at her birth.

Roscoe never stopped trying to get Blue to come forward and accept the Lord in baptism. Blue supported the church, he came to most of the meetings, but he would ignore Roscoe's out-stretched hands to come forward, and accept the Lord as his Savior. When Blue first started coming to church, he only wanted to see Sarah and hear her sing, which he truly did enjoy, but he also loved to see Sophie get happy, and this really was hilarious to him to see this woman run around the church, and to see the little dance she did.

Cassandra was devoted to the children she taught, she was always trying to do things that would keep them interested in coming to school. After Kenny went off to the war, she had plenty of time to devote all of her time to doing things for the children. When Kenny was home, Cassandra had to spend a lot of her time trying to keep him straight and to help him keep his mouth shut, which always seemed to keep him in trouble. He did have one smart mouth, and she was afraid he would get hurt by the way he would run his mouth so much.

The Douglases asked Cassandra to attend the meeting with them in the valley, but Cassandra refused, her only excuse was she didn't have time, but she felt guilty around Sarah, especially after Thomas made Sarah move out of her home after Thaddeus died, and he fixed the home up for she and Kenny to live in. Cassandra was never able to feel comfortable around Sarah, and Kenny was never happy living in the beautiful home Thomas fixed up for them. Kenny was always telling Cassandra she had no right to accept this home from Thomas without first asking his permission to move to the Ovington's servant quarters that Thomas had offer her.

The residents in the valley were really nice to Cassandra while

Kenny was away at war. They were grateful to her for all of the time she devoted to their children. She not only taught them basic educational courses, she taught them to do creative things and she took a lot of time to see what their talents were, and then, she would encourage them to pursue these talents. Cassandra hoped to see them grow up to do what they were best qualified for.

Kenny wasn't a educated person, he wasn't able to write very interesting letters to Cassandra, but she could understand them enough to know that he missed her very much, and was lonely for her. Kenny wanted Cassandra to go home to her people until he came home, he wasn't too happy with his wife staying on the Ovington's estate alone and having to walk the steep hill from the school in the valley to the Ovingtons.

The Bollings allowed the workers to cut branches away from the creek so all of the residents of Ovington could enjoy walking the road around the creek that led down the mountain again. They worked hard for weeks as they even cleaned out some of the bigger rocks that had fallen down into the creek, most of the children loved to swim in the creek. The people from the valley were grateful to Roderich for letting them use the road again to travel off the mountain, because it was so hard for them to climb the steep hill up from the valley through the Ovington's estate.

Jane Elizabeth had to slow up some since the new baby was on the way. Although the frail Beth was trying to visit the Bollings almost everyday, she wasn't much help, and most of the time, she only got in the way. Jane and her friends tried to include Beth in most of the things they did, but Beth was in no shape to run around Ovington the way they did, and get in involved with all of the activities they had going. Thomas tried to persuade Beth to slow down, and to stay at home more, but she trusted Estella to run the Ovington's house while she hung out at the Bollings.

The Newmans were pretty quiet these days, they were letting Sarah do most of the nursing care. Betty Jean went to the Bollings occasionally to be with Jane and Beth, but there wasn't a place in Ovington she loved better than the Ovington's house, and all of the attention she received when Sarah and Sophie was there waiting on her hand and foot.

Dr. Newman was getting a little old and feeble, but Betty Jean was still full of spunk, she never let up on the cussing, and some of the residents preferred not to be around her at times. The workers on the Bolling's farm despised her and got out of her way when they saw her.

When Beth wanted to upgrade her rock garden, as she did sometimes, she sent for Blue. This would always make Thomas angry, and he never would welcome Blue at the estate, but Beth Marie would have no one else working on her garden, Thomas tried to give Steven the job of working Beth's garden, but he knew nothing about any rock flower garden, in fact, Steven wasn't too good with flowers at all. Beth believed that Steven would damage some of her beautiful flowers that she took such pains to have planted. Beth was almost as nervous with Steven breaking something in her house as she was with Thaddeus.

Beth Marie would always talk to Blue as he worked, she knew how smart he was with his hands working with the mortar. Beth wished that Thomas would forget the bad feelings he had for Blue, he would never change, and he was getting on in years, and should forget the past. Thomas was so partial to the people in the valley, and he was especially partial to Thaddeus, the one person he treated like his own son, and when he saw how cruel Blue was to him, he never forgave him for his cruelty, and Thomas always blamed Blue for the men in the valley being arrested for making the moonshine.

Sarah helped Betty Jean as she delivered a lot of babies in Ovington. Sarah would hold the newborn baby, and she would wish for a child of her own sometimes. The Bennetts did wonder why they weren't blessed with a child. The Bennetts enjoyed a healthy sex relationship, but Sarah never became pregnant. Roscoe was a passionate person, and Sarah certainly never had to beg Roscoe to love her as she did have to beg Thaddeus, who seemed to completely ignore her at times.

During the years of World War II, Thomas never traveled very much as he did before the war. Thomas had promised the men that had families in Ovington he would make sure they were well taken of, and that included Cassandra. If there were any major problems with the wives of the service men, Thomas tried to do his best to correct them.

The Bolling's second girl was born during the war; they named her Kathryn Diann. Nearing the end of the war, another girl was born, the last of the Bolling's children, and she was named Tina Rebecca. This was quite a family for Jane Elizabeth and Roderich. There were no problems with the help they needed, because there was always someone around to help take care of the children and all of the other things that were going on at this farm.

29

After the war ended, most of the residents who had gone off to fight came home, and there were jubilant wives all over Ovington. Kenny came home to Cassandra, and he was so happy to be with his wife again, he was in tears. Kenny realize that Cassandra was the best thing to happen to him, and the war had finally made him grow up and accept his responsibility as a husband.

Kenny had traveled a lot and had seen a lot of the world he never knew existed. After being away from Ovington, he planned to move to another city, and he planned to move to a northern state where he would be able to make a decent living, and Cassandra would not have to work, and his dreams were that they would be able to start a family.

Cassandra was shocked when Kenny told her of his plans to move from Ovington. Kenny Williams' people still thought of him as a bratty kid, and could not believe he was all grown up now. One thing that Kenny wasn't about to do, was to continue to live in the servant's house on the Ovington estate. Kenny told his wife he was moving back to the valley the first night home. Cassandra was disappointed, but after hours in her husband arms, and to have her husband home after so many months, she was willing to do whatever he asked.

Thomas was glad to see the husbands come home, but there were a few that didn't come home, and some of the husbands came home to get their wives and they moved to the town where they were stationed in service. Thomas was glad that Kenny was home, but he could see that he was a changed man, and he even talked more mature, none of the silly stuff he used to talk about, and he wasn't as aggressive as he was before being inducted into the military service.

After shaking hands with Thomas, Kenny told him he planned to move from the estate back to the valley he grew up in. Of course,

Thomas was shocked and very disappointed, especially when he told him he was moving his wife to another state. Kenny knew he would never be happy in Ovington again after traveling so much and seeing so much, and being in all of the fighting he had been through, he was lucky to be alive. Kenny wanted to settle in a bigger city where his children would have a better chance than he did. Thomas acted happy for Kenny, but he was thinking of Cassandra leaving the school, and this was devastating to him.

Thomas tried to forget everything but his many investments. He was ecstatic now that he was showing a profit in his money he invested, and was free from borrowing from his wife's money. The many acres of land that he had bought before the war were now paying off for him, since he was selling the land at a enormous amount of money. This was unbelievable to Thomas to see how the price of land had jumped.

Sarah was surprised to see Kenny move Cassandra back to the valley, and she could see that Cassandra wasn't to happy, but Sarah knew that the Williams were leaving Ovington soon, and believed that Cassandra was trying to cope with this new living arrangement. Kenny's people were happy to have him home, and in one piece, there were a few of the men that weren't the same when they returned home.

After the Williams moved back to the valley, Sarah would see them often, and Kenny always greeted Sarah with a hug and kisses. Kenny never felt good after he moved Sarah to the Ovington's house, and Thomas allowed them to move into her home that she and Thaddeus shared together. After Thaddeus' death and Thomas moved Kenny and his wife into Sarah's home that she was forced out of, Kenny always felt guilty and unhappy, and he wondered how his wife could agree to move to the Ovington's estate behind his back.

The Bollings had their hands full with five children, but as busy as the house was, all seemed to have their own special thing to do. They were even able to travel some after the babies were able to walk on their own.

Judith Holman wasn't able to come to Tennessee when the last two babies were born, she wasn't up to par for traveling so far, so the Bolling family would travel to New York to see their families. It made no difference how many children there were, the Bollings always packed their belonging and the children, and they would travel wherever they wanted to go.

Getting off the mountain was no problem for the Bollings since Roderich was the one to buy a new car, in fact, he first purchase a station wagon to hold his family so they would be comfortable, and soon after he brought Jane a new car.

Thomas never brought another car, and his one vehicle left over from the two he brought years ago wasn't running too good, but he had Steven to wash and polish this car as if he was taking the car on the road each day. Thomas still had the Phaetons parked in the shed that he kept them in, and Steven had to polish these carriages periodically the same as the one car. Poor Steven cussed these vehicles every time he had to do the jobs, he never could understand the reason since Thomas rarely used them.

It seemed strange to everyone that Thomas never bought another car, and he always had someone else drive him most of the time in later years. Thomas would still ride the horses when everyone else was driving around Ovington. Jane always drove Beth whenever she wanted to go. Thomas could well afford a car now, more so than when he went to purchase two vehicle years ago in Lawsonville, but he never had any desire to buy another car for the estate, he was always haunted by the wreak that Thaddeus had in one of his cars.

The Williams came to the meeting, they was with Roscoe and Sarah, they wanted to tell everyone good-bye. The couple had planned to leave Ovington when school was out. Cassandra had tears in her eyes, she loved the children and had taken a lot of her time trying to teach the children many things to keep them interested in school. The Williams clan were all there, and were rather sad. Kenny had been the one that kept the valley from being dull when he was home, because he was always into something to keep him into trouble.

Thomas was beside himself with worry, wondering who would teach the children in the valley. When Cassandra left this valley, there was no one qualified to take her place. Thomas could not understand why Kenny wanted to leave Ovington, he knew how the parents depended on Cassandra to run the school, she was so efficient, and the children improved under her special care that she gave them.

The next gospel meeting, the Bennetts looked for Blue, he had missed, and that was unusual for him to do, because he was always at the meeting, he was afraid he would miss something. Sophie was sitting content with the Douglases, Steven was always right up under Estella, he could not sing, but he belted out the songs louder than anyone. Roscoe would sort of smile to himself when he saw the Douglases, they were sort of funny to him, Steven looked like Estella's child when he would see them walking together. Roscoe was concerned all through the meeting about Blue, and he asked the Williams if they had seen him during the day. For some reason the meeting didn't seem right without Blue attending them.

No one was happy when the Williams were ready to leave Ovington, but Thomas was the one that was the most unhappy, he continued to worry about the school, his first priority, and he wanted a teacher that was as devoted to the children as Cassandra had been.

Ovington was growing bigger with each new residents that brought land from Thomas. The community was expanding on down the mountain as Thomas sold off his real estate. Most of the people that brought the land, they planned to build. There was a decent road built that connected the land so that the perspective buyers wasted no time building on their land.

Everyone that knew Thomas Ovington respected him in a way you would a parent, you may not agree with them all of the time, but you went along with them out of respect. Thomas Ovington was well known, and once the people came to Ovington and saw the town, they liked what they saw, and wanted to be a part of this community. Although Thomas was hard to bargain with, when doing business with him, no one seemed to mind paying his price. Every once in awhile, Thomas would meet a hard nosed business person as himself, but he tried to ease away from them in a nice way.

The main reason Thomas was selling his land to people that would build in Ovington, he wanted to have more residents, and that meant more businesses would have to be opened in Ovington. Thomas' whole life, beside Beth Marie, was the business world. He liked to wheel and deal in the business market. The money was plentiful for Thomas now, he had worried for so many years about losing his wife's money. There were many times he had to borrow from his wife, and unable to pay her back, of course, Beth never wanted him to repay her anything, but Thomas felt guilty, and worried until he felt like he could replace the money.

Though Thomas was up in years, and should have been thinking of retiring, he remained active, and still tried to do things he always did, and that was run this community. The only one he could not rule and control was Blue, and they continued stay out of each other's way.

The more people that moved to Ovington, the more trouble there was going to be, so they began to look for law officers to run the now empty constable seat. Since Roderich gave up this position, there was to be a election for a sheriff to run Ovington. There was enough people in the community to have a good turn out, but there was only one man that wanted to run.

One family of the new residents that built further down the mountain, the Chambers, Chad and his wife Ruby, were a young couple that had three girls, and seemed to be real close. Chad talked to the residents of Ovington, and he expressed his desire to be the elected sheriff of this community. Chad Chambers looked like he could handle the job, since he was a pretty big man. As far as this town was concerned, Chad was welcome to the job.

Chad assumed the job would be pretty easy. There wasn't a lot of rough stuff that went on in Ovington, everyone seemed to mind their own business. The Chambers wanted to make a good impression on the people in this community. The Chambers went around Ovington making acquaintance with the residents. Chad even went into the valley to make himself known to these people, but he went by himself.

The seemly, friendly Chad Chambers talked to the residents in the valley with his little grin he usually wore. Bluntly he told the men in the valley he didn't know who the moonshiners were at this time, but he would certainly find out, and he would waste no time putting them in jail right here in Ovington. Chad meant every word he said, if he caught any bootlegging going on here in this valley, because he wasn't afraid to travel any parts of this mountain. At one time, Chad had lived in the most treacherous parts of this mountain, and wasn't afraid to go anywhere around these part of Ovington as the other law officers.

Of course, the men that were guilty, looked a little surprised and were very hurt, they knew of nothing else to do here in the valley to make a living, since there was very little work, this bootlegging moonshine was their way of life, and they didn't consider themselves hurting anyone. This was the first time they seemed afraid since the law came down on them years ago. Chad didn't want to be so hard on these people, but the first thing some of the residents of Ovington wanted stopped was the bootlegging the moonshine liquor in the valley.

Dr. Newman insisted that Beth stay at home more and rest in the evening. He didn't like the way she looked these days, and her blood pressure was higher than usual. Dr. Newman went to Thomas to warn him about his wife's health, that she should stop trying to run to the Bolling's house everyday.

The parents worried along with Thomas about the future of their children attending the school in the valley. The only school for their children to attend was miles down the mountain. They looked for a qualified teacher to teach in the valley, but no one wanted to take this job that was so far to have to travel to the valley. They felt like it was a job itself just to get down into the valley.

During the war most of the men in the valley left this mountain to work jobs where they made good money, but these jobs were eliminated after the war, and these men came home to their families. The moonshiners always knew that when they were out of work, they could always make a few dollars selling their moonshine. But with this new sheriff walking this mountain, the chances were slim for them to continue this bootlegging operation.

Chad Chambers was as bad as Thomas walking this community. You never knew when you would look up, and there he was, always wearing his famous grin he had on his face, but underneath his grin, you could tell the man was rough and tough, and he had the muscles to match his body.

Blue was still missing the meetings when Roscoe began to get curious about Blue. He cornered the man, and asked him the reason for missing the meetings. Blue's only response was that he was too weak to walk to the church, plus sit through the meetings. Roscoe didn't believe Blue, and assumed Blue was worried that he would come forward and accept the Lord as he would try to get him to do.

Roscoe was more happy when Sarah and Sophie seemed to back him up as he pounded the floor, jumped up and down getting his word across to the people, and he would sweat so much as he got so carried away at these meetings.

The Ovington seemed to like the Chambers, but Thomas was getting a little concerned with the way Chad walked this community, he felt like he was only doing his job, but he looked as if he was looking for something to arrest these people for; however, Thomas was trying to see just how far this man was into law and order. Thomas was hoping Chad wasn't one of these men from the old days of beating up on the arrested men and abused them when they were helpless.

Steven wasn't as happy in Ovington as Estella, especially after Cassandra left, and he wasn't as good on his job as his wife. Every time Steven tried to talk to Estella about his unhappiness, she would shoo him away from her, she had no time for his whining. Estella knew that the Ovingtons were pleased with her performance at the estate, and she could not understand what the problem was with her husband.

Thomas wasn't able to find a suitable person in Ovington to teach in the school in the valley, now that Cassandra was no longer living there. Thomas knew that he would have to teach in the school again, rather than to see the school to be without a teacher, and the children unable to attend school. Thomas wasn't able to take on this big responsibility, but he would never see this school, that he had worked so hard for, be closed, and the children miss out on their education in this valley.

Beth Marie was very upset with Thomas taking on this time-consuming job, and he never was paid for his time he spent teaching these children. It really was just too much for him to do with all of the other businesses he had to see after, not to mention all of the bookkeeping he did. Although there were many people in Ovington qualified to teach in the valley, they refused to take the job, because of the hard time they would have getting up and down the steep hill to the valley.

Steven wasn't too happy with his wife having to get up earlier, because she made him arise early with her, and he had to walk to the estate with her, Estella was a little afraid to come such a short distance in the darkness so early in the morning. Since Thomas had to go the school and take care of so many things, the Ovingtons had to start earlier in the day. Steven was sorry he had moved to Ovington. He hadn't adjusted as well as Estella, and he felt like the people in this community made fun of him, because of his size, compared to his wife.

Sarah was distressed at times by the way she tried to save a patient, and see life just slip away from them. Betty Jean was glad she had taken the time and patience to train Sarah, she was a great nurse, and she was becoming real popular among the residents of Ovington. Sarah felt like she had a good life now, she loved Roscoe more so than words could describe, but Thaddeus had been a comfort to her at times, but she knew Thaddeus did not love her in the same tender and passionate way as the love and marriage she shared with Roscoe, and he always let her know, how special she was to him.

Ovington was enjoying a rapid growth. Though Thomas was busy with the school, he still had time to keep up with his enormous gain in his business and the stocks and bonds that he owed seem to flourish beyond belief.

Chad Chambers was considered to be a good elected sheriff, and he did his job well, Thomas would see him walking in the valley as he had classes in the school house. Ovington residents believed that Chad was doing a good job, they trusted him, but something about this young fellow bothered Thomas, as if he was waiting for something little to happen, so he could make something big out it.

Blue was able to come back to the meetings with Roscoe and Sarah, although he was missed, he still only came to see what was going on, and who was getting happy in the little church. Roscoe never let up on his dynamic meetings he had with the residents in the valley, sometimes Sarah would have to make her husband sit down, he was so worked up.

Although Thomas wasn't able to have the school plays, and to take the time to do things outside of the basic schooling to keep the children interested, he did try his best to give the children a good education. Thomas was getting up in age, but he still walked to and from his estate to the valley to make sure the children were in school each day.

Estella, with all of her weight she had to carry around every day, seemed to be able to do whatever Beth asked her to do. Sophie never did mind doing what Estella asked her to help out with, and on rare occasions, Estella would have to have her husband help them out when Beth was having one of her elegant dinner parties, where as, only the most important residents of Ovington were invited.

Sophie loved to see the Douglases together. Poor Steven wanted to be the dominant one over his wife, and Estella would let him rule her at times, until she would tire of him trying to show authority, and that is when she would sit him down in a hurry.

30

It was ironic the way Roscoe Bennett and Daniel "Blue" Johnson died within weeks of each other. The shock was on the faces of all the people in Ovington. What a tragedy to lose the only preacher ever to be in this valley. Blue was known by his bad reputation when he moved to the valley years ago, but he was a good family man, and always made a good living for his family. Blue was bad as could be at times, but at the same time he was noted for helping some of the residents in need, and had elped build the little church in the valley. Even with all of his faults, he was considered one of the smartest men in the valley.

Roscoe was the first to pass on. He was still a rather young man, but he lasted only a week after becoming ill. Sarah had no idea Roscoe was feeling so bad when she came home after a hard day herself working with Betty Jean. First, he refused to eat, and this was unusual for Roscoe. He always used so much energy practicing his sermon and preaching to the people, he needed to eat to keep up his energy for his vigorous meetings he had for the people who attended his church.

Sarah was horrified to see Roscoe so sick, and sent for the Newmans to help her with her husband . The Newmans wasted no time coming to the valley to see about Roscoe. Although Dr, Newman was getting feeble himself, he tried to do what he could for Roscoe, but he was gone after about a week of illness.

There are no words to describe the grief and antagonizing pain Sarah suffered during this period of her life. She was in a state of shock, the one person in her life she believed truly loved her for herself, was gone forever. Roscoe had been the most loving and warm-hearted person anyone could know, and Sarah thought that they would grow old together.

Sarah had been devastated when she lost Thaddeus, but Roscoe had filled that hurt. Although Sarah never forgot Thaddeus, she knew that Roscoe's love for her was different and was more mature than Thaddeus', and it was going to take her a long time to get over Roscoe Bennett's sudden death, and accept this great loss in her life.

There were many people that came to see Sarah and comforted her in her hours of mourning for Roscoe. Sarah knew that Roscoe had relatives somewhere in Alabama, but she had no idea how to locate them, so she buried him in the valley. Thomas was there with Sarah all the time until Roscoe was buried, ignoring Blue, who wasn't letting Sarah out of his sight. Beth was feeling sorrowful for Sarah, she knew how much she had been through in her life, and this was just another sadness in her life.

Sophie was beside herself with grief. Besides Sarah, Sophie loved Roscoe with all of her heart, she even had a secret love for this man, and to lose him, was a devastating blow to her as well. Sophie and Sarah were together again, trying to comfort each other. They not only lost a good friend and husband, but this whole valley had lost the only minister, plus, he was friends with most of the people in the valley. Sophie begged Sarah to move back to the Ovington's estate, so she would not be alone. Sophie didn't say the words, but she wasn't happy with Sarah living alone in Blue's home, since she never trusted the two together.

Everyone was wondering what would happen to the little church. There was no other minister around close, and no one could fill Roscoe's place, or stir the people the way he did.Sarah and Sophie tried to have meetings with the people in the valley, but they weren't the same, even though they would sing the same songs and tried to read the Bible, the people weren't able to have the same feelings as when Rev. Roscoe Bennett was leading the meetings.

After everything had settled down in the valley and Sarah had gotten herself together, Blue came to see Sarah and they talked about her staying in Blue's old house. Blue assured Sarah that she was welcome to stay in his home as long as she needed to, and there would still be no charges to her. Blue told Sarah she didn't have to move, in case Vera said something to her about moving. Vera wasn't one to talk ugly to her husband, but she sure had been bitching to Blue about Sarah moving since Roscoe had died.

Blue really wanted to take care of Sarah, the same way he had wanted to for so many years. Blue let the Bennetts stay in his house rent free, because he was always hurt by the way Sarah was shifted from so many homes as she grew up, and she never knew what it was to have a real home of her own.

When Sarah came home from her jobs with Betty Jean, since they worked together now, she hated to face another lonely night in this house without Roscoe, sometimes she never lit the lamp in her bedroom, just burned a small light in the kitchen. Sarah knew she shouldn't lay in the dark thinking about Roscoe, because it only gave her grief, and the tears were always heavy on her face.

Blue would come over sometimes in the evening to try and cheer Sarah with his making all kinds of jokes with her, and would encourage her to sing with him, he only wanted to sing his low down blues songs, he was forever singing, and he still did his little tunes on his harmonica. Sarah never thought of Vera getting jealous, but she started following Blue when he went to see Sarah. Sarah didn't seem to mind and Blue didn't seem to care about Vera following him, but Blue came over anyway and he never paid any attention to Vera and her pouting, he just kept trying to make Sarah happy.

Sophie and Sarah continued to hold the meetings, although the crowd was thinned out without Roscoe. The Douglass still came and Sarah noticed Steven getting a little restless. The biggest shock came when Steven jumped up like lighting had struck him, and did he ever preach. Steven must have memorized the same style as Rev. Bennett, even the wording he used when preaching, because he had the same mannerisms as Rev. Bennett, and he even quoted the same verses he would use in his text.

Estella was sitting glued to her seat; this was one big shock to her, she never knew her husband had this type of memory, she knew he wasn't a literate person, and could only write his name poorly. Sarah could not believe her ears, to see Steven in her husband's pulpit preaching the same way he did was mind-blowing to her, and Sophie almost fainted right in the church.

When Steven stepped down from the pulpit, he was all smiles to see the shocked faces, but he knew he wasn't far from stirring the people as Roscoe Bennett had done. This was something important Steven had done, and the people looked at him with a new respect. Estella was jubilant as she ran to hug Steven, even though he had to struggle to breathe after she got a hold of him, but she let him know how proud she was of him.

After Steven's little showing he did in the church with his memorized sermon, the people had a little more respect for him, and Estella seemed to let Steven "wear the pants" now, and she was less critical of him since he was getting some praise from the residents in the valley. When Estella told the Ovingtons of her husband's ability to preach a sermon, only Thomas looked at Steven and smiled.

Thomas was trying to find a teacher to teach in the valley. He was completely worn out from the pace he was trying to keep. Thomas was sitting in his chair, almost out of it from the worry and hard work, when Vera came to the school, in hysterics and saying words that Thomas could not understand right away. Vera kept repeating "my husband, please come quick," Thomas was stiff and unable to move right away, and Vera had run some distance ahead of him to her house, Thomas didn't know what to expect, but he had a feeling this wasn't anything good he was about to face.

Blue was stretched out on the bed, sick as he could be, his long lean body looked rigorous as he stared at the ceiling. Thomas almost had a fainting spell himself, he never liked this man, but to see him in this condition, made him feel only sorrow for him. Thomas tried to calm Vera, he sent for the Newmans, but only Betty Jean came along with the hysterical Sarah. Dr. Newman was too feeble to make the trip to the valley, and Sarah wasn't much help to Betty Jean.

Betty Jean tried to save Blue, but she felt like his heart had given out on him. Vera kept running to the bed trying to speak to her husband, and hoping he would answer her, but Blue never spoke another word, and probably never heard anything his wife said to him.

The Johnson children, along with the Williams clan came to be with Vera. Betty Jean had worked hard doing all she could for Blue all during the night, but before day break, Daniel "Blue" Johnson was gone. No one could comfort or calm Vera down. She wailed for hours, her eyes were swollen and red, she wouldn't let the children touched her, and she would only cry out Blue's name.

Sarah tried to put her arms around Vera, she was wailing herself, and Vera sort of pushed her aside. This really hurt Sarah, because she thought she could comfort Vera since she had been through the same thing herself only weeks before, and she could understand the hurt she was going through.

The valley was really shaken with the loss of two of their residents so close together. The two men were really outsiders, who came to this valley and became a part of the people that lived in this valley for generations. Although Blue was one of the most hellish men in this valley when he first came to Ovington, but in later years, he had earned the highest respect in this community, and they had to admit, he was very talented and always did a good job when he was hired to do anything pertaining to working with mortar.

Beth was the most distressed person among the residents of Ovington. It was a great loss to her when Blue passed; she loved Blue, and hired him when Thomas didn't want him to set foot on his land. Beth always sent for Blue when she needed anything done to upgrade her rock garden. Beth admired the hard work Blue had did when he built her garden years ago.

Thomas went to see Vera everyday for awhile to help her settle herself after Blue died. Vera was moved by the benevolence of everyone to her and her family. Vera knew Blue had his faults, but she knew she would never have found a better husband and father to their children than Blue anywhere in this valley.

Sarah was hurt over the death of Blue, and she felt sorry for Vera, and she wanted to comfort her, but Vera acted sort of hostile toward Sarah, she seemed like she wanted nothing to do with her. This act of hostility from Vera hurt Sarah, and she knew it was only a matter of time before Vera would ask her to move from her home.

The valley was quiet these days with two of its residents buried within weeks of each other, and there was still a look of sadness on the faces of the people in this valley. The valley didn't seem the same, they missed Roscoe and Blue so much.

Thomas hated to come to the place he loved so much, this valley was his heart, but he was so worn out, and he still tried to find someone to teach the children, plus the steep hill that he was so used to walking, was getting the best of him. Thomas had the worry of Vera and Sarah on his mind, he had a feeling that Vera was going to kick Sarah out of her home, he could see the way Vera acted toward Sarah.

The moonshiners were worried, too. They were running scared because Chad Chambers was doing his job well, Thomas was afraid he was getting to be too hard on these men in the valley. They weren't criminals, they only wanted to make a few dollars selling the bootleg moonshine they were used to making, and they always had the liquor when there was any type of celebration in the valley.

When Chad Chambers made his campaign pledge, he swore to the people he would clean up the bootleg moonshine in the valley. The residents of Ovington wanted to get rid of the bootlegging ever since William Harrison was the Constable of Ovington, but no one was successful, because they were afraid to go in the dangerous parts of this mountain after the men who had the stills.

Chad would pass the school when Thomas was trying to teach the children; he always stopped to chat when he found Thomas available to talk to him. He never stopped his grinning, but he looked like he would turn that grin to something less friendly if he was given a reason, like finding someone breaking the law.

Not all of the stills that Chad Chambers found hidden in the tough and dangerous parts of this mountain belonged to the men in the valley, but Chad would walk the path leading to the site of these stills, and bring in men to destroy them. Chad never arrested anyone in connection with these stills, because no one was around when he would find them.

The servants' quarters were empty that Kenny and Cassandra lived in, and Thomas had not let anyone else move into this house that was sort of special. Thomas was so disappointed in Kenny being so negative toward his wife's feelings, when he made her move back to the valley before they moved from Ovington, Thomas felt that Kenny was unreasonable to do this to Cassandra, but he knew not to say anything to him, he was known to have a big mouth, and Thomas didn't want to deal with Kenny and his smart mouth.

Thomas really missed the Williams, especially Cassandra, how Kenny thought that they didn't belong in this house was only his excuse to move back to the valley. The furniture was still in place, and shined to perfection since Estella always took great pride in this place, which was much nicer than her own house that Thomas allowed the Douglass to occupy, and she was tempted many times to ask him if they could move into this nicer servant's quarters.

Thomas was thinking of Sarah and her future in this community, she was so alone, and still living in the Johnson's house, and he felt like she should move before Vera made her move from her house.

Vera had mentioned to Thomas that she wanted one of her children to move in her old house, because she was lonely. Vera felt that her children close to her would be a comfort to her. Thomas listened to her repeating this same thing over and over, and he took this to be a hint for him to find Sarah another home to live in.

Although Thomas felt guilty about asking Sarah to move from the servant's quarters that she had lived in when Thaddeus died, he had never asked her to move back to the estate, when she was married to Roscoe, even when the Williams moved out of the house. For some reason, Thomas only let his special people live in this house he fixed up for Thaddeus and Sarah when they were first married, and Thomas didn't understand himself, asking Sarah to move out, when she had no place to go, but he thought of Thaddeus as a son, he felt just that close to him.

The school was about out, and Thomas was elated that all of the children had done real good in their classes. He hadn't been able to teach them to do school plays, and take the time with them that Cassandra did, but he was so worn out from all of the things he had to do, he was happy, that he was able to finish teaching the whole school year.

For the first time in his life, Thomas was completely exhausted, and worried that he would not be able to make the steep hill home some days, but he was hoping Beth would not notice how exhausted he was when he came home.

Ovington was showing prosperity as a few of the residents began to open small businesses, and community activity was established. This was a beautiful town, everyone cooperated to beautify the surrounding grounds, the mountain view was breathtaking, and Thomas Ovington beamed with pride to see the change in this town.

The Bollings were all jubilant when Roderich decided to open his business that he had been thinking so strongly about opening in Ovington. Roderich wanted to open a modern type of retail store that would sell food items, this type of business would be better than the old country store that you had to weigh and measure everything you brought. This was a big event for the Bollings when this became a reality, and the big and beautiful store was opened in Ovington.

Thomas never opened a business in Ovington, he was more of an investing type of businessman; he had learned most of his knowledge from James Cannon. He never stopped learning all he could from other sources, including the Bradleys, although he didn't trust everything they said, he did take their advice sometimes, and he was able to make money from some of these investments they advised him to take a chance that they would make money one day.

Thomas was always afraid of a cat fight between Sarah and Vera. The two were hardly speaking, and Thomas had no idea that Vera had so much hell in her. Vera would speak harshly about Sarah every time she saw Thomas, and always wanted her to move, and Sarah had to move to Suzette Adams' house to get away from Vera. Thomas understood that Vera was lonely for Blue and missed him, but he never thought she would be so cruel to anyone, especially to Sarah.

Sarah wasn't too happy to move by herself to Suzette Adams' house, but she decided to make the best of her life, and staying away from Vera, was one of them, she seemed to take all of her trouble out on Sarah.

The Adams children welcomed Sarah to use the house as long as she wanted to stay there, since the Adams had passed on, the house had stood empty and was run down, and in dire need of repair, but it was a roof over her head, and Sarah decided to live in the house temporarily.

Betty Jean was always trying to persuade Sarah to stay with her, but Sarah knew this was a bad idea, because she knew there would be no rest living with Betty Jean. However, she did spend the night sometimes when she was too tired to go home in the valley.

The men were tearing down the old shacks in the valley that had been abandoned or left standing as Suzette's house was. These houses were an eyesore, and the relatives never did anything to improve them, or tear them down when the parents, or relatives were deceased. Thomas knew Sarah was staying in Suzette's old house; the guilt was eating inside of him, he was worried about Sarah, especially when he knew she was in the old Adams house.

Between Thomas and Chad Chambers, the valley was becoming a rather clean place to be. Chad had cleaned out the stills, and Thomas had the old houses torn down. The residents of this valley were inspired by Blue to upgrade their home site; the few residents to stay on in the valley were proud of their heritage, although they were a mixed race of people, they tried to hold on to the life they were used to living in this small community. The valley was isolated and inconvenient to most of the residents, especially those responsible for making the living, they wanted to remain in the valley, and had no desire to live no other place on this mountain.

Steven continued to get out of hand with his inability to keep up with the duties he was assigned to do on the Ovington's estate. Of course, he always took his anger out on Estella, being a loving wife, she tried to keep him calm and assured him he was doing his best. The Ovington's had no complaints about Steven, he was well liked in this community, and Estella told him to be thankful for the job and a place to stay.

Jane Elizabeth didn't have much time for Beth Marie since she was helping Roderich so much in the store. Beth still went to the Bollings as often as she was able to make it; she did the shopping herself, she always let other household members do the shopping, but she preferred to shop herself since Roderich opened this modern store, she was excited that Ovington had such a store in this town. For the first time in Beth's life, she wanted to own some kind of business on her own. Business was something she always let her father and Thomas worry about, she felt like she was to old open a business herself, but she did desire to do something she liked.

After World War II ended, Ovington became a bigger community with new residents that moved to this town, and the expansion of homes on down the mountain, Most of these families had children, so the school in Ovington had to be upgraded, built bigger, and sports were a part of the school's program.

After all of the hell Vera raised trying to get Sarah to move out of her house, the house remained empty. Vera begged the children to move home; all refused, because of their wives, who had no desire to move close to their mother-in-law, though they had no bad feeling toward Vera, they preferred to stay in their home that they occupied.

The old Adams' house would be too cold during the winter, and Sarah knew she would not be able to stay there during the winter months. Sarah would go the church to pray; she felt close to Roscoe during these times, and it was a comfort to her to sit quietly alone in the church Roscoe loved, and to know the residents still loved the church he built and pastored. The church was always cleaned and kept in the good condition it was when Roscoe was alive.

Sarah was leaving the church, feeling the loss of Roscoe Bennett.

Vera had seen Sarah enter the church, and was waiting for Sarah to come out. Sarah was surprised to see Vera, of all people, but she spoke kindly to Vera. Vera was looking sort of sad, but she wanted to apologize to Sarah for the way she had treated her these past few months. Vera told Sarah she knew her feeling of the loss of a loved one, because she wasn't able to get over the loss of Blue, and this was a very painful time for her too. Sarah was numb for a few minutes, but she put her arms around Vera, and they each forgot their bad feelings toward each other, and became friends again.

31

Like a bolt out of the blue, Thomas was speechless as Beth stood in front of him to tell him she would like to open a business in Ovington of her own. Beth was getting up in age, and opening a business would be too strenuous on Beth's frail body. Thomas listened patiently to Beth as she excitedly told him of her desire to have a little boutique shop like the one Vickie Lynn owned in Lawsonville.

Vickie Lynn's boutique really was a business that belonged to Thomas before Ledia Summer sold out to Vickie Lynn. This was a blow to Thomas when Beth told him of her love of the boutique in Lawsonville, and he felt a little guilty, that he had opened the business for Ledia to help her out as a friend, and to give her a better start in life than the street woman she was before she became his friend. Thomas was proud of Ledia during those years, and had paid a lot of money to open the business, but Ledia did all of the hard work to make the business a big success, and she was able to sell the business for a big profit.

Thomas wasn't eager to open another boutique. Most of the people in Ovington were down to earth people. There were a few of the women that shopped for better clothes off the mountain, but he didn't see any big profit in opening a fancy boutique in this community. Thomas didn't know how to tell his wife, he didn't think a dress shop for women only, was a good business to have in Ovington.

The Newmans made Sarah move to their house when the weather became too cold for her to stay in the Adams' house. Sarah didn't want to move in with Betty Jean, but she had no choice. Sarah would not have survived the winter where she was.

Every time Thomas saw Sarah, he had a guilty feeling. He wanted to amend the hurt he had caused her, when he had asked her to move out of the only real home she ever had. Before Thomas had a chance to tell Beth she should forget the boutique business in Ovington, Beth and the Bollings came to Thomas all smiling and talking excitedly at once. They told him they had decided to open the Women's Apparel Shop, the name the store would be called, and Jane Elizabeth would be the manager. Beth would sort of be a silent partner. Jane would hire some of her friends in Ovington to help her in the shop, and Beth would not have to work or worry about operating this business.

Thomas slapped his head in despair, this was one wild scheme these three had thought up, and he didn't go along with them. Beth had made up her mind, this was what she wanted to do, and of course, money was no problem. The same way Beth wanted Jeffrey Carter to have the farm, she also had Roderich to make the necessary arrangements to open Ovingtons only Women's Apparel Shop.

Sarah was making herself content living at the Newmans, Betty Jean stayed with Dr. Newman most of the time, because she knew she wasn't going to have her husband very long. Sophie would visit Sarah and always wanted to talk to Betty Jean so that she could say something to get her all riled up. She would say something to make her angry and then Betty Jean would cut loose with some of her nasty words she often used. Sophie always got a good laugh when she visited the Newmans and Sarah.

Roderich wasted no time making the necessary arrangements to build the building for the Women's Apparel Shop. It would be the size of a three room house, and designed like a cottage with picture glass windows on the front. Beth and Jane were excited as the building was being built. The two ladies worried the carpenters each day, you would have thought they were the builders.

The Ovington's house was run by Estella while Beth was involved with the building of her little shop. She depended on someone each day to take her to the site of her shop. Thomas walked in a different direction while the shop was being built, he wasn't happy with Beth getting involved in a business, he wanted her to stay home more, and he didn't believe this business was a good one for Ovington.

Sometimes Thomas would pass the empty servant quarters. Estella kept the small house spotless, but the house looked so lonely. This was the time that Thomas would think of Thaddeus. He had loved the Williams so much when he was growing up, and he would never forget

Mattie. He had looked after Thaddeus since he was in his early teens, and he missed Thaddeus.

When the shop was completed, and Jane made the trips to New York and several other places to shop for this store, she wanted to make sure she would have a huge selection for the ladies to choose from. The opening day was jubilant to Beth and the Bollings, and they had a big celebration at the shop.

This new shop was suppose to be a Women's Apparel Shop, but you could buy some of everything else, including a huge stocks of picture frames, every size and color, but it was one of the finest shops for miles around, and they had customers to come from other towns to shop in Ovington. The shop was the talk of the town, and Thomas had to admit this shop was better stocked, and seemed to be a thriving business from the first opening day.

Thomas was walking near the Newmans on his way to see how Dr. Newman was doing these days. Sarah was on her way home and ran into Thomas. He looked at her, and felt so guilty and sorry for her. Thomas wasn't able to speak clearly as he asked Sarah if she would like to move back to the estate. Sarah looked at Thomas for a moment, seeing the hurt in his eyes, Sarah ran to Thomas, and put her arms around his waist, as sobs shook her body.

Thomas was emotional himself as he hugged Sarah close to him. He kissed her smooth brown cheeks as he told her the worst thing he had ever done was to make her move from the house she shared with Thaddeus. Thomas also assured Sarah he loved her too, he loved Thaddeus, and he was like family to him, and she was his wife, and he wanted to take care of her as long as he lived.

Thomas and Sarah stood together very emotional and trembling as they held each other tightly; this moment he only felt love for Sarah. Thomas remembered the time Sarah was born, how he went out into the blackness of the night, very frightened, to get Suzette Adams, but he was too late to save Sarah's mother, but he was the one to help pull Sarah to safety into this world from her mother's dying body.

After the emotional Thomas and Sarah calmed down, Sarah looked around to see if Betty Jean was in sight, she knew she would have one of the worse cussing fit seeing her and Thomas together this way. Sarah felt like this was private between her and Thomas, and she didn't want anyone to spoil this moment for her.

Thomas took Sarah to the house to talk to Beth. When the household staff saw Thomas holding Sarah's hand and tears in her eyes, they were bewildered, unable to understand what was causing this emotional dolor. The household staff stood frozen, but they followed Thomas when he took Sarah to see Beth Marie.

Before Beth had a chance to say anything, Thomas told her he was moving Sarah back to her home in the servant's quarters she moved out of after Thaddeus died. Of Course, Beth was elated, but surprised at this moment. Beth knew she would be much happier with Sarah living in the servant's quarters than she was with Cassandra living there. Beth welcomed Sarah home, and she put her arms around her and hugged the tearful Sarah as Sophie looked on with a smiling face.

Everyone gathered around Sarah, joyful that she would be moving to the estate, just like old times. Estella was a little disappointed, because she wanted to move into the nicer servant's quarters, she didn't understand the reason for one being nicer than the other one. Estella would spend time there sometimes and wish this house belonged to her. No one knew Estella's disappointment, not even Steven, because this was her own private wish to change her housing, but she decided to be thankful for the roof she had over her head.

Everyone recovered from the shock of learning Sarah was moving home, and no one except Sophie was more excited about this than Thomas, who felt relieved now that he knew Sarah would move back to her own home, and would not have to depend on others for a place to stay.

The Women's Apparel Shop was a huge success, and Jane was very busy. She talked so much with her sales pitch, she was too tired to do much talking when she returned home.

The daily trips Beth made to the shop kept her busy, although she did very little beside get in the way, but the shop kept Beth from thinking about herself and her loneliness at times. Beth knew Thomas wasn't one to sit very long, but she wished her husband would stay at home more so they would have a chance to be together more.

The worst thing Sarah ever said to Betty Jean was that she was moving back to the Ovington's estate. Betty Jean told Sarah she was surely crazy for even thinking such a thing, not to mention really moving back to the Ovingtons after the way Thomas threw her out of her home.

Sarah sat down and cried tears of despair, but Betty Jean kept on with her words of ridiculousness against Thomas Ovington, and only let up when Dr. Newman got up to see what was causing his wife to be so upset. When Betty explained to Dr. Newman why she was acting so boisterous with Sarah, he didn't take sides with Betty Jean. He thought it was a good idea, and forbade Betty Jean from saying anymore on the subject.

The next time Thomas went to Lawsonville, he visited the Carters as usual, but this time he had news for them. He wanted them to know about Beth Marie being partner with Jane Elizabeth, and the little boutique they open up in Ovington. Jeffrey was really surprised to know that Beth opened a business of her own, since she had inherited many business investments from her father. The Carters thought this was a good business to start, since women loved to shop for the latest fashions, and they promised to visit Ovington to browse around and shop in Beth's new shop.

Betty Jean tried to make up to Sarah for the way she upset her, telling Sarah she didn't want her to be hurt again by Thomas Ovington. Sarah knew Betty Jean was thinking of the hurt she suffered the time Thomas moved her from her home after Thaddeus died, but Sarah believed Thomas was sincere, and wanted to make amends for the way he had hurt her. Sarah didn't want Betty Jean to be angry with her, because she did give her a better chance in life when she trained her to be a nurse, and this was more rewarding to her than just trying to take care of a house, and it did give her a chance to meet some of the people she never knew in Ovington.

Estella spent the afternoon in the little house Sarah was to occupy, she wanted to have one last time in this house she admired so much. When Steven came looking for Estella, and asked her why she stayed so long in this house, Estella told him of her desire to live here. Of course, Steven was annoyed with Estella, and shouted, "Come on out of this house foolish woman." Estella knew Steven would never understand her desire to have a home of her own, and she would go into this house, and pretend it was her own.

Everyone assumed that Sarah was going to work for the Ovingtons in their home again, and so did Beth Marie, when they asked Thomas about Sarah, and if she was going to be doing her same duties she did in this house before she left the estate. Thomas looked surprised, and he said Sarah was a nurse and she would still be nursing. The shocked household staff was disappointed, because they were planning on Sarah being with them in the Ovington's house again.

Beth Marie had no idea what her husband was up to now. She was glad Sarah was going to be a part of the Ovington's staff again, but Thomas plainly stated, "Sarah is still a nurse." It made no difference to Beth if Sarah moved to the estate, she felt like Sarah was family, she was born on this estate, and Thomas should have let her stay here and Anna take care of her. Sarah, beside little Judith Bolling, were the only babies born at this estate.

Beth knew Anna would have been happy in Ovington if Thomas had let her keep Sarah as her own, and raise her, since she never had any children, and she wanted Sarah so bad. Beth felt like Anna's problem was having no family, and she knew that she was too old to have a baby herself. Anna just gave up after Thomas took Sarah away from her, and she began to hate him more as the years went on, and this mountain was lonely for her, she even paid no attention to Fred in later years.

Beth had Steven to take her to the Newman's house to get Sarah. Beth knew Betty Jean and how she would make a person feel so unhappy, and she suspected Betty Jean would try to keep Sarah from coming home to the estate. When Dr. Newman opened the door, he was elated to see Beth, but was alarmed, afraid something had happened to Thomas.

The Newmans had no idea Beth Marie would be the one to come to move Sarah to her old home on the Ovington's estate. Sarah was as surprised as the Newmans to see Beth. Sarah rushed to get her few belongings and was almost out of breath as she quickly gathered her clothes. For once, Betty Jean was at a loss for words; she would rather Sarah move anywhere on this mountain but to the Ovington's estate.

The Women's Apparel Shop was a thriving business, the shop was making a profit, but Beth took time out from running there every day to stay at home for awhile. Sophie and Estella were doing a good job helping Beth, but she needed to make sure everything was up to par, in case she decided to have another elegant dinner party. Beth thought it would be a good idea to have a big party for some of their best customers.

Sarah was still doing nursing jobs with Betty Jean, and they never mentioned anything about her living at the Ovingtons. The Ovington's household staff would see Sarah leave for work in her starched white dress, and they seemed a little envious of Sarah. She was living on the estate, but was allowed to work elsewhere.

Sophie would come to see Sarah in the evening and it seemed like old times as they would talk about the times with the meetings, the songs they sang, and how Roscoe Bennett would preach to the people. Sometimes sadness would be too much for them, and they would shed a few tears, but most of the time they tried to talk about happy events to keep from being sad.

Estella was a little shy around Sarah at first, but she soon found out she was a beautiful person to be around, and she became as close to Sarah as Sophie. Steven would see Sarah in her starched white dress, her voluptuous body walking proudly around the estate, and this would cause him to compare his wife with Sarah, but he knew better than to say anything to Sarah, knowing what Estella was capable of doing to him, and he knew that she was a little jealous of him, and he wasn't about to make her angry by looking at Sarah too long.

32

The school year was about to began, and there was no teacher to teach the children in the valley. Thomas was so busy, and still did a moderate amount of traveling with his businesses, he had no time left for the strenuous job of trying to go to the valley each morning to teach the children.

The laws had changed, and unless you had a teaching degree to teach, no one was capable of teaching with no degree. This valley had no one with such a degree. None of the residents of Ovington wanted the job, Thomas didn't even have a teaching degree, but he did do a good job teaching the children, even with all of the other things he had to do.

The residents in the valley were worried, because they would have to send their children off the mountain to attend school. There were no mixed school, and it was a great distance to a Black school.

Some families with children moved from the valley, but the few that could afford to have their children boarded out during the school year would do so, and they would bring them home on the weekends and the holidays. Of course, there were a few children that didn't get to school, and this caused great problems. Thomas was trying to help the residents do all he could to have a school teacher in the valley. He was as devastated as the residents to see the children having to go through so much to get an education.

There wasn't much for Chad Chambers to do since he had cleaned out the stills in the valley. He would still go out in the dense wooded areas to see if there were any new stills. The men in the valley hated this man, he never failed to greet them with his grin he kept on his face. Chad was forever sneaking around the houses in the valley.

The church was sitting idle, and so was the school, there were few residents left. Vera was living in a nice modern house, with the old house empty, but she stayed home and spent half of her time on the front porch trying to see some of the neighbors, but few of her family came to see her. When she would see Sarah in the valley, she always called to her, and would talk to Sarah for a short time. Sarah would always come to the church to sit alone for awhile, and Vera would see her and wait until she came out to greet her, and asked her how she was doing.

Jane Elizabeth was busy with the shop. She helped her husband in the business he was operating, and she still had to take care of five children. Jane had little time to go to the estate everyday to pick up Beth, and sometimes she had to stay home if Thomas was too busy to bring her the short distance to the shop.

The Carters made the trip to Ovington to visit and shop in the Women's Apparel Shop. Beth was ecstatic to see Jeffrey Carter and his family. This was a big surprise to her, but she loved them so much. Beth insisted they stay at the estate. The Carters didn't bring their children, but they brought the grandchildren. This was a treat for Beth to be able to see the grandchildren of the Carters, and spend some time with them.

Thomas was elated by the Carter's visit to the estate. When Thomas saw how happy his wife was with the Carters, he was glad he had invited the family to visit, and to make Beth happy by shopping in the shop she loved.

The household staff had to work overtime to keep up with Beth's demands, She treated the Carters like royalty, and there was nothing left undone, as far as doing their best for the Carters. Beth wore herself out trying to make sure the family was comfortable. When Beth took the Carters to the shop, Jane gave them a good dose of her sales talk, plus she talked them to death trying to find out all she could about this family her aunt Beth loved so much.

The Carters stayed a week in Ovington, and Jeffrey hated to leave Beth, she was so lovely to him and his family. Of course, the Carters spent a lot of money shopping, there were many things they could use beside the dresses that could be found in Beth and Jane Women's Apparel Shop.

The Bollings children were smart. They participated in sports, and Kathryn must have been born with a tennis racket in her hands, because she was one champion tennis player, and the best in Ovington. Roderich, Jr. was just like his father, he went to law school, and fun loving James liked to play around a lot, but he was a rather level-headed businessman. Beth thought the world of the Bolling children, and referred to them as her grandchildren.

There was no better place to live anywhere in the eastern Tennessee state than in the town of Ovington. Thomas was proud of his town, and the people that lived in this community. There was always talk for miles around about Ovington, and the man Thomas Ovington. There were few people living that knew the name Willie Monroe Ovington, and if they were, they never mentioned the name. Willie Monroe had disgraced the name Ovington, but Thomas had changed the bad image his father left in this town. Thomas' success was the result of meeting James Cannon, the kindness he showed him when he was alone and desolate when he left the mountain, and ended up in Lawsonville.

The friendship Thomas had with the Cannons changed his whole life. Marrying Beth Marie Cannon was the best thing he ever did. He loved the frail and unpopular woman; Thomas and Beth seemed to share the same loneliness, and they both had no other close family members, but they always had each other. Of course, having full control over the Cannon's wealth, enabled Thomas to build a town from the poorest resident who survived the harsh winters on practical nothing to wealth and prosperity among some of the residents in this town many years later.

Thomas would think about the Williams family sometimes. He loved Mattie Williams so much, and he was so hurt the day that she died in his arms. The robust woman had been a comfort to Thomas when he was trying to survive the years when he was growing up and trying to live with parents that had lost love for each other, but Mattie was there when he needed someone to lean on. The jug she always gave him, her "medicine" as she called the jug of moonshine, must have been good for him because he never suffered any sickness in his whole life.

Thomas was determined to do something about the children's schooling in the valley. He almost went crazy trying to have money appropriated for a school to benefit the children in the valley. The school would be built near Ovington and the small counties near Ovington for these children that lived in these small counties. There were to be two schools built, one a grammar school, and the other a high school. The problems of getting these children to school would come later. He was trying to assure the families, schools would be built for their children.

Ovington was a small town, but considered to be one of the best places to live, there were some ignoble people still livong in the community, but not enough for Chad Chambers to worry about. You didn't have to go out of Ovington to shop anymore, there were enough business places to get your money, if you needed something. Farming was still a priority in some small areas, and was a way of life for a few of the residents.

Sarah became well known and popular in Ovington, as well as in the valley. She had a good reputation as a nurse. She was devoted to her patients, was always on the job, and stayed the limited time caring for the sick. Sarah even sang and prayed with her patients that requested this part of her treatment.

Betty Jean and Sarah became real close, and Betty depended on Sarah, especially, when Dr. Newman became totally disabled. If not for Sarah, Betty Jean would have to employ professional help to help care for her husband. Dr. Newman told Sarah he doubted his wife when she wanted to train her, but she was the best nurse he had ever seen, Dr. Newman added with a wink and a smile, "beside my wife, she was the best."

Beth lived longer than Dr. Newman thought she would when he first came to Ovington. Dr. Newman wondered what would happen to Beth if he died. His years he had lived in Ovington was devoted to caring for Beth Marie. It seemed like Dr. Newman would pass on before Beth.

The love Beth shared with Thomas kept her fighting many illnesses to stay with him, she wanted to spend as much time as possible with the man she gave her whole life to. Thomas Ovington was a lean man, but a strong one, he never suffered from illness as most of the residents in Ovington. His lean body remained straight, his walk still whisked as he walked some parts of this community each day. Most of the residents were used to seeing Thomas, whether they spoke to him or not. His presence around Ovington seemed to make the residents proud that they were a part of this community he lived in and bore his name, Ovington.

The Ovington community had many good years. The town had not suffered too many devastating times in the years that Thomas Ovington moved back home. The Ovingtons themselves lived good. They were always respected, and were the pride of this community, but the time was running out for them. They were getting up in years, and knew they would be put to rest very soon.

The Cannon's wealth was helpful in building up this town, and Thomas was thankful he never lost the money he was trusted to oversee. James Cannon depended on Thomas to take care of his daughter, and he tried to do what his friend, the best friend he ever had, asked him to do. He did his best to care for Beth, and he loved her with all of his heart.

Sarah's moving back to the estate was the best thing she could have done to help her and to benefit the Ovingtons, because they needed her as a nurse, because Beth was showing signs of illness, and Thomas trusted Sarah to comfort his wife, and depended on her. Beth had not been able to leave this estate these past few months and Thomas was feeling real nervous, believing she was in real trouble with her health.

Jane hired full-time help to work the shop, which was still a thriving business, and required long hours of hard work. Sometimes the Bolling girls would work the shop to give their mother a rest. Beth had given her part of the shop to Jane sometime ago, when she became unable to go to the shop. Beth wanted Jane to keep the shop open, this was the only business she had that was of interest to her.

The Bolling girls married close together. They married nice men who were in business, and two of them moved to other cities. This left more time for Jane to be with Beth. Jane tried to do things that would make Beth happy, she even kept up with the most popular plays in New York theater, and even read the reviews to Beth as soon as they became available.

The long fight for the children in the valley to have decent schools for them became a reality. The day the new shiny school bus came to Ovington to pick up the children was a proud day for Thomas. He shed tears of happiness as he waved to them as the parents put their children on the bus.

33

The Ovingtons enjoyed many good years together. To most who knew them, they were surprised to see Beth Marie live to be in her 80s. Beth had always been frail. Her petite body was stronger than you would think; she seemed to have no fat on her thin frame. Beth's love for Thomas and her desire to be with him brought her through many trying times health-wise, and she endured many pains and suffered many illnesses to stay with him.

During the last days of Beth's long illness, she would have her husband to take her to her piano. She weighed so little that Thomas had no trouble carrying her in his arms. Beth was too weak to play the piano, but she would ask Sarah to play some of her favorite music, which she had taught her to play. Sarah would play as best as she remembered, but wasn't very good with the classical music Beth taught her to play that Beth loved so much. Thomas wasn't into any classical music at all, but for Beth Marie, he would listen to the music faithfully.

Dr. Newman had long passed on, and there was another doctor that had set up practice in Ovington. Beth never sent for this doctor because she was comfortable with Betty Jean and Sarah waiting on her. The Bollings were at the estate almost every day, at least one of the other would be there to help out any way they could. Thomas knew very little about the new doctor; but he wanted to have him look at Beth and see if he could help her, but Beth refused. She wanted to be left in peace. She didn't know this doctor, and felt like Betty Jean was as good as any doctor, since she was always at her husband's side the long years he practiced medicine.

Beth, weak and trembling, asked to sit in her rock garden, which was her favorite place to be and relax when she felt strong enough to sit up for a long period of time. Beth would think of Blue, as she enjoyed her favorite place around this estate.

James Cannon was on Beth's mind, since she would think of her parents almost every day in her pain and suffering. James Cannon was her heart; Beth had not married or had a serious relationship with a man until he passed on. Beth was always with her father, regardless where he went. Beth had plenty of time to think these days, and she only thought of her family and the good years she enjoyed in New York.

Fred and Anna had long been gone, but Beth would wonder if she had done the right thing letting Thomas take them back to the farm in Lawsonville to die alone, when she was all they had to depend on. Anna was so unhappy when Beth moved her to Ovington, she had cared for Beth for many years, it was Anna who tried to keep her happy when her parents were away, or most of the time. Mrs. Cannon didn't have the patience to cope with her spoiled and pampered child, and she left Anna to do the best she could to keep Beth happy.

Jane Elizabeth did her best to make Beth comfortable, no one believed Beth and Jane were only cousins, they were so close, and seemed like mother and daughter. Jane did miss her mother, Judith. Jane wasn't one to sit for very long, but she was always there when Beth needed her.

The Carters heard the news of Beth's illness and they came to Ovington to stay a few days with Beth. This was a pleasure for Beth to have Jeffrey Carter and his wife stay at the estate, and as usual, waiting on her and making her feel so special to them.

During the last days of Beth Marie's life, Thomas never left her side, neither did Jane or Sarah. Beth wanted for nothing; someone would be there to attend to whatever she needed to make her comfortable. Although Thomas tried to act relaxed and cheerful around Beth, he was grieving so much inside to know he was losing her.

Beth wanted to hold Thomas' hands, she told him she knew she was dying and hated to leave him. Beth knew she wasn't able to hold on much longer; Thomas began to cry openly, and begged Beth not to leave him. He became so emotional he had to leave the room, he didn't want to upset his wife, but he was so overcome with grief he wasn't able to control himself.

Betty Jean and Sarah were beside Beth's bed; she asked for Jane, but Jane was to emotional, and she had left the room with Thomas. Beth asked Sarah to take care of Thomas, if possible to move back inside the house. Beth wanted Sarah to see that Thomas would eat regularly, and to see that his clothes were kept up to par for him. Although Estella and Sophie were still living at the estate, she trusted no one but Sarah to take care of her husband after her death.

The day Beth Marie closed her eyes forever, she just went to sleep and was gone, although Thomas had left the room, he came back to Beth's bed when Betty Jean came for him. Thomas held his wife's lifeless body in his arms. The tears were heavy on his face, as all of the other household staff. Betty Jean was the only one to have dry eyes, but she was very upset.

They all tried to comfort Thomas, but he shooed them away from him as he walked to Beth's rocked garden. Sitting among the beauty of this garden, he felt relieved and close to his loving wife. He knew the many people that came to the estate were preparing his wife for her burial, and his body shook with sobs.

Looking over the estate, Thomas continued to sit in the garden, he wanted his beloved Beth to be buried close by, so that he could visit his wife's grave. Thomas had buried his parents on the other side of Ovington, but he wanted Beth Marie to be buried close by the estate. Thomas sent for some of the men in the valley to help him prepare a place on the estate to bury his wife.

The few days between the time it took Thomas to find a special place to bury his wife, and have the men from the valley clear off this Land, he grieved hard for his wife. Thomas found a large tree, and a few small trees further up the mountain, surrounding this area, and he thought this was a beautiful place to lay his Beth to rest. The burial plot was facing the beautiful home Thomas built for his wife years ago, and this was the place he wanted Beth to be buried. Although it would be a steep hill to have to walk and carry Beth, this is what Thomas wanted for his wife and himself one day.

Thomas had Beth's body brought back home to the estate until she was taken up the mountain to the site where she was laid to rest. There were few people at the gravesite, because it was painful seeing Thomas so hurt and grieving for Beth Marie so much. Sarah was beside Thomas side during the whole funeral and burial of his loving wife. Betty Jean and Sophie walked slowly behind the Bollings and the other household staff, and the few people that came to be with Thomas Ovington; he had no other relatives. There were a few people from the valley that came to watch from a distance.

The next few weeks were a sad time in Ovington, because the residents were disturbed to see Thomas so lonely looking and seemly unaware of the things he was used to doing. Thomas walked very little and he stayed in the Ovington house most of the day, something he wasn't accustomed to doing when Beth was alive.

Sarah did move back inside the Ovington house as Beth had asked her to do before she passed. This wasn't something she wanted to do, but felt like she should since she promised Beth on her last hours of her life. Sarah was used to moving from house to house, and she always had a grieving feeling when she had to leave a home where she was living.

The Ovington house was run just as smoothly as when Beth Marie was alive. Estella was still particular with the cooking and the housekeeping and all of the things Beth had taught her to do for the up keeping of this house. Although Thomas hardly touched the special meals Estella prepared for him, she still took the time to do little special dishes.

Steven was still doing his job, but he was getting burned out with the polishing a car that didn't half run, and carriages that had rusted from years of weathering the harsh winters in this mountain. The fine horses the Ovingtons owned for years had died, and Thomas refused to replace them, since this town had more than enough transportation, and there were few people that kept horses to ride anymore.

The first house and doctor's office Thomas had built for the Newman's when they first moved to Ovington, was still standing in front of the Bolling's property, and directly across from the Ovington's estate. This little house had been kept in prestigious condition, and most of the time it was empty. Sometimes a family or a person working the Bolling's place would live in the house, if they had no other place to live.

For reasons unknown, Thomas began to take all of his time remodeling this house, and the surrounding ground was cleaned. The few things that Thomas had stored were taken out and he moved furniture out of the servant's quarters where Sarah moved into the house across from his estate. Most of the residents were used to Thomas doing unreasonable things at times, and assumed he was doing something to occupy his mind.

Sophie was ecstatic that Sarah was living in the Ovington house again, she had someone to talk to at night, and she wasn't so lonely these days, but she missed Beth so much, and she felt sorry for Thomas. At night Thomas would walk in the rock garden, or sit alone in his bedroom, rarely did he have company or go to any of the residents' houses. The Bollings would invite him to dinner occasionally, but he preferred to stay at home.

34

Everyone passing the Ovington estate, would always look to see if Thomas was within speaking distance or, where they could wave to him.

The proud figure of Thomas Ovington could be seen walking around the estate, his tall lean body was still strong enough to walk on his own, and it was rare for the residents to fail to see this man they called, "The Patriarch of Ovington".

Thomas Ovington lived many years beyond Beth Marie. Although he became unable to walk the valley anymore, he still would ask about the people in the valley he loved so much, and he would send for the ones he was fond of from time to time, just to see them.

In later years, there were many that would come to work the estate since, the Douglas' finally moved back to Spalding. Steven could not live with the stress of trying to keep up with all of the things he had to do daily, and could really see no sense in doing the same thing over and over. Estella had a fit the day Steven walked up to Thomas, and he told him he was moving home, and he would not be working for him any longer. Estella had no choice but to move back to Spalding with her husband.

Sophie lived to be pretty old. In later years when she became ill, she was taken to a convalescent home when she became totally helpless, and confused in her mind. Sarah was devastated, but she was unable to care for her, if only she was ill, Sarah would have taken care of her, but Sophie's mind was also deteriorated.

The time finally came when there was only Thomas and Sarah living at the Ovington estate. Sarah was getting up in age herself, and had gave up the nursing care when Betty Jean passed. There were people that still worked for Thomas around the estate, but he had no other people to live in the house that worked for him. Thomas was always doing something around this estate to improve things, or, just to make sure everything was kept up to par. The landscaping was beautiful, and the house always was repaired when anything was deteriorating.

The strangest thing Thomas did, was to have the servant's houses on the estate torn down. The servant's houses were in good condition, plus, he had the stables he built where he kept the fine horses when he brought the Cannon's horses to Ovington, and his favorite one he owned himself in later years, he had all of these buildings torn down, he only kept the carriage house standing that he kept his vehicles inside. The old carriages and his one car was always kept in the best condition, and was still his pride, though they were of no use to him anymore.

Ovington was quiet a thriving little town. The residents that lived in this community were living very well, the ones that had businesses were prosperous with them. There were a couple of good doctors, a hospital close by Ovington, and two good lawyers in the Bolling family. There were no more bums that came up the mountain looking for handouts. There was enough work for the people.

The proudest day for Thomas in Ovington, was the day the children in the valley walked around the little creek, through the Bolling's place up to the Ovington community to attend the school in their own town. No more being transported off the mountain. The dangerous trip they took each day to school always made Thomas nervous. Thomas lived to see the day he could stop worrying about a teacher in the valley for the children, or trying to see that they had a school to attend.

Thomas Theodore Ovington lived to be up in his nineties. His weary body remained straight; he never suffer a sick day, as far as taking to the bed, but Sarah watched him closely. Sarah knew Thomas was getting weaker each day as he tried to keep his daily pace he always tried to keep each day. The days were long for Thomas since, he was unable to walk beyond the few steps he took around the estate. Sarah was always afraid of him falling, and she began to walk with him. At first, Thomas protested and refused help as he some- times stumbled, but as he grew weaker and sometimes unsure of his step, he welcomed Sarah to walk by his side, the two could be seen walking the estate.

Sometime the residents would come up to speak to Thomas, he always seemed to recognize those that would visit. The Bollings would come to visit and chat with Thomas. The day came when Thomas sent for Roderich as a lawyer, and this is the day, he put in writing the way he wanted his estate to be disposed of at his death. Beth had left Thomas the bulk of her estate, except the Cannon's farm and her interest in the Women's Apparel Shop. Thomas wanted to will his wealth to those he wanted to share in the huge estate he owned.

Sarah faithfully stayed with Thomas, as Beth had asked her asked her to do, she had never lived anywhere beside Ovington. She was born in the Ovington's house and had lived the last few years taking care of the man that helped her into this world. Sometimes the loneliness was unbearable for Sarah, she missed Thaddeus, but her greatest love was Roscoe Bennett. Sarah would often think of Blue and Vera. She and Vera had become good friends in later years.

There were many people that came for miles around to pay their last respect to "The Patriarch of Ovington", Thomas had lived a long and rewarding life. Thomas was able to continued the job his forefathers set out to do, and that was to build up a town for the people.

The off-spring of the many people he knew, and had out lived, they came to pay their last respect doing Thomas sickness and his passing. The Carters, the Smithsons, and many others who knew this man and knew how powerful he was throughout the long years he lived. Thomas was a compassionate person, although he did some harsh and regrettably things in his life, but he always thought he was doing right at the time.

Thomas was buried by his loving wife, among the trees and the mountain side he loved so much. There were few tears among the mourners. Sarah stood alone, tears in her eyes, she had a sinking feeling, this was going to be another traumatic time in her life.

Sarah was sorrowful, and mourned for the Ovingtons, but as she gathered her few belongings, she was wondering where she would go from here, she had no home to go to, and she didn't want to go to the valley to live. Sarah had a little money, but not enough to live very long on.

Roderich Bolling came to the estate to see Sarah, she felt like she was about to be evicted from the Ovington estate, but Roderich told Sarah to get all of her belongings together. When Roderich saw Sarah's shocked face, he quickly explained to her that Thomas Ovington had given her the house across from his estate, the Newman's old house, and where Doctor Newman had his office when he first came to

Ovington. Sarah knew her furniture was carried to this house, but she never knew that Thomas had planned for her to move to this house at his death.

The wailing could be heard for a distance in Ovington as Sarah cried tears of joy and sadness. Sarah had been so worried, she would be was without a home again. The smiling Roderich told Sarah she had nothing to worry about, because Thomas had provided for her, and she shouldn't worry for a long time.

Thomas Ovington, not only provided for Sarah, he left his wealth to the town, that bore his name, his estate would belong to Ovington. Although Thomas Theodore Ovington was buried atop this mountain, his present would always be visible among the residents of Ovington.

THE END